EXPAT BLUES

Erin Eldridge

Gotham Books

30 N Gould St.
Ste. 20820, Sheridan, WY 82801
https://gothambooksinc.com/

Phone: 1 (307) 464-7800

© 2024 *Erin Eldridge*. All rights reserved.

No part of this book may be reproduced, stored in a retrieval system, or transmitted by any means without the written permission of the author.

Published by Gotham Books (May 31, 2024)

ISBN: 979-8-88775-890-9 (H)
ISBN: 979-8-88775-888-6 (P)
ISBN: 979-8-88775-830-5 (E)

Because of the dynamic nature of the Internet, any web addresses or links contained in this book may have changed since publication and may no longer be valid.

The views expressed in this work are solely those of the author and do not necessarily reflect the views of the publisher, and the publisher hereby disclaims any responsibility for them.

Contents

Prologue vi

Chapter One: Departure, 1972 1
Chapter Two: In Flight.. 7
Chapter Three: Landfall 10
Chapter Four: Livingstone 25
Chapter Five: Interim 51
Chapter Six: School 61
Chapter Seven: Maids, Borders, and Blue 79
Chapter Eight: On Safari, Tragic Loss, Life Goes On 101
Chapter Nine: Work and Play, A Brush With Witchcraft,
A Close-Run Thing. 124
Chapter Ten: The Italian Connection, The Mother of all Safaris,
A Brush With Death.. 156
Chapter Eleven: Monkey Bay, The Borders Curse Strikes Again,
Apartheid Angst 202
Chapter Twelve: Felled Again, a Wise Move, Back to Rhodesia
.... 240
Chapter Thirteen: Loves and Betrayals, Soccy Rules the Roost, an
Errant Priest, Luangwa Valley 256
Chapter Fourteen: Homeward Bound 287

Epilogue 295

For my son, Ben...morning has broken.

"The past is a foreign country; they do things differently there." L P Hartley.

Prologue

I was in Form Three (Year 9, as it's called now) at St Mary's College, my first year of high school, and it was our religious education time, RE as we called it. We had a period devoted to this subject every day and it was our Form Teacher, Sister Mary Gemma, who was responsible for our Catholic edification. She was young, probably only about 9 – 10 years older than her fourteen-year-old students, (in my case, thirteen-year-old) and we all liked her because she was sweet and gentle, unlike some of the fire-breathing dragons amongst the order of nuns that taught us (Sisters of *Mercy*…right!).

On this particular occasion, the topic under consideration assumed a personal note when Sister decided to go around the class asking each girl what she planned to do with her life (hoping, of course, that at least a few of us might voice a desire to take the veil). Most of the girls mentioned fairly mundane professions, eventual marriage, and children. When it was my turn, I stated quite confidently that I was going to go to Africa and work with the black babies (that was the term we'd been raised with whenever the Catholic Missions in Africa were mentioned. We frequently had coin trails at primary level, competing in our appointed school Houses, to raise money for 'the black babies'). The other girls tittered, giving me bemused looks, and Sister nodded with a twitch of the lips and a raised eyebrow before moving on to the next student. I quickly intuited the reaction of patronizing amusement and burned within. They may all have found my avowed ambition far-fetched and fanciful, but there was never the slightest doubt in my mind. None at all.

Chapter One: Departure, 1972

I was twenty-four when I told my parents that I had a new job – in Africa. They looked mildly surprised, smiled indulgently and then gave each other that sideways glance I remembered so well from my childhood when, as one gifted with an over-fertile imagination, I would regale them, along with members of my peer group, with the most preposterous stories, never for a moment suspecting that they would disbelieve me. I believe the apogee of my flights of fancy was achieved on the day I roared into the house to tell them that a plane had crashed in our street. I hastily assured them not to waste their time rushing out to check on this catastrophe for themselves, as the fire and rescue services had done a splendid and lightning-swift job of removing every trace of maimed humanity and smoldering debris. My parents tried to mitigate my flair for mendacity by describing me to appalled relatives as 'a great romancer'. Life can be tough for adventurous romantics. They almost always come to a sad end. Witness some of the most famous ones: Amelia Earhart, Ernest Hemingway, David Livingstone himself. Not wishing to place myself in such illustrious company, I nevertheless hoped I might beat the odds.

But I was no longer the child with the febrile imagination. This time it was the truth, and I had the letter to prove it, one of those flimsy little blue aerogrammes that people used back then, and which had to be carefully opened with a knife. Slit the wrong seam and you had a dismembered missive! This insubstantial epistle was the culmination of many months of wrist-cramping letter writing and anxious vigils by the mailbox.

It had all started – or been rekindled, I should say – when I met a young Englishman, Robin Parker, who'd taken up a position in the English Department of the school I happened to be working in at the time, my very first teaching job after completing my Master's degree and post-graduate teacher training. Before coming to New Zealand, he had worked at a mission school in Tanzania, run by an order of German Catholic monks. After school, and over a pint in the local pub, I listened with rapt attention to his stories about his time there. He told me about the occasion when he joined some local Masai warriors in a lion hunt. The hunt was traditionally conducted in bare feet as befitting true warriors, a rigorous rite of passage into manhood. Then there was his story about the monk who was recovering from an attack by a spitting cobra, which had occurred while he was gardening and had almost blinded him when he took the sprayed venom full in the face. With his eyes still extremely sensitive and painful but recovering after a quick-thinking colleague had poured milk into them, the standard bush cure, he had deliberately left the light off while answering the call of nature in the communal bathroom and had removed his protective dark glasses. Unfortunately, when my young English friend breezed in and, quite understandably, flicked on the lights, the monk's screams of torment could be heard all over the monastery.

I bought a chess set from Robin, the pieces carved from (I'm ashamed to admit it now) ivory and ebony, and I, too, dreamed of things African. Old longings tucked away were reawakened.

My English colleague gave me a list of addresses from the Times Educational Supplement to apply to for teaching jobs and I began my quest. Some did not answer, some told me they only hired British nationals, some said they weren't recruiting right now, but would bear me in mind and then, out of the blue, came a reply from an organization called the Catholic Secretariat based in Lusaka, the capital of Zambia, formerly the British colony of Northern Rhodesia. They'd changed the name to Zambia when they gained independence in 1964. The letter confirmed that I had been appointed to a Catholic girls' boarding school, St Mary's, (same as my old alma mater – it had to be an omen, a good one, I hoped!) in a town called Livingstone, that they would send me a plane ticket, a baggage allowance and a school prospectus. As soon as I had been granted a work permit by the Zambian government and fulfilled the medical requirements, I could be on my merry way. Finally, they added, the principal of the school would be in touch with me to let me know what classes I would be teaching, the nature of my accommodation and anything else they deemed it necessary I should be apprised of to prepare me for my thirty-month contract. I read the letter several times trying to let it all sink in. Livingstone! The very name was redolent with the mystique and romance that was Africa.

As word spread through my family and friends, I received mixed reactions. I was assured that I would not survive the culture shock, snakes and other predatory wildlife, crazed, white-hating, machete-wielding natives, a multitude of potentially life-threatening diseases, an extreme climate, or the sub-standard food. I was humbled by the depth of knowledge about Africa acquired by so many people who had never actually been there. It was all pretty depressing and had the effect of strengthening my already firm resolve to go into an adamantine hardness. My brother, Mike, gave me a fairly typical reaction.

"Africa!" he snorted derisively. "What on earth do you want to go there for? You're supposed to do your OE in the UK, lose your cherry, work in a pub, then come home and settle down with a nice, boring carpet salesman."

My mother seized gratefully upon the settling down bit while frowning at the rude bits. My older sister had married at 20, had two children and was expecting a third. My mother considered this to be the norm for all young women to emulate.

"I'd just like to see you, well, *settled*," she sighed. "You know, like your sister."

"But I don't *want* to be settled, Mum," I tried to explain soothingly. "I don't want domesticity, not yet anyway. Plenty of time for all that." (Not like my parents had set a great example of marital bliss!). "There's a whole, huge, fascinating world out there and I want to be part of it. I want adventure."

My mother sighed again. I had just demolished her *weltanschauung*, her *raison d'être*: women were inferior to men, and they found fulfillment through giving birth and subserving themselves to spouse and progeny. Then she did what she did best: withdrew behind a rampart of wounded, accusatory silence. My father didn't really care what I did, so long as it didn't inconvenience him in the slightest. I'd always been the black sheep of the family, anyway, its scapegoat and least valued member. I needed to detach myself, to seek my own path and identity, free from pressure to conform and negative judgement when I didn't.

The letter from the principal duly arrived. She was called Sister Carmel and she said she looked forward to meeting me. My newly built, fully furnished house a convenient short walk from the school awaited me, she said. I would be teaching English and history to secondary-school-aged African girls. She insisted that the school had no discipline problems, (really heartening after two years spent with hulking, insolent teenaged Southland boys), had a roll of 400, mostly boarders, and that there were several other expatriate teachers working alongside the nuns, who were mostly Irish and belonged to the Franciscan order. Well, after 13 years of convent education I was used to nuns and their ways.

I wrote back immediately, assuring her that I was really looking forward to teaching at the school and would be on my way as soon as the work permit arrived. There were a couple of documents to do with contract terms I had to sign and return and there was a list of inoculations that had to be completed before I could enter the country: smallpox, yellow fever, typhoid and cholera. I also had to have a chest x-ray to prove that I was free from tuberculosis, which was apparently endemic amongst the local Africans. All these vaccinations were to be recorded in a small yellow passport to travel with me. Fortunately, I had no bad reactions to any of them, and only a faint scar from the smallpox jab.

I completed all the paperwork and sat back to await the arrival of my work permit. During this hiatus I completed all my shots and organized my passport. As the weeks dragged by and no work permit materialized, I lost confidence and began to wonder if I had actually imagined the whole thing. I re-read all the letters to reassure myself.

My mother said things like, "Never mind." and "Perhaps it's all for the best."

Then, finally, about three months after the initial letter offering me the job had arrived, the unprepossessing work permit came. With mounting excitement, I booked my flight for early July. It was really happening. I was on my way. I bought a suitcase, resigned from my interim job as a waitress, used the modest luggage allowance to send off a crate of favorite books, nick-nacks, and my tramping gear, purchased a brand-new camera, transferred my meager savings, bought some travelers' cheques, good-naturedly fielded the inevitable jibes and innuendoes about pith helmets and house boys with extra duties and was ready to depart. My workmates at the restaurant, a hard-bitten bunch at the best of times, surprised me with a little farewell party and presented me with a leather-bound photo album and a small paua and silver brooch in the shape of New Zealand. I pinned it to the leather jacket I'd bought and which, by some perverse logic, believed would come in handy in the jungle. Mary the breakfast cook, of whom we were all terrified, a large, raw-boned woman as tough as goat's knees and the product of a hard life with an alcoholic husband, gave me a spine-buckling slap on the back and told me to let her know when I'd sampled 'a little bit of black velvet.' I duly promised her a missive to that effect, while she roared with laughter at my megawatt blush.

Other than that, I left New Zealand with little fanfare. My sister hosted a quiet farewell dinner for immediate family, but considering I was going away for the best part of three years, little was done to acknowledge the event. Fortunately, I was well used to such familial disinterest in my endeavors.

Erin Eldridge

It was a Sunday evening in early July, a typical cold, wet, miserable, mid-winter Christchurch day when I finally set off on my great adventure into the heart of darkness. My mother wore an air of martyred betrayal, my father was grumpy because he wanted to be at home in his pole position by the heater watching the news on the telly, and my siblings and in-laws regarded me with a mixture of bemused interest and thinly disguised pity. At the airport, my father, who'd ignored me all day, drew me to one side and told me that if anything unpleasant happened to me 'over there' he wouldn't help me – financially, I assumed he meant. He also warned me that I should not write anything in my letters that might upset my mother. In this way he absolved himself of all responsibility for me. For my part, I detached my arm from his grip, looked him in the eye and assured him that I would never call on him, however desperate my circumstances. Thus, my complete lack of value in my family was brutally confirmed. I felt suddenly, terribly alone.

I had a revenge of sorts when, part way through my tour, I sent him and my mother a contrived photo of me in the embrace of a large African male with a set of piano key teeth exposed in a face-splitting grin and informed them that he was my fiancé. My sister later told me they were in shock for days.

Goodbyes were made, my mother snuffled accusingly, my young nephews pressed their small noses and palms against the glass panels separating well-wishers from the security area, a final flurry of waving and I was aboard the plane ready to depart on the first leg of my journey, to Sydney. A long, daunting odyssey lay ahead of me: Sydney, Perth, Mauritius, Johannesburg, Blantyre, Lusaka, and finally, Livingstone. But I didn't mind. My appetite for adventure was fully whetted.

Chapter Two: In Flight

The flight to Sydney was memorable for two reasons. I was seated next to a crazy person on the plane, and I was welcomed at Sydney airport by two relatives I had never met before – my father's eldest sister, my widowed Aunt Tui, who had scandalized the family by running off to Australia at sixteen with a young man, and the fruit of that liaison, her only child and son, Pat, who was a Catholic priest and Apostolic Delegate for Australia. Perhaps, I wondered, he was over-compensating for his parents' licentious past.

The crazy person on the plane started off being quite amusing and quickly progressed to being intensely scary. She was, to all appearances anyway, a woman, perhaps in her late fifties, who was returning to Australia after completing one of those blue rinse brigade geriatric bus tours of New Zealand. I remembered the breed well from the motor lodge where I'd worked as a waitress. They were whiny, demanding, and difficult to please.

This particular example was immaculately dressed in an expensive looking fur coat, strands of pearls at her throat, her makeup elaborate and expertly applied. She was keen to make small talk and I was instantly struck by the disparity between her voice and her appearance. She spoke with a heavy accent and her voice had a guttural, gravelly quality. I looked at her harder. Was she in fact a man? In between fluttering her fingers delicately and calling out gushy greetings to fellow bus tour participants who were on the same flight, she told me a remarkable story. She was, she said, a German by birth who'd emigrated to Australia after the war. Leaning closer so that her perfume enveloped me in a fragrant miasma, she confided that she had a deep and abiding hatred of all things related to Hitler and the Nazis. To this end, she said, she had joined an underground movement, which aimed to subvert the fascist government and war effort by whatever means possible. She had dressed each night in the stolen uniform of a Wehrmacht soldier and frequented parts of Berlin popular with the armed forces on leave or merely socializing. Once a drunken camaraderie had been established with her intended victim, she would lure the unfortunate young man into an alley where her co-conspirators would quickly and expertly dispatch him with a knife. I instantly spotted a flaw in this story and said I thought it should be much easier to lure young men wherever if one was vamped up as a female. She studied me coolly for a few seconds and insisted somewhat condescendingly that it was, in fact, infinitely easier to get closer to her prey disguised as a man and a soldier.

To emphasize her point she leaned closer and with a conspiratorial air explained, "I rubbed hair-restorer into my face every morning and night to give me a beard. Now I have to shave every day, even after all these years."

I suppressed a shriek as she suddenly grabbed my hand closest to her and drew it across her jawline. Sure enough, there was no mistaking the prickly furze of male stubble beneath the heavy makeup. She leered triumphantly.

"There, you see! This is what I did for our cause."

When she slid a hand inside my leather jacket on the pretext of fingering its quality I reacted sharply, batting her away. She was beginning to make me feel decidedly uncomfortable. To this day I remain convinced that 'she' was indeed a man and wondered if the poor woman she would have shared sleeping accommodation with on the bus tour ever suspected anything. To my relief, she nodded off shortly after recounting her disturbing story and left me in peace for the remainder of the flight.

At Sydney airport I was recognized by my hitherto unseen relatives from a photograph sent them by my father, who'd organized the rendezvous, and I received a warm welcome. Aunt Tui hugged and kissed me while my cousin, Father Pat, delivered a manly handshake. We just about had time for quick refreshments and a chat before my flight left for South Africa via Perth. While Aunt Tui nattered away happily, Father Pat fetched a tray with three steaming cups of tea. He was a big man, ex-navy, serene and self-assured. Although no longer resembling the handsome young chap in an Australian naval officer's uniform that used to grace the wall in my grandmother's house, he was still an imposing presence. He patted my knee and told me I was doing a great thing, something I would be able to tell my children and grandchildren about. He believed I would have a wonderful time and never regret my decision to go to Africa. I felt a rush of confidence and thanked him for his encouragement.

"You'll have a marvelous time," he declared. "Wish I was going with you."

All too soon it was time for further hugs, kisses and handshakes and, feeling buoyant after such positive affirmation, I was off on stage two of my odyssey – Perth, Mauritius, Johannesburg.

This time, I was seated next to a young Indian man who smiled shyly at me and whom I instantly considered a vast improvement on the sinister, knife-wielding anti-Nazi of dubious gender. We exchanged greetings and he told me he was from Uganda. His family had sent him to Australia to further his education, but home sickness had ravaged him, and he'd decided to return home, without parental permission and more than a little anxious as to what kind of reception he could expect from his disappointed family. Much later, in the light of Idi Amin's takeover of Uganda in 1973 and his subsequent expulsion of all Asians, I recalled the young man and wondered what became of him.

By this time, it was late at night, and after the dinner service was completed the cabin lights were dimmed and the passengers hunkered down to try and sleep. Issued with a blanket and a miniscule pillow, this became the first of my many fruitless attempts to sleep on a plane during long distance flights. Matters weren't helped by the fact that my young Indian friend curled up on his seat in a fetal position and proceeded to kick me regularly in the small of my back, throughout the long, sleepless night.

Chapter Three: Landfall

As a magnificent sunrise washed colors of peach and coral across the sky, we landed on the island of Mauritius in the Indian Ocean. Everybody was encouraged to disembark for a leg stretch before re-boarding for Johannesburg, and so I sleepily trundled after the other passengers toward the Port Louis air terminal. I clearly remember two things about Port Louis; swift, brightly colored little birds darted about inside the terminal building and the toilets smelt very bad. As I struggled towards full wakefulness, it was time to leave again, and this time I found myself seated beside two young white South African women, one blonde, the other brunette, who had been holidaying in Mauritius. They were friendly in a restrained sort of way and exchanged enigmatic glances when I told them my destination was Zambia. Breakfast was served, poached eggs on a bed of spinach, and then the plane touched down in Johannesburg. I was officially on the continent of Africa. The travel agency had explained that because of tense relations between Zambia and South Africa there were no direct flights between the two countries. Malawi, on the other hand, found it expedient to preserve peaceful relations with its rich and powerful, white-controlled neighbor while maintaining ties with Zambia also. I therefore had to detour to Zambia via Malawi (formerly British Nyasaland before independence, 1964). This was my introduction to the convoluted world of African politics versus economics.

When I reached the front of the immigration queue, an unsmiling man in uniform thrust out his hand and barked, "Passport! Tickets!" I handed over both items and waited while he perused them with an impassive expression. Eventually he looked up and asked coldly, "Why are you going to Zambia?"

"To work there," I replied somewhat naively, "as a teacher. I have a—"

He cut me short. "You can get these back when you leave."

He swiveled his chair, tossing both tickets and passport onto a counter behind him.

"But my next flight leaves in less than an hour and I have to check in."

I was shocked by his overtly hostile behavior, but as I stammered my protests, he craned his head around me and snapped. "Next!"

One or two people in the queue who had witnessed our interchange looked at me pityingly as I drifted away aimlessly, unprepared for this train of events and unsure how to handle the situation. The state of physical weariness I found myself in didn't help matters. I saw an empty chair and sat down to gather my thoughts. I'd only been in Africa five minutes, and already I was in trouble! Not a propitious start.

In the world of international travel, I was a complete greenhorn. Now I would know exactly what to do in such a situation, but back then, sitting in Jan Smuts airport, I simply felt lost and bewildered. As I looked around, I couldn't help noticing that although the terminal was teeming with travelers, nobody seemed to be going anywhere. It looked totally chaotic, even to an inexperienced voyager like myself. At this point, I spotted some people talking to a woman in an SAA stewardess uniform; they appeared to be asking for her assistance and, after a brief exchange, she pointed them towards a particular destination. With a surge of hope, I scurried across to her, grabbing her by the arm.

"Can you help me, please? The man at immigration took my tickets and passport and I'm supposed to catch a plane to Blantyre in forty minutes."

"He did *what*?"

She shot me an incredulous look, so I blurted out the story a second time, trying to sound as desperate as possible. The ground stewardess studied me for a second or two, then took me gently by the arm, apparently convinced by my obvious distress.

"Sit down here and don't move. I'll be back in a minute. What's your name and where are you from?"

"Erin Anderson. I'm from New Zealand and I'm travelling to Zambia to work. I have to catch the plane to Malawi at two o'clock."

"Just stay here," she repeated firmly.

Then she disappeared into the mêlée of milling travelers while I resumed my seat, wondering if I'd ever see her again. I watched the clock tick relentlessly onward, wondering what became of passengers stranded in foreign airports. Perhaps they just became wizened, little anonymous skeletons and were swept into a cobwebby closet somewhere. I anxiously scanned the throng of people hoping for a glimpse of my ground stewardess savior. At last, she reappeared, smiling, and I leaped to my feet with relief.

"Here!" She flapped my plane tickets in her hand. "I've got your tickets and confirmed your connecting flight. That's your boarding pass and they'll call you to board shortly. All our flights are delayed because today's a national holiday and we're operating with as skeleton staff."

I started to thank her effusively and then stopped in midstream.

"Um, where's my passport?"

She gave me a sheepish grin. "They appear to have lost it. But don't worry," she added quickly, seeing my appalled expression, "I'm just off to try and locate it now."

With that she plunged back into the mêlée, and I slowly sank back into my chair feeling like the star billing in a very bad nightmare and hoping I'd wake up soon.

After what seemed like an eternity, the stewardess reappeared and handed me my passport. I felt like kissing it before I carefully stowed it away in my bag and thanked her over and over for her kindness. Looking back on this incident, I don't believe my passport was ever 'lost' but was probably photographed and its details recorded as part of a security procedure. This was not the only run-in I was destined to have with the South African authorities during my sojourn in Africa. Apartheid was firmly entrenched at this time and a white woman volunteering to work in a black African state hostile to South Africa was considered betrayal.

No sooner had my precious documents been returned to my safekeeping and I'd bade goodbye to my deliverer than my flight to Blantyre was announced. All passengers were instructed to form

Expat Blues

two queues, men in one, women in the other, in order to undergo some kind of security check. I queued with the other women and eventually came face to face with a barrier consisting of two green curtains pulled together. As I'd seen the others before me do, I swept them aside when a voice called "Next!" and stepped into a narrow cubicle to be confronted by a tall young woman in uniform, smiling fixedly at me through a mask of particularly garish makeup. Without a word, she stepped towards me and began to vigorously frisk me. I was so astounded at having my person so rudely accosted in this manner with no foreplay or forewarning, so to speak, that I simply froze while she ran her hands firmly over me, but when she thrust one hand into my crotch and then down my inner thighs it was all I could do not to haul off and thump her one. She stepped back, her large, vivid red lips mouthing a "Thank you" before she pushed me out through a similar set of curtains on the other side. I stood momentarily stunned, my face burning, before I was able to restore my equilibrium and head for the plane. Thankfully, airport security is now less intrusive!

Once aboard, just to add to my general state of confusion, they seated me in first class. I mumbled about having an economy class ticket, but nobody was taking any notice of me, so I slumped into my seat, wondering what other surprises South African Airways had in store for me. I didn't have to wait long. No sooner had I adjusted to the idea of enjoying the comparative luxury of a first-class berth than a voice crackled over the intercom, apologizing profusely and asking all passengers to disembark as the flight was delayed. By this time, I was pretty well inured to suffering and so apathetically trudged back to the terminal with the other disgruntled passengers, found a vacant seat, flopped into it and prepared to languish for an indefinite period of time. I resigned myself to the fact that my itinerary was now completely skewed. I'm never going to get to Zambia I told myself peevishly. They'll probably give the job to someone else.

Eight hours later, when darkness had fallen, and we'd been given some food vouchers to placate us…during which I'd witnessed a middle-aged white man savagely berate the colored assistant in the airport terminal café because the food item he wanted was no longer available…we were finally back on the plane and en route to Blantyre. I'd whiled away the time reading the instruction manual for my new camera and now felt pretty confident about using it. I was disabused of this notion when I got back the first set of photos I took with it. It would take me some time to become proficient with the split image focusing.

I noted with amusement that I was now back in economy class and SAA told me I'd be accommodated in a hotel in Blantyre for the night, courtesy of the airline, since I'd missed my connecting flight to Lusaka by some hours. I was very happy to be leaving Jan Smuts airport, but my adventures in South Africa were destined to continue, at a later date.

After we'd been served a rather sad meal of limp salad and dry, curled up luncheon meat, we arrived in Blantyre, named for David Livingstone's Scottish birthplace. The airport was small by comparison, but the natives were friendly, and the paperwork was expedited smoothly. We stepped out of the terminal into a balmy night, the sky a ferment of stars, and in the air a distinctively sweet, musty smell which struck me as being very exotic, very African. A minibus delivered about seven of us to Ryall's Hotel and I felt a surge of excitement as I recalled that Laurens van der Post had mentioned this hotel in his wonderful book *Ventures into the Interior*. I was indeed following in some illustrious footsteps.

The hotel staff swiftly dispatched us to our rooms, and I discovered I was sharing with a young, native-born, white Zambian woman, about the same age as me. We wearily exchanged introductions as we prepared for bed, and she apologized because she didn't have a 'robe'. I wanted to say I didn't give a rat's heinie, but was asleep before I could form the words.

At breakfast the next morning I learned that there was no flight to Lusaka until midday the following day, so I sent a telegram to my employers to reassure them that I was on my way, giving them the new flight number and ETA. The other half-dozen or so Zambia-bound people seemed a reasonably affable bunch, most of them white residents. One large, florid-faced gentleman in his fifties, or thereabouts, safari suit jacket stretched perilously across an expansive abdomen, proved to be a proficient whiskey drinker, and although he came across to me as a harmless, gregarious type, he appeared to have a very negative effect on my roommate, who read all sorts of sinister implications into, what seemed to me anyway, his fairly innocuous remarks to her.

"I *know* what he's trying to do," she declared dramatically, when we were alone in our room, which was more than I did, so I concluded that I was just too unsophisticated to appreciate the social nuances of these people. They all seemed part of a different era really, a time and place that no longer existed for most people, as if they had failed to move on or adapt to the new-look Africa, but were trapped in a time warp, clinging to their outdated elitist colonial culture, hanging on to a way of life that no longer had any relevance in the modern world. I was to encounter many such people in the course of the next three years, each one a separate story. At independence, not so long ago in 1964, there were 70,000 Europeans in Zambia.

I was eager to explore Blantyre and its environs, but the nation of Malawi had a strict law that a woman's legs must be fully concealed in public, right down to the ankles, and I had no clothes that fit the bill since long pants, like jeans, didn't qualify. It had to be a skirt, dress or the native 'chitenge' – wraparound sarong. So, I idled away the day reading and napping until my roommate pointed out that it was 'time to dress for dinner'. I straightened my jeans and shirt, grinning happily at her, while she gave me a disdainful look in return. For her part, she disappeared into the bathroom and reappeared ten minutes later in a frothy little number, reeking of perfume, and heavily bejeweled. I felt rather outshone. The evening meal was apparently something of a formal occasion in colonial etiquette.

Dinner was a drawn-out affair punctuated by lots of alcoholic drinks and conversation that grew increasingly in volume and merriment in such a bibulous atmosphere. They told me that Livingstone was very hot, too hot for them, they said, as they preferred the climate in the north, or in Lusaka. They hastened to assure me that it was a 'delightful town', though, 'a bloody good place before that lot took over', as my whiskey drinking friend assured me. I was enjoying the conviviality and company until the florid-faced gentleman made one seemingly pointed remark too many to my hypersensitive roommate and she snarled a few choice epithets at him before flouncing off. For his part he looked quite unabashed, shaking his fleshy jowls sadly, and said she had a lot to learn, being young and intolerant. It was midnight by this time, so I excused myself and went to bed in anticipation of who-knew-what traveling hazards the following day. I believed I was jinxed at this stage.

Breakfast the next morning was a tense affair, with my roommate glaring at the whiskey drinker and refusing to acknowledge his enquiries as to her wellbeing. But I didn't really care. I would be in Zambia in a few hours, relaxing in my new, comfortable house, and everything would be fine.

We reached Lusaka at about 2 p.m. Father O'Riordan, from the Catholic Secretariat, welcomed me at the airport with a big smile and a hearty handshake, and I was equally pleased to see him. A tall, benign, middle-aged Irishman, he seemed very au fait with the protocol and a word from him to the customs men saw us promptly on our way with no baggage search. I guess his height, confident demeanor and priestly garb all helped to create an air of authority.

"She's a teacher," he announced magisterially. "She's come all the way from New Zealand to work here."

The customs men nodded deferentially, eyeing me curiously, and stepped aside as Father O'Riordan swept past, carrying my suitcase and beckoning me to follow him.

"Is this all your luggage, Erin?"

"I have a small crate coming by sea."

"By *sea*! Sure, and it might get here just as your tour ends!"

I grinned sheepishly.

Once on the motorway, he filled me in on the remaining segment of my journey to Livingstone as we traveled towards the impressive, western-looking capital of Zambia, with its striking boulevards and tall buildings glittering in the sun. "Got you on a flight about noon tomorrow," he informed me. "Tonight, you'll stay with the sisters in the Ursuline convent. They'll take good care of you."

Expat Blues

We turned into an entranceway somewhere on the outskirts of the city and stopped in front of a pair of massively manacled chain link gates, which were part of a formidable concrete security fence the height of two men, topped with concertina razor wire and jagged shards of glass set in the cement, the whole surrounding the impressive two-storey building that was the convent. Two enormous German Shepherd dogs, raised hackles augmenting their already impressive bulk, bounded up to the gates, barking fiercely, and Father O'Riordan chuckled as he sounded the horn a couple of times, while I slid down into my seat in terror. A plump, diminutive nun in a white habit appeared from somewhere to our right, hurrying along the driveway towards us. She shooed the dogs away, both still growling deep-throatedly, and opened the gates, smiling apologetically.

"Is this kind of security typical?" I asked as we drove through, with the dogs gamboling alongside, bright, dark eyes fixed on me, the intruder.

Father nodded. "Oh yes, but don't worry, they won't hurt us. They're trained to attack Africans." While I looked at him in horror – *not just bloody fierce...bloody racist!* – he wound down the window for the little nun, who peered in curiously, a large canine head shoving in either side of her, huge paws dwarfing the tiny pair of hands gripping the door sill, glistening pink tongues flecking drops of saliva onto the dash and upholstery while exposing impressively large fangs and gleaming carnassials. I shrank over against my own door as far as I could go.

"Good afternoon, Sister Margaret," said Father O'Riordan cheerfully, seemingly unfazed by this odd simulacrum of the three-headed Cerberus, "I've got Erin. From New Zealand."

I lifted a hand, wiggling my fingers. "Sister," I squeaked.

The little nun smiled at me. "We've been expecting you," she said in a strong Irish accent. "Drive on in, Father. I'll close the gates and be along. Down now, Finn, Bran. Good boys. Away wit' ye."

I had a sinking feeling. This place was scary.

When Father stopped the car in front of the convent's main door, I looked around warily before stepping out. The dogs had apparently accepted that I was not to be torn to pieces on this occasion and had disappeared. I was relieved. I loved dogs, but those two mutts were seriously intimidating. By the time father had lifted my suitcase from the boot and closed it, Sister Margaret came huffing up and flung open the door before ushering us into the convent's cool interior. "Come along, dear."

Father planted my suitcase on the gleaming tiles of the foyer and said goodbye, promising to catch up with me later. Right on cue, a tall, imposing sister arrived, and I was introduced to the Mother Superior of the convent. She was accompanied by a shy young African man who seized my suitcase and fairly sprinted off upstairs with it as Reverend Mother barked instructions after him.

"Room 9, Zachary."

Sister Margaret hurried off to resume her duties, gatekeeper, presumably, and Mother showed me upstairs to my overnight accommodation, a compact room with a single bed, washbasin with mirror, and a small bureau. My suitcase was waiting within. After making sure I knew the location of the bathroom and toilets, situated further along the corridor, she bustled off, calling over her shoulder that I should come downstairs when I was ready.

Once she'd left, I closed the door, hoisted my suitcase onto the bureau, and wandered over to the only window, gazing out. This wasn't my idea of Africa. A big western-style city with gleaming high-rise buildings dominating the landscape. Even on the second floor, the windows had burglar bars. There was something raw and unsettling about the place. Feeling despondent, I flopped down on the bed without even removing my shoes, and shortly began to doze. I drifted in and out of a semi-waking state for I don't know how long, feeling the effects of jet lag, no doubt, but this was no restful nap. My slumber was punctuated by terrifying visions of huge, slathering dogs and Africans with machetes clasped between their teeth scaling the security fences and the convent walls like cats to leer threateningly at me through the bars crisscrossing the window of my room before wrenching them asunder like wet noodles.

Expat Blues

I awoke with a start when somebody tapped on my door, and I recognized Mother Superior's voice. "Come on down now, Erin. Dinner's ready."

"Coming!"

Feeling discombobulated but relieved to find that the scary phantoms had been just that, I rolled off the bed, pulled myself together and followed Mother downstairs to the dining room, where a group of nuns, African and European, were seated around a large communal table, tucking into piled plates of food that smelled very appetizing and reminded me how hungry I was. Breakfast had been a long time ago and I'd missed lunch. The diners paused momentarily when we entered, looking me over curiously, apart from Sister Margaret who gave me a little wave of recognition, and then resumed their eating and conversation. Reverend Mother ushered me to a chair and poured me a large glass of milk from one of a cluster of pitchers before gliding off to seat herself at the head of the table, where she clapped her hands and, once she had the chattering group's attention, introduced me and explained my temporary presence at the convent. The other sisters all bobbed and nodded, murmuring various versions of 'welcome' while I smiled back, feeling pretty awkward and out of place. I was rescued by the appearance at my elbow of a young Zambian girl wearing a blue smock who placed a laden plate in front of me and left me to study its contents. It all looked very familiar, no surprises here. There was a large pork chop, some peas, a slab of pumpkin and a big dollop of white stuff which I didn't recognize. It wasn't potato as it had quite a different texture and color.

"That's nshima; mealie-meal," explained the nun seated next to me who'd observed my tentative jabbing with the fork. "It's the staple food in this part of the world. Maize porridge," she added in response to what must have been my blank expression. "Traditionally, you eat it with your fingers, but no need here. Usually comes with relish, if you're lucky." She chuckled.

I looked at my naked portion. Not lucky tonight, then. No sign of any, um 'relish', or gravy on the chop for that matter. Mum always had a delicious gravy for pork chops, but, hey, we're not in Kansas anymore!

Oh well, I thought, time to sample the indigenous tucker. My verdict was that the nshima was fine, if a little bland. Knob of butter and some salt and pepper would make it more palatable, I decided. As it turned out, that was the one and only time I ever ate the stuff while I was in Africa. 'Relish', I learned, was a broad category and could be anything from soup, meat, fish, chicken, offal, bush tucker, stewed greens, pumpkin to just plain sauce e.g., tomato. Starchy staples, whether made from maize, manioc, cassava, millet or sorghum and called by various names, were to be found all over Africa. To eat nshima the traditional way, you scooped up a piece of it in your fingers, formed a ball which you indented with your thumb and then used it as a scoop for the relish. In genteel company like nuns, you used a spoon or fork!

Another nun had joined us, a big bonny-looking woman, who sat down opposite me, and we smiled at each other, exchanging greetings across the table.

"Sister Judith," Mother called, "we gave your chop to Erin, from New Zealand. She's with us tonight en route to Livingstone to teach at St Mary's. There're vegetables and nshima left, though."

Sister Judith's friendly smile faded, and she turned a rather baleful look on me. I gulped with embarrassment, shrinking down in my chair. Her bulk indicated a hearty appetite, and I watched in horror as the serving girl placed a supper of crushingly meagre proportion in front of her. I'd eaten her dinner! I knew nuns were supposed to make sacrifices but this one had been forced on her by ME! She'd probably done a hard day's work while I was snoring in the sack. They'd said they were expecting me, yet they couldn't organize an extra chop?

"Sorry," I muttered lamely as Sister Judith poured herself an almost overflowing glass of milk – desperate for every smidge of nourishment flashed through my mind – before she picked up her cutlery with a resigned sigh, ignoring me. To my great relief, Mother stood up at that excruciating point and said that since I was finished eating, she'd show me into the lounge for a cup of tea. I lunged gratefully after her as she swept out.

Expat Blues

No sooner was I settled in an armchair in the nuns' little sitting room, sipping my tea and reading the communal copy of *Lusaka Times*, while trying to erase the image of Sister Judith's starvation rations from my mind, when Reverend Mother returned with Father O'Riordan in tow.

"Erin, Father's come to take you out for the evening. He has another teacher he wants you to meet." A woman of seemingly flagless energy, she sailed out again.

I recalled Father's words when we'd parted earlier in the day, that he would see me that evening, so I obediently abandoned my tea and newspaper and followed him out to his car. On the way into the city, I pumped him about the stringent security measures that had unsettled me.

"There is a high crime rate here, no doubt about that," he replied seriously. "They come in from the villages with nothing and they see the white expat workers with nice cars, houses and money and they want a piece of that, too, so they rob, and they murder as well, if you get in their way. Everybody takes sensible precautions – dogs, security fencing as you've seen. Often a watchman. Some people keep a gun as well."

"Is Livingstone like that, too?" I asked.

"Not as bad as the city here," he replied reassuringly. "The Copperbelt towns in the north are the worst, the Wild West. People in Kitwe and Ndola, for example, they chain their car to their house at night and put a dog in it for good measure. If they go out at night, they leave an armed watchman on the stoop. The thieves can buy cheap guns from the Congolese army. It's tough up there."

I felt a deepening sense of dread creeping over me. This all seemed terribly remote from my safe, predictable little world back in New Zealand. Maybe those naysayers had been right. Maybe Africa was too dangerous and risky for this Kiwi.

"Anyway," said Father O'Riordan cheerfully, slapping me on the knee, "You'll feel grand and safe in Livingstone. All the teachers live in a very secure compound."

'Compound'??? I looked at him in alarm. Sister Carmel had not mentioned a 'compound' in any of her correspondence. Was I destined to spend the next two and a half years living in fear and trepidation inside the confines of Stalag Luft St Mary's? Would it have dogs, guns, and a watchman? My tireless imagination went into overdrive: Erin's version of Rorke's Drift, standing shoulder to shoulder in serried ranks with my fellow teachers, (Yes, I'd seen *Zulu*, with Michael Caine screaming 'Fiarr!) shooting through the chain link fencing at rampaging hordes of Africans hellbent on rapine and murder, Sister Carmel directing the fire. Amongst the documents she'd sent me, had been a Zambian tourist brochure. It was titled 'Zambia in the Sun' and included within its folds photos of the spectacular Victoria Falls, wild animal safaris, smiling natives in traditional costume pounding drums, and fabulous sunsets over the Zambesi. There'd been no suggestion it was crime central. Obviously.

Father brought me back to reality as he swung the car into the kerb and announced, "Here we are. The best Chinese restaurant in Lusaka. Hope you're hungry. My treat, of course."

I opened my mouth to reply that I'd just eaten rather a large and fraudulently obtained dinner, but, as we got out of the car, Father continued to wax lyrical about the food at the restaurant and I didn't have the heart to dent his enthusiasm.

We climbed some narrow stairs into a traditionally decorated Chinese restaurant featuring lots of red and gold furnishings and were shown to a table where a young woman was already seated, sipping on a lemonade. Father introduced us as we joined her.

"This is Anne. She's a teacher at St Joseph's Primary here in Lusaka. Anne, this is Erin, the New Zealander I told you about."

He didn't seem to bother with surnames, I noticed. The young woman and I duly exchanged greetings. Anne was also Irish, a slim, serious-looking girl with bright auburn hair secured in a ponytail. I assumed father had invited her along for propriety as much as anything else. He thrust a menu into my hands and told me to ask Anne, over dinner, anything I wanted to know about what it was like working and teaching in Zambia.

"She's been here a year already, so she knows the ropes."

A waiter arrived and, to my relief, Father took charge as Anne and I dithered over our menus, ordering several dishes and more soft drinks. I just didn't feel right ordering large plates of food for myself with the specter of poor, deprived Sister Judith still hovering before me. At least with some shared dishes I could just pick a bit here and there.

The food arrived, all looking delicious as Father had promised, and, while I nibbled daintily, hoping my chocker tummy wouldn't start making sounds of protest, I quizzed Anne to keep Father happy.

"How do you find the kids here?"

"Oh, they're lovely. I teach the primers, both boys and girls, and they're very sweet, keen as mustard. You'll be teaching girls only, I think."

"Yes," Father replied for me. "Only girls at St Mary's. Some of the government high schools can be tough, but you'll find that the Catholic colleges are all pretty good. Sister Carmel is a fine principal who has a firm grip on things. She's been working in Africa a long time." He stabbed his chopsticks towards my bowl. "Eat up, Erin. You've the appetite of a bird."

"Sorry, Father." I sighed inwardly as I plunged back into my chow mein.

As I chewed half-heartedly, I thought of my own education. Most of the nuns who'd taught me had Irish backgrounds and they'd ruled us with rods of iron. Same in the Catholic boys' schools with the Marist priests and brothers. Clearly, the Irish Catholic clergy had a big influence in Africa as well through their missionary work.

Anne wanted to know more about New Zealand, a country she longed to visit, she enthused, and I answered her queries, feeling increasingly homesick as I digressed. We didn't return to the topic of life in Zambia again, and I thought perhaps the less I knew the better.

After dinner, and after making our goodbyes to Anne, who kindly wished me all the best, Father drove me back to the Ursuline convent. The two enormous German Shepherds romped into the headlights' beam when we pulled up at the gates, barking wildly until a burly African watchman armed with a large torch arrived to quell them and open the gates for us. Clearly, the dogs made an exception and didn't attack *him*!

I thanked Father for a nice evening, and he said he'd pick me up around 11 a.m. the next morning for my flight to Livingstone.

After a few wrong turns I relocated my room, undressed, and crawled into bed feeling horribly bloated and more than a bit conflicted. *Oh, God,* I thought before sleep claimed me. *Have I done the right thing?*

Chapter Four: Livingstone

The following morning, after a surprisingly good night's sleep, I awoke feeling refreshed and a lot more positive. Tonight, putting aside qualms about living in a compound, I would be sleeping in my own newly built, fully furnished house. It had been a long, often fraught journey, but my odyssey was almost over. I looked at my watch and saw to my surprise that it was almost 9 o'clock. I found the showers, dressed quickly and went downstairs. Breakfast was over, (I hoped Sister Judith had filled her boots!) the long table deserted, but the African girl who worked in the kitchen made me some toast and tea, which she brought into the dining room on a tray. She also handed me a copy of that day's newspaper so I could browse as I ate. There were lots of photos of President Kenneth Kaunda. Some research I'd done before I left home had revealed that Zambia had not become a democracy post-independence. It was a one-party state where the dominant tribe, the Bemba, were backed up by an ill-disciplined military, and it was hostile to both white-ruled Rhodesia (now Zimbabwe) and South Africa, at that time also white-ruled under the segregationist apartheid system. Russia and China were gaining influence within the context of the Cold War. Tribalism and Marxist leanings were the hallmarks of newly emergent African countries.

After breakfast, I went back to my room and repacked my suitcase, before lugging it, since there was no busboy in attendance, down the two flights of stairs to the foyer. There was still nobody around, so I ensconced myself in one of the two capacious armchairs in the foyer and read my book until father O'Riordan arrived. Fin and Bran came gamboling up, satisfied by now that I was part of the furniture, even permitting farewell pats.

There were no hiccoughs at the airport, and when it came time to board the plane, Father shook my hand warmly, wished me well, and told me I could contact him to talk over any problems or difficulties I might have, at any time. He also assured me someone would be there to meet me in Livingstone.

"You'll arrive in time for lunch. The nuns will look after you."

"Please pass on my appreciation to the sisters at the convent for their hospitality. I couldn't find anyone this morning."

"I will."

Father had impressed me as a genuinely kind and caring man, and I thanked him sincerely before I took a deep breath and headed off on the final, thankfully short, leg of my odyssey.

I had a window seat for the first time in daylight on the African leg of my journey, and as the plane started its descent on the short flight from Lusaka to Livingstone, I stared down at a topography that was nothing like the Africa of my imagination. For miles all I could see was what looked like bush and trees punctuated by patches of savannah. There was no steaming jungle, no convoluted vines of the sort that facilitated Tarzan's travels. It all looked vast and uninhabited, almost drab rather than enthralling. Obviously, I was not a geographer. We'd only done bits and pieces at school as part of the Social Studies curriculum.

When the plane had taxied to a halt and the passengers had been cleared for disembarkation, there was a short walk across the tarmac to the terminal, a small but attractive building surrounded as it was by trees and brightly flowering shrubs. Standing behind and leaning on the low netting fence bordering the tarmac perimeter, were two figures clad in identical tropical white, two women. They had to be from St Mary's, sent to meet me. One was a slightly built European, the other an African, her white nun's smock contrasting dramatically with the black sheen of her skin. The Franciscan African habit, adapted for the tropics, consisted of a white cotton knee-length short-sleeved dress belted at the waist and included a shoulder-length veil attached to a headband that clasped behind the head revealing the hair at the front. This was quite different from the heavy black garb worn by the Sisters of Mercy who had taught me. For them, the veil had been a long, pleated affair falling most of the way down their backs; hair, forehead, cheeks and throat had been concealed by a headdress comprising stiff white bandeau, coif, and guimpe. Only an oval of face from the eyebrows down had been visible. We had always pitied them during the summer months.

As I drew closer, I gave the nuns a tentative wave and they straightened up, waving back. They pointed to the terminal building, indicating, I supposed, that they'd meet me inside and I veered off in that direction, following the other arrivals.

The interior of the terminal building was cool and attractive, potted plants dotted about and overhead fans spinning lazily. I made my way to the baggage claim area and the two nuns promptly appeared at my side. After verifying that I was indeed Erin from New Zealand, they introduced themselves. Sister Nora was of course Irish, a softly spoken, middle-aged woman with glasses that magnified her blue eyes, of slight build with little wisps of grey hair curling about her temples. The African nun was Sister Frances Mooya, Deputy Principal of St Mary's and, as I later learned, the first woman to graduate from the University of Lusaka, making her a precious asset to the school. She regarded me coolly as she shook my hand, and I sensed a certain reserve. I felt she would take her time to make up her mind about me. I'd already grasped the fact that everyone in Africa was conscious of race. And I was a descendant of British colonial usurpers, like the ones who'd ruled her country up until eight years ago. (Ironically, I am in fact 45% Irish, according to a DNA test).

The sisters gamely insisted on hauling my leaden suitcase to the car and between them managed to lift it into the back of the station wagon.

"Is this all your luggage?" asked Sister Nora. "Have you anything coming by freight?"

"No," I replied. "This is it." I tapped my crossbody bag that held all my documents. "And this, of course."

The two nuns raised their eyebrows and looked at each other.

"I have some books coming," I added, "and my tramping gear."

They nodded slowly. "Tramping gear?" echoed Sister Frances, breaking a smile for the first time.

"Hiking." I thought perhaps I'd better use the British English for the activity. I'd spent many an enjoyable weekend with the school tramping club in Southland.

Sister's smile broadened.

"They're coming by sea," I added lamely, and the nuns' eyebrows shot up again.

"Sure, and that'll take months," said Nora, "if they get here at all."

"I know," I replied, feeling foolish. "That's what father O'Riordan said."

The nuns shrugged in sympathy. (My packing case *did* arrive, about three months later. I didn't do any tramping, though. Nobody did).

Sister Frances held open the door to the back passenger's seat for me. Sister Nora drove, and Sister Frances sat in the front with her. At least it's left-hand drive here, I thought with relief.

The road from the airport descended through a tunnel-like vista of tall green trees and then we turned right into the township itself. I gazed out the car window, anxious to take it all in. This was where I'd be living for the next 30 months. First impressions were that Livingstone, with a population of around five thousand, was a neat-as-a-pin township with lots of brightly painted stucco shop and business facades. The broad main road through town was in excellent condition, as had been the road from the airport, the median strip dividing the two lanes planted with tall leafy trees that Sister Frances said were jacarandas in response to my question. The overall effect was one of cleanliness, orderliness and attractiveness, a pretty little provincial town with a touch of class – after all, it had been Zambia's capital until 1935. I was enchanted.

Sister Nora turned left off the main street and away from town, crossing a narrow bridge. After a mile or so she turned left again, off the seal and up a narrow gravel road that curved around past dozens of tiny identical stucco houses in differing vibrant colors, featuring corrugated iron roofs and a flourishing garden (shambas, as I learned) alongside each one. I saw there were many Africans in attendance, men and women, along with chickens, goats, pigs and sundry other animals. This was Maramba township, Sister Frances explained. We drove on, through an archway of towering green trees past a church on the right towards a long low building I thought might be the school. Finally, we glided left off the road at an angle, pulling to a stop in front of an imposing two-storey building, dark cream in color, surrounded by a high wall, studded with glittering shards of jagged glass, same as the convent in Lusaka, and fronted by an archway bearing a large cross. *Don't think this is my house.*

Sister Nora cut the engine and turned her head to address me. "We'll have lunch first, at the convent and you can meet Carmel. Then we'll take you to your flat. Your suitcase is safe here in the meantime."

'Flat'??? I thought as I clambered out of the car after them. Surely, she means 'house'.

At that moment a bell tolled, and I glanced over to my right. That single-storey white building directly opposite the convent was indeed the school. A babble of chatter broke the quiet and the girls began to stream out of the classrooms, heading across the lawns and the dirt road to the boarding side of the convent to get their lunch. They wore dark blue pleated skirts and short-sleeved white blouses that contrasted with their black skin. So, these were the kids I'd be teaching. It was starting to feel real.

I followed sisters Nora and Frances into the cool, dark recesses of the convent down a corridor with columns on one side giving a view into an attractive inner courtyard that featured a well-laid-out garden with a central fountain and regularly spaced bench seats on which I could picture nuns sitting quietly, reading their daily office. Convents always seemed to be beautiful, peaceful buildings, I mused. The sisters' convent on the grounds of my old school back home had been a stunning greystone Gothic structure with marble floors. Going into it was daunting, like entering another world as austere and ascetic as its dwellers. Sister Nora gave a polite cough to hurry me up as I dawdled and then ushered me through a doorway into the sisters' dining room. I sat where she indicated at the single long table, and almost immediately a very thin nun with freckles and tufts of gingery hair framing her face put a plate in front of me on which was a thin slice of toast topped with a poached egg. A tiny poached egg, pullet size. I stared at it bleakly. Hope I'm not nicking anyone's food again, I thought.

"We have our main meal at night, said Sister Nora, with a hint of apology in her voice. "We only have a light lunch."

I smiled. "It's fine, Sister."

She pushed a cup and saucer towards me, along with a jug of milk and an enamel teapot. "Here, help yourself to tea."

As other nuns arrived, I was introduced to each in turn, trying hard to remember all the names, after which they took their seats, studying me keenly. Everyone tucked into their meagre fare, and I tried to eat, too, feeling like an insect under a microscope. The toast was very hard to cut through, but I felt it would be bad form to eat with my fingers.

"You're our first New Zealander," said one nun, exposing her large teeth in a megawatt smile.

"Really? That's nice," I responded lamely.

I felt surrounded by nuns, which I was, and having endured 13 years of convent education I wasn't all that keen on them as a species, although this bunch seemed nicer than most of the ones I could remember. I caught Sister Frances' eye. She sat with a cup of tea half raised to her lips, her gaze upon me steady. I kept my head down, and hacked away doggedly at my meal, feeling more than a little uncomfortable. Then all heads swiveled towards the doorway and several nuns chorused, "Here's Carmel!" The principal had landed.

I swallowed my egg and toast with a gulp, and, as seemed appropriate to the moment, – meeting the boss – I rose to my feet. I was looking at a diminutive woman, older than I expected, probably in her late fifties or early sixties, with tiny features, wearing strong-lensed spectacles that magnified her intense blue eyes to an unsettling degree. What hair I could glimpse was steely grey and pulled back severely under the band of her wimple. She looked me over briskly, and then her face broke into a welcoming smile as she stepped closer, extending a hand in greeting. That was when I noticed that she tottered on a pair of toeless white strapped sandals with ludicrously high, albeit sturdy, heels.

"Isn't she nice and young?" she enthused, clasping my hand in both of hers.

Expat Blues

I blinked at this odd remark addressed to her assembled nuns, and wondered if it meant all the other expat teachers were geriatric. Sister Carmel took her place at the table and lunch resumed, me painfully aware that I was once again under scrutiny, this time by those intelligent blue eyes of hers as opposed to Sister Frances' inscrutable dark ones. Despite Sister Carmel's grey hairs and the lines on her face, she had a youthful air about her and an aura of energy. Over the next 30 months I would learn to appreciate this wise, cheerful little Irishwoman again and again. Sister Carmel McGill was a remarkable person, a dedicated missionary who had spent 40 years of her life in Africa, many of them in British Uganda, bringing education to African youngsters. Nothing escaped her attention. She was fair-minded, diplomatic, compassionate, and the staff and students had immense respect for her. In fact, the girls were terrified of her. Statuesque African adolescents twice her height who'd earned her disapproval would drop to their knees before her, quailing under the censure of those steely blue eyes. "Car-mel! Car-mel!" they'd hiss to each other in class whenever they saw her tottering across from the convent to her office. Yet, she had a heart of gold, too, and a self-effacing warmth that endeared her to everyone. She was the best principal I ever worked for.

As lunch concluded, one of the nuns pressed a bright green orange as solid as a billiard ball into my hand, apologizing for its atypical appearance, but insisting that the taste, once it was peeled, would be pleasant. I thanked her, assuring her I'd eat it later as I thrust it into a pocket. Sister Carmel excused herself to return to the school, promising to catch up with me later, and my, by now familiar, escort of Nora and Frances drove me a couple of hundred yards further down the road to the teachers' compound. I'd picked up pretty quickly that the nuns called each other by their given Christian names without the 'sister' title. They didn't use adopted saints' names like the nuns I'd grown up with. Having also finished lunch, the girls were standing about in groups in the sunshine, enjoying a break before afternoon study. They watched us curiously as we drove by, those in the road moving quickly aside.

The teachers' compound did indeed resemble a concentration camp, with its massive chain link gates and fencing, all topped by angled metal battens supporting rows of barbed wire. As we drove through the gates, I could see a cluster of houses, all similar in style and color, white stucco with corrugated iron roofs, randomly dotted about, seven in all by a quick count. I scanned them eagerly for a glimpse of my house, standing out like a brand spanking new edifice from the rest. Then Nora stopped the car beside a rather dilapidated building with drab green paint, badly faded in patches, and looking as if it had seen better days. It seemed long and low in contrast to the bungalows, and I soon learned why. This rather odd little building comprised two one-bedroom flats adjacent to each other with a narrow brick lattice wall protruding at right angles from the center to clarify their semi-detached nature. A rusty kerosene tin stood in front of the one we'd parked alongside, a sad little plant drooping over its rim. No way could this be my new house.

"Here we are," said Nora cheerfully, dispelling any doubt, and she and Frances opened their doors and scurried around to the back of the car to wrestle out my bulging suitcase. Feeling dazed, I slid out of the back seat and followed them. Nora lifted my suitcase onto the stoop and Frances said evenly, "This is your flat. This is where you'll be living."

"No." I shook my head vehemently. We weren't even inside, and I already hated it. "Carmel said I would have a brand-new house. It was in the letter she sent me. She never mentioned a 'flat'."

Frances and Nora exchanged a patently guilty look, then Frances drew herself up and stated regally, "Carmel probably forgot to explain it to you. We had to assign the Mullins to the new house. They have two children and have just transferred here from Chikuni. Peter's a badly needed science teacher." She smiled. "You'll be comfortable here. The girls spent all Sunday cleaning it for you. It's spic and span. Single teachers normally get the flats," she added, the smile markedly absent now, the dark eyes resolute, and the message a clear one: not up for debate.

Years of Catholic education had taught me that it was pointless to argue with nuns, and I looked away with a sigh. Inside a little bell of impending doom was tolling. So far, my grand adventure had been a series of missteps, this development just the latest in the saga, and it was probably going to get worse, not better. I was right about that.

Nora unlocked the front door that faced out onto the tiny, tiled stoop (also spelled 'stoep', a Dutch word widely used for a porch in Southern Africa) with its solitary outdoor chair, the black plastic lattice binding cheerfully unravelling, and I followed her inside, Frances close behind me. We were in the living/dining room which featured a red lounge suite comprising a shabby couch and two equally shabby matching chairs, a stained coffee table topped with an ashtray positioned in front of the couch, and a solid old fashioned wooden dining table with seating for four. On the right-hand side of the room, against the wall, was a glass fronted cabinet containing glassware and crockery, its top adorned with a crocheted doily. Set in the wall opposite was a small fireplace with a mantelpiece and an arresting bright pink brick façade. A fireplace? In Africa? Bright pink bricks? I took note of a small bookcase beside the fireplace. In the center of the dining table was a plastic bowl holding a cluster of green oranges identical to the one I'd been given at lunch, so I took it from my pocket and added it to the pile.

There was a strong odor of floor polish and disinfectant permeating everything, the aftermath of the girls' cleaning spree, I assumed. The concrete walls were painted a sickly green hue – my least favorite color – much like the exterior of the building and the door frame at the end of the room was thick, white-painted steel, which, along with the low ceiling, gave the place all the ambience of a German WW11 bunker on the Atlantic Wall.

Heart steadily sinking, I followed Nora into the rest of the house. Off a narrow hallway were the bathroom, furnished with bathtub, toilet, handbasin and mirror (No washing machine, Nora clarified. You used the bath for handwashing and rinsing out laundry); next, a tiny separate shower room (cupboard) with all the plumbing brutally exposed; to its left, a utility cupboard with storage shelves for cleaning equipment like floor polish, and a broom, mop, and dustpan as well as ironing board and iron; to my right a bedroom with a single bed, neatly made up with a counterpane and plump white pillows, a mosquito net knotted above it, a bedside table, a chest of drawers, and a free-standing wardrobe; finally, the kitchen, which featured a small white wooden table and two chairs, a dolls' house sized fridge, an equally compact little electric stove, the hob crowned by a non-electric kettle, a sink standing on four spindly metal legs, again with exposed plumbing, and a wall-mounted pantry above the stove with pots and pans nestled on top and drawers beneath for cutlery, cooking utensils, tea towels etc. On top of the fridge, squatted a pink and white lidded plastic box prosaically labelled 'Bread' in chipped gold lettering. All the windows in the house had burglar bars and insect netting. Between the bench and the table there was a second outside door but no steps. Nora chattered away throughout the viewing, while Frances hovered to my rear, no doubt ready to tackle me if I tried to do a runner. Now I understood why they'd all been watching me so closely since my arrival.

Nora pointed out the can of insect spray, fire extinguisher, (I stifled a manic cackle. I couldn't imagine this oppressive chunk of steel and concrete ever catching fire!) and opened the fridge to reveal the basic foodstuffs placed within: milk, eggs, butter, marmalade, sugar – sugar?

"Keep the sugar in the refrigerator," she advised, pre-empting me. "Ants, you know?"

She closed the fridge and opened one of the pantry's small glass doors to list off other basics like cooking oil, salt and tea. Finally, she whipped the lid off the bread box to reveal a loaf.

"Fresh this morning. The bread here's not wonderful, but you get used to it. (I recalled the rock-hard toast). Use the oven grill to make toast. Someone will take you shopping for anything else you want. People go into town every day. There's a butcher's and supermarket. Oh, and make sure you boil all your drinking water. Sometimes it goes off, but not for long, usually. The power can go off, too, especially during a storm. Keep candles handy."

I nodded, trying hard to process everything, and not to shame myself and my country by throwing a massive, fists-beating-on-the-floor tantrum. *Take a deep breath.* "Thank you both. For all your kindness."

The 'house' was not what I had expected at all, and I felt a crushing sense of disappointment. Whoever the Mullins were, I hated them on principle.

"Well," said Nora, "that's that then. We'll leave you to unpack your things and settle in. No doubt people will be dropping by to welcome you. Elizabeth's right next door. She's the other single one."

"Older, though," said Frances.

"Yes," replied Nora. "She's older."

"There's only one other single person here?" I asked, feeling even more depressed.

"Yes. Miss Coughlan. Our typing teacher." Frances pressed the keys for the flat into my hand. "Now we must be going."

As we began to retrace our steps, I pointed to a door almost concealed in the gloom at the far end of the passage.

"What's in there?"

"That's a little closet, for storing things, like your suitcase once you've emptied it, and" – she smiled – "your hiking gear, when it arrives."

I escorted the nuns out and intervened before they could begin wrestling with my bag again, insisting that I'd take it from there. Nuns doing luggage detail didn't sit well with me. Frances paused as she opened the car door, turning back to address me, her face serious.

"We don't expect you to start work immediately," she said. "You'll need time to recover from your journey. Tomorrow's Thursday, so take tomorrow and Friday, then you'll have the weekend as well to get thoroughly rested and you can start work next Monday. I will call in at some stage to discuss your classes with you."

I nodded miserably, putting on a brave face. Then the two nuns drove off, leaving me alone for the first time since I'd left New Zealand. Alone, disoriented, bewildered.

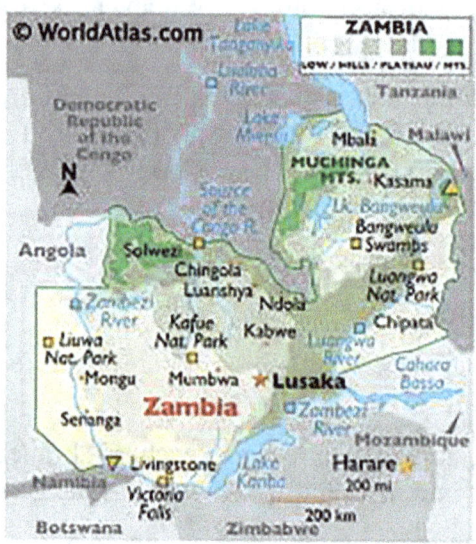

Looking around the fenced compound, I noted that it was rectangular in shape with just the one entrance gate and a roughly discernible gravel track, interrupted by grassy patches, running centrally through the interior. There was a respectable distance between the flats and houses so that we were by no means living on top of each other. There were also some shrubs and trees dotted about, including a lovely shade tree with a bench seat underneath it opposite my flat, and what looked like a banana palm outside one of the houses to my left. Off to my right there was an open-sided shelter on poles that apparently served as a communal car port, although there was only one vehicle parked under the rusted corrugated iron roof, a blue Datsun. Other vehicles were parked outside houses. At one end of the carport was a sagging clothesline I assumed I'd be sharing with Elizabeth.

This was not how I imagined my living arrangements would look, but there was little point dwelling on that now.

Expat Blues

I humped my suitcase into the sitting room, set it down, and stood for a moment looking around the odd little flat, trying not to linger on the bizarre pink fireplace bricks. I observed there was no grate in the hearth, but there was a hearth brush and dustpan to one side. *This is my home for the next two and a half years.*

The thought sank like a stone to the bottom of my heart. Oh well, nothing for it now but to go and unpack. I hefted up my suitcase, instantly listing to starboard with the weight of it, took a deep breath, and headed for the bedroom where I hauled my worldly possessions up onto the bed, and stood scratching my head, trying to remember where I'd put the keys to gain access to them. They were tucked away safely somewhere in a zipped pocket of my crossbody bag that held my passport, vaccination certificate, travelers' cheques and other sundries.

As I unpacked, I thought about my meagre savings that I'd transferred to a bank in Livingstone, wondering if they'd arrived safely. I was going to need a car since the school and teachers' compound were some distance from town, and I hadn't observed any buses on the way in. Carmel's original letter had stated that I was entitled to a loan to buy a car under the terms of my contract. I filed those concerns away for the time being and concentrated on getting my clothes and personal items stowed away.

The wardrobe provided ample space for my clothing with shelves on one side, closet compartment on the other, and there were plenty of coat hangers. On one shelf, the nuns had kindly provided spare sheets and pillowcases, and there were extra bathroom towels beside them. I used the small chest of drawers to accommodate nighties, underwear etc. It didn't take long for me to sort my belongings. I'd never had much in the way of clothes or possessions, anyway, having been mostly a poor student up to this point in my life. I hoped I'd be able to purchase some extra clothing in Africa to supplement my modest wardrobe.

When I'd finished unpacking, I changed out of my travelling clothes (I'd worn skirt, blouse and lace up shoes to meet my employers), into more comfortable jeans and a T-shirt, slipping my feet into jandals (called flip-flops outside New Zealand, I was to learn) and then thought about making myself a cup of tea to lift my spirits. I also thought I'd better write to my family and let them know I'd arrived safely. It was all snail mail back then, or telegrams and phone calls. My house didn't have a telephone as far as I could see. Something else on my mental list to ask about. If I could get to town I could send them a telegram, but the hurt from my father's cruelly dismissive farewell at the airport, which my mother would have approved, was still raw. Either Mum made the bullets, which Dad then fired, or Dad made the bullets and Mum rubber-stamped them. That's how they worked. I decided they could wait for a letter, which would take about two weeks to get there, depending on how soon I could post it.

Before making my restorative cup of tea, I carried my empty suitcase from the bedroom down the hallway to the storage closet Nora had indicated. When I opened the door, it was so dark inside the small, windowless space that I couldn't see anything. A quick grope around the doorframe revealed the light switch, and I flicked it on.

For a moment, I stood rooted to the spot, the suitcase falling from my hand, then I retreated slowly backwards away from that grim cavity and the denizens dwelling within, now so brutally exposed in their lair. Four or five very large spiders, roughly saucer size, were dotted about the walls of the narrow, rectangular concrete box. They were thin and flat, legs splayed around their roughly circular bodies, mottled grey in color, and visibly twitching in the sudden invasion of light. Once the initial shock subsided, I sprinted for the kitchen and grabbed the can of insecticide. Sidling back up to the closet door, I sprayed liberal amounts into the interior, then shoved the suitcase in with my foot, yanked the door shut and switched off the light. I've never liked killing creatures, but this was a them-or-me scenario, and I'd always suffered from arachnophobia, anyway. God, were they poisonous? All sorts of beasties had probably taken over the place, given its age.

To calm my nerves, I made some tea in a pretty pink and white china teapot I found in the glass fronted cabinet along with matching cups and saucers, and wandered back into the sitting room, where I studied the furniture as I sipped and thought that things might be improved if I moved items around a bit. Placing my tea on the dining table, I started with one of the drab red chairs, pulling it away from the wall with the intention of sliding it further along to the right, since it was somewhat oddly jammed up against the china cabinet. To my horror, I saw that it had been concealing a reddish-brown stain that stood out starkly against the pale green wall. The stain resembled a multi-branched tree that protruded a couple of millimeters or so beyond the wall's surface and seemed to be heaving with some kind of living creatures. Peering closer, I saw dozens of tiny white translucent bodies scurrying about the weird structure. Termites, I guessed, backing away in disgust. Wasn't the whole purpose of concrete meant to deter such critters? I slammed the chair back against the wall to conceal this latest nightmare and sank down onto one of the dining table chairs, groping for my steadying cup of tea. What other unsavory creatures dwelled within these walls? As if in answer, I caught a movement from the corner of my eye and swiveled my head to see a little lizard darting across the ceiling. Its splayed toes told me it was a gecko. We had lots of those in New Zealand and I thought them beautiful. I was okay with lizards. One time I saw a chameleon in a tree near the school, rolling his eyes independently as they do, and performing his weird little forwards/backwards rocking motion. I was enchanted.

At that moment, there was a knock at the door, and I opened it to find a painfully thin middle-aged woman standing on the stoop.

"Hello," she said, extending a hand, "I'm Elizabeth Coughlan, your next-door neighbor."

I greeted her, shook her hand, and ushered her in, inviting her to join me in a cup of tea, which she accepted. I made a fresh pot, and once we were both seated, she asked me how I liked the place so far. I told her I was feeling pretty miffed because some people called the Mullins had scored my new house.

Elizabeth drained her cup and replaced it on the saucer. "It was never going to be a house for you," she explained in her soft Irish accent. "It was to be a flat like ours here, only much newer, one of two on the other side of the compound." She waved a hand languidly to indicate the direction. "The Mullins are in the flat because *their* new house is still being built. You can see it from your kitchen window. It's almost finished."

Okay, I'd missed that one. "But Carmel definitely said I'd have a *house*."

Elizabeth smiled. "Well, it's a moot point, I suppose. You and I are in flats, that's for sure. The single people get flats, the couples get the houses. The Mullins went into the newer flat because Maureen, the teacher you've replaced, was still in here when they arrived."

"How could a married couple with two kids fit into one of these, even temporarily?"

Elizabeth chuckled. "With great difficulty. Their kids are sleeping on tiered bunks in the hallway. Mind if I smoke?"

Elizabeth lit up and I passed her the ashtray. "Perhaps I'll be able to transfer to the new *flat,* then?"

"I wouldn't count on it." Elizabeth blew a cloud of smoke towards the ceiling. "And anyway, those flats are a bit isolated in the far corner of the compound, too close to the fence for my liking. We're more secure here."

"So, who's in the other new flat?"

"Rahnee and David Paul and their little girl, which is also a squash. The school's expecting a new girl from Ireland who should be here soon, another English teacher. She'll move into the flat the Mullins vacate."

So, the Irish girl, even though she's arriving later than me, a no-account Kiwi apparently, gets a new flat! My bitterness reached critical mass, but before I could express it, there was another knock on the door, and I opened it to find two more women who introduced themselves as Nora Mullins and Mary Browne. I did my best not to be too icy towards this second Nora. After all, it wasn't her fault that she and her kin had stolen my house/flat from under my nose, but that did nothing to ease my hurt and the sense that I'd been totally conned – in the most charming way, of course.

Elizabeth excused herself and the two younger women sat down on the settee, while I went off to make yet more tea.

"Early days, but settling in okay?" asked Nora between sips.

I decided to avoid any mention of my housing rancor. "Well, I was pretty shocked by the size of the spiders in the storage closet."

Both women laughed.

"You'll get used to them. Are they the big flat ones?" Mary asked.

I nodded.

"Well, no worries. I was scared of them at first, too, but now I don't take any notice of them. They're totally harmless old house spiders. They just stay up on the walls and they're your best friends, really, because they keep the other insects down, like mossies. Same with the geckos."

I sighed. "That's what Elizabeth said." I felt like a hysterical neophyte, not to mention mean for trying to kill my apparent allies, however repulsive. I also wondered how many insects those spiders could dispatch skulking in the closet, not that I wanted them joining me in my living quarters.

I wasn't having my grievances dismissed altogether, though. "What about this, then?" I leaped up and with a flourish whipped aside the chair covering the weird bronchial structure and its seething inhabitants.

Mary and Nora leaned in closer for a better look.

"Nasty," said Mary.

"Termites," said Nora. "They won't hurt you either. Tell the sisters to let Brother Joe know. He's in charge of all the building and maintenance, so I'm sure he could remove the nest."

"You'd think they would have been removed before my arrival," I retorted grumpily. "Did Maureen never complain about them?"

Nora shrugged. "Just cover them with the chair for now," she advised. "Probably won't get any bigger."

I did as she said, and both women stood in unison. "We're going into town to do a bit of shopping," announced Nora. "Would you like to join us, have a look around?"

"Is the bank open?" I asked. "I'm keen to check if my savings transferred okay."

"Afraid not," replied Mary. "Today's half day at the banks."

"Is there more than one?"

"There's the Standard and Barclays. Which one are you with?"

"Pretty sure it's Standard."

Mary frowned. "Barclays is better. All the teachers are with Barclays. I work there, actually. Once you've tracked your money down, we could change you over, if you like."

"Sure."

I fetched my keys, locked the door to the flat, and followed Mary and Nora to the car, a nice station wagon belonging to the latter.

"Is it easy to get a car here?" I asked, sliding into the back seat. "Carmel said I could get a loan."

"You need to talk to Nell Gibbons," replied Nora over her shoulder. "She works at the Mazda dealership in town. That's if you want a new one. It can be difficult to find good secondhand cars, unless you know of some expats who are leaving. Don't buy a car from an African. They never service them."

We drove past the convent and school. The girls were standing around in groups or strolling together, waiting for afternoon study to commence. As they'd done previously, some waved as we drove past.

"They know there's a new teacher coming," said Nora. "They'll be dying to meet you."

After we'd passed by the little multi-colored 'council' houses and turned onto the seal, I noticed for the first time the huge concrete drains on either side of the road.

"What are those enormous gutters for?" I asked.

"They're stormwater drains," answered Mary. "There's a really big catchment here during the wet season."

"Wet season?" I braced myself for more depressing news, mindful of Carmel's 'Zambia in the Sun' brochure. "When's that?"

"From November through to April," Mary explained.

I did a quick calculation. "Six months!"

"Yes, that's the climate here. Six months dry, six months wet."

"So, we're in the dry now, right?"

"Yes, it's sort of their winter at the moment. Chilly mornings and balmy days around the low- to mid-seventies Fahrenheit."

"Then in August it starts to get *really* hot," chipped in Nora, "and September is called 'the suicide month'."

"Why's that?" I asked wearily, not really wanting to hear the answer.

"Because it's so darned hot the locals go loopy and top themselves. Hanging's the favorite method, although others jump off the Falls. They feel the heat worse than we do, you know; their black skin absorbs it more."

I subsided into the car's upholstery with a despairing sigh. *Swell. Dead Africans swinging from the trees or floating down the Zambesi. Six months of deluge. Giant spiders leering from the walls of my dismal 'house' while termites gnawed their way through those walls. My cup runneth over.*

By the time we reached the little township, the commercial hub of Livingstone, Mary and Nora had explained that, in addition to the banks closing every Wednesday afternoon, all the shops shut every day from 12 'til 1.30 p.m. for a siesta. It was common to have lunch and then rest or even nap a while, a colonial hangover, I supposed. They also explained that most of the shops and businesses were owned by Indians, a reality that created considerable tension with the locals, increasing since independence. Like most African countries, Zambia had a large Indian community.

Nora parked in one of the many angled car parks fronting the shops, and as I got out, I glanced up at the sign directly in front of us. Livingstone Meat Supply.

"The meat here's not great quality," said Mary, heading for the shop's door, "but it's all right if you know the best cuts to buy and your cook's a good one."

'Cook'? People actually had cooks?

We stepped inside and my nostrils baulked as they tried to process the overpoweringly stale smell of butchered animal flesh and sawdust. There were lots of African customers queued in front of the white-tiled counter, and much haggling going on with the servers.

"Trying to get meat scraps," whispered Nora, behind her hand, "but they're not easy to come by. The butchers take most of them home for their own families. It's part of their salary. Before independence, they could only shop from a side door of the building under a sign saying, "Dogs and Africans"."

"Mother of God!"

As Mary and Nora were making their purchases, I gazed idly around, and suddenly froze when I saw the large poster that adorned one wall. It was a striking advertisement for New Zealand lamb! The very last thing I had expected to see deep within the interior of the southern African continent. I felt a lump rise in my throat and my eyes prickled.

"Do you like a curry?" asked Nora suddenly from beside me. "You're welcome to come and have dinner with us tonight."

"Thanks, I'd love to," I said, swallowing hard and blinking furiously. I pointed to the poster. "They sell New Zealand lamb here," I squeaked.

Mary, having joined us, wrinkled her nose. "Ah, it's not good quality, third grade perhaps, and it's deep frozen, takes days to thaw." She laughed. "Not trying to put you off or anything."

We left the butcher's and went a few yards along the street to the supermarket, which was bright, spacious and well-stocked. I browsed the shelves while Mary and Nora took baskets each and made their purchases. They offered to pay for anything I needed, but if I was going to Nora's for dinner, then I was alright for the moment, so I declined. I had no Zambian money and no way of obtaining any with the banks closed. Nora kindly offered to bring me back to town the following day so that I could find out if my funds had arrived.

Expat Blues

In the check-out queue, a European woman ahead of us had a little monkey, wearing a collar and leash, perched on her shoulders, its bright inquisitive eyes darting around and over the other people in the store as it nibbled on a treat. The supermarket sold an intriguing array of non-food products as well: old fashioned style Chinese made bicycles, a variety of black enamel and cast-iron pots and pans ranging from witch's cauldron size to smaller ones, and formidable non-electric cast metal irons with flip-up lids to enable you to put your hot coals inside. Clearly, the local women, like the ones living in Maramba township, had to contend with some pretty primitive domestic conditions, no electricity, for starters.

The little town center impressed me with its wide, clean streets and leafy boulevards. It was beautifully laid out with some impressive buildings, like the museum and post office. I wasn't on the wild frontier here, not by a long stretch, but it still had a homely smalltown feel to it. My overall impression of Livingstone was that it was a thriving, smoothly run community with a diverse population. Dodgy domestic arrangements aside, I felt certain I'd like it here.

Quaint and peaceful, Livingstone township.

"How far is it to the Falls?" I asked as we drove home, shopping completed. I was keen to visit one of the seven natural wonders of the world.

45

"About twelve kilometers from town, out the Falls Road," answered Nora. "They don't look much at this time of the year, though."

"Why not?" I asked, surprised.

"Well, the river's so low with it being the dry season that there's just a trickle of water flowing over. You can actually walk right across the top of the Falls, if you're brave enough. We'll take you for a tour on Sunday, if you like."

"Thanks, that would be great. Give me a chance to use my new camera."

Nora turned out to be an excellent cook and the beef curry was outstanding. She even had Bombay duck to sprinkle on top of it, and I hadn't seen that for ages. I met her two lively children, Helen and Angela, who'd been born in Zambia, and her husband, Peter, who taught science at the school. He was a skilled, amateur photographer, as it turned out and promised to help me with my new camera, a Miranda Sensorex, something of a prototype with split image focusing as well as a prismatic viewfinder. The family was indeed badly cramped in their temporary home, a flat identical to mine in layout, but contrastingly new and fresh in appearance. I made no mention of the housing confusion.

After dinner, once the kids were in bed, we were joined for coffee by Mary and her husband, Brendan. They brought along their three-month-old daughter, Sarah Louise, sleeping peacefully in her carry-basket. Brendan, a painfully thin Irishman, taught Math at St Mary's. He seemed to enjoy teasing the newcomer from New Zealand.

"Mary said you were scared of the big old house spiders." He grinned. "Wait 'til you meet the snakes."

"Snakes?"

"Did you meet Elizabeth yet?"

"Yes."

"She had one in her house, under her sofa."

Expat Blues

"God, was it poisonous?"

"Big spitting cobra," said Brendan smugly, extending both arms to full stretch to convey some idea of its length.

I gulped and asked the obvious question. "What happened?"

"The maid discovered it while cleaning, told Elizabeth, and they both ran screaming into the compound. Kuta, one of the houseboys, came running and hacked it up with his machete. Then he hung the pieces on the fence to scare other snakes away. Superstition, I guess. Africans *hate* snakes."

"Why?" As an avid animal lover, part of me felt sorry for the snake, sliced and diced in the middle of his nap.

Brendan delivered a pitying look. "Well, imagine if you live miles out in the bush and you get bitten by a venomous snake, nearest clinic a couple of days' walk away. Horrible, agonizing death. Snakes kill hundreds here every year."

For the remainder of the evening, Peter and Brendan vied with each other to see who could instill the most terror in the newcomer, as they described the hazards of life in the compound and Africa in general. The one I remembered mostly was Peter's story of the putsi fly. This was, he explained, an insect that liked to lay its eggs in the seams of your clothing while it dried on the washing line. It was, therefore, essential to have a reliable housemaid or houseboy who would iron every inch of your clothes meticulously, the hot iron destroying the eggs before they could hatch into larvae and burrow into your unsuspecting body while you were wearing said clothes. I was skeptical, but Nora assured me it was all true. She had discovered a strange blister on Peter's back, and when she looked closer, there was a putsi larva wriggling about in the fluid.

"I gave our housemaid a big rark up over that. Peter couldn't believe it when I squeezed out the worm and showed it to him."

On that note, I excused myself, saying I was rather tired, which was the truth, and thanking them for their kindnesses and hospitality. Brendan, who had a decidedly spiteful streak, mustered a parting shot.

"If you think those house spiders are scary, wait until you meet the hunting variety!"

I hurried away, not wanting to hear any more horror stories.

Nora, who had come out to see me off, called after me, "You must buy a good torch! It's dangerous to walk about at night without a torch."

I called back a thank you for the advice and picked my way carefully across the inky black compound in what I hoped was the direction of my flat, nearly falling into a bush in the process. It was with great relief that I found my front door and then almost jumped out of my skin when a torch was shone full into my face as I fumbled my door

keys. It turned out to be the night watchman, a stocky, middle-aged African man, who gave an apologetic grin. "Sorry, mad-um." My flat had been vacant for a while, so he was checking on the unaccustomed activity. I told him no harm done and that I was the new teacher/tenant. He grunted, nodded solemnly and shuffled away on his rounds. It was reassuring to know he was out there and being vigilant.

Following a quick wash, I undressed, got into my nightgown, and prepared for bed, closing the curtains and checking the doors one last time. Before I retired for the night, I did a tentative check on the hallway closet only to find the cluster of spiders still clinging happily to the walls, none the worse for being sprayed; in fact, I'll swear they leered at me triumphantly. I closed the door with a shudder. Clearly an inferior brand of insecticide. Okay, compromise; they could stay in there so long as they didn't come into my living quarters.

Back in the bedroom, I fastidiously tucked my mosquito net tightly around the perimeter of the mattress, leaving only a tiny aperture through which to crawl into the bed. The light switch was on the far wall, so I took a deep breath before plunging the room into darkness and scurrying over to the bed. After some fumbling, I found the opening and dived through it to slide between the sheets. Once I'd made sure the last bit of netting was safely secured under the mattress, I wiggled myself down into a comfortable position, made a conscious effort to relax, and began to mull over the events of the day. Had I been duped into coming here? What other surprises were in store for me? I'd find out soon enough, I guessed.

Outside, there was a deafening cacophony from the local insect population, and I wondered how I would ever manage to sleep through such a racket. But then a new sound emerged, swelled, and steadied into a rhythmical beat that formed a deep bass underlay for the shrill insect chorus, an unvarying, urgent tempo that throbbed through the night like the driven pulse of some savage beast – of the dark heart of Africa itself. In my already fragile state, to me the relentless drumming summoned up images of raw menace: gleaming spear points, spilled blood, dark magic, and I burrowed deeper under the bedclothes, my own heart pounding, feeling wretched and wishing I was back home in New Zealand amongst safe, familiar things. A disturbing poem called *The Congo* that I'd learned at school for a class recital sprang to mind, and I couldn't help but dredge up the terrifying imagery in excruciating detail.

> *Then along that river-bank*
> *A thousand miles*
> *Tattooed cannibals danced in files;*
> *Then I heard the boom of the blood-lust song*
> *And a thigh-bone beating on a tin-pan gong.*
> *And "BLOOD" screamed the whistles and the fifes of the warriors,*
> *"BLOOD" screamed the skull-faced, lean witch doctors,*
> *"Whirl ye the deadly voodoo rattle,*
> *Harry the uplands,*
> *Steal all the cattle,*
> *Rattle-rattle, rattle-rattle,*
> *Bing!*
> *Boomlay, boomlay, boomlay, BOOM!*

Despite my increasing neurosis, and the nocturnal clamor, I must have begun drifting off to sleep, because suddenly I was wide awake again, my ears acutely attuned to a scratching noise that was undeniably coming from *inside* the room. I sat bolt upright, fertile imagination running wild. Was it my arachnid 'friends' from the closet, approaching in tight formation, fangs glistening and hellbent on exacting a terrible revenge for my having doused them in insecticide? The light! I had to turn on the light, but in the same instant I remembered it was on the opposite side of the room and I had to cross that vast expanse of bedroom floor to reach it.

Mouth dry, heart pounding, I tore the netting loose and launched myself across the room, trying to execute the maneuver on tiptoe, expecting any second to make contact with something very nasty. I hit the wall with a gasp, groping frantically for the light switch. As I found it and light flooded the room, I pivoted around, ready to be terrified by what I might see. There was nothing. Not a thing. I almost laughed with relief, but at the very moment that my body, taut as a piano wire, began to relax, I saw it. It came out from under the bed, ambling along as if taking a routine midnight stroll. It didn't look that scary. I peered closer. It was some species of brown beetle with long, feathery feelers. I recoiled in disgust. Cockroach. It was an enormous specimen, so big that it was making the rasping noise I'd heard as it scuttled along. Then, another one, equally as large, emerged from under the bed, following in the wake of its companion.

I watched them for a few seconds, then lunged forward, stamping my foot hard on the tiled floor. The sudden movement and vibration had the desired effect, and they broke into a run, disappearing into the closet through the gap between the door bottoms and the floor.

Well, all we needed now was for the burrowing termites to break through the wall in a shower of ochre-colored plaster and the day was complete.

Feeling somewhat beyond caring at this point, I doused the light, groped my way back to bed, repeated the net tucking and flopped down on my pillow where I fell into deep, exhausted sleep.

I guess the cockies had the last word, though. I found their droppings, the size of mice excrement, liberally dotted about amongst my folded clothes in the wardrobe.

Chapter Five: Interim

The next morning, I was awakened by the sounds of people moving about the compound, calling greetings to each other, their footsteps crunching on the gravel. The teachers were heading over to school, spouses heading off to work in town, cars drove out, nannies and house servants arrived. I could hear children squealing, a dog barking.

I dozed for a while, then got up and made some tea and toast. I also ate one of the green oranges. It was tough to peel, but the flesh was pleasant enough, if a little on the astringent side. Were all the oranges here green, I wondered? I'd imagined there'd be all kinds of delicious exotic fruit available, but this turned out not to be the case. In Zambia, anyway.

There were now two of the big flat spiders in the kitchen, high up on the wall. I ignored them. "Must be gay spiders," I said to myself. "They've come out of the closet." This made me laugh out loud. I had quite a bit of hysterical laughter waiting to be released, I think. *Oh, come on, bit early to go troppo!* Why had they all been congregated in the closet in the first place? I never did figure that one out. Once I'd settled in, they spread themselves throughout the house and stayed there.

Breakfast over, I hunkered down back in bed for a while and read my book until it felt like time I was getting up, at which point I ran a bath and enjoyed a good soak. No way was I ever going to use that grim cupboard-cum-shower. Small house geckos with splayed toes and bright, bulbous eyes darted across the bathroom ceiling. I liked watching them. "Catch those bugs, guys!" I called.

Once refreshed and dressed, I made my bed, washed my dishes, tidied up a few odds and ends, and then looked at my watch. I sighed. It was still only 11 0'clock and I wondered how I was going to fill in the day stretching ahead. I opened the living room door as it was another brilliantly sunny day with no trace of cloud or breath of wind, and warm by antipodean standards. I decided I really liked this mild climate, for now anyway. I'd assumed I'd be coming to stifling heat, and I am not a person for high temperatures. Feeling pleasantly cool and comfortable in my jeans and T-shirt.

I settled myself at the dining table with a fresh pot of tea and wrote for a while in the diary I'd brought with me. This kept me busy for about half an hour, following which I made a light lunch of a boiled egg and buttered bread. I recalled that Nora Mullins had said she'd take me to the bank in the afternoon. Perhaps I'd be able to organize my car loan at some point, too. I was keen to be independent and explore my environs.

I sat mindlessly drumming my fingers on the table and at that moment Sister Frances appeared in the open doorway, a brown manila folder clasped to her breast.

I stood up to welcome her, and she inclined her head in that dignified manner of hers as she entered the room. Settling herself opposite me at the dining table, she declined my offer of tea.

"I've come to discuss your classes with you," she said, taking documents from the folder and spreading them out on the table.

For the next hour or so, she went over the classes I would be teaching and explained the timetable to me. The school day commenced at 7.15 a.m. in the winter, or dry season, and finished at 1 p.m. In the hot, wet season, school started and finished half an hour earlier. The day was divided into eight periods of forty minutes each, with half an hour for morning tea. Every school day began with a form time for each class, where a teacher checked the roll and led the class in prayer and a hymn. There were sometimes assemblies for the individual forms, she explained, and these would be called at a time that suited the principal. A full school assembly might be called for something like a special visitor. There was no assembly hall, she explained, so chairs were brought out onto the verandah for staff and the girls stood in ranks in front of them. Sister Frances informed me that I would be teaching twenty-nine periods out of the forty in a five-day school week. This was a heavy load, she elaborated, as most teachers taught only around twenty-four. She studied me for my reaction, but mindful of the heavy workload imposed on New Zealand teachers, where your few precious non-contact times were invariably used up covering for absentee staff anyway, I shrugged and smiled.

"Keep me out of mischief."

Sister nodded approvingly. "That load will be reduced when more teachers we are expecting finally arrive. You'll also be rostered on for afternoon and evening studies. It's only about once a fortnight or so. The roster is posted in the staffroom each week and staff are responsible for checking their duties."

With that out of the way, Frances gave me a breakdown of my actual classes. I had senior modern history, intermediate history, junior and senior English, and junior religious instruction. My eyebrows shot up at that one and I had to suppress a grin. Me, taking religious instruction? Okay, I'd been raised a Catholic, but I was hardly an exemplary one. I was going to feel a tad fraudulent.

Sister Frances rose to her feet, gathered up the documents, returned them to the folder, and slid it across the table towards me. It contained, she said, not just the information we'd discussed, but curricula for each of my classes clearly annotated to show me where they were at, a school handbook, and other material I needed to familiarize myself with. She advised me to visit the school, perhaps the following day, Friday, to pick up copies of the textbooks and resources the students used for each subject, and to familiarize myself with layout and classrooms before commencing work next Monday. Then, for the first time, she flashed me a smile, quite a warm one at that, and sailed out as proudly erect as a ship's figurehead.

I'd heard the bell ringing for end of school while Frances was with me, and she'd no sooner left than Elizabeth stood framed in the doorway. I invited her in, offering tea again, but she shook her head.

"Thanks, but my lunch is waiting. I've just popped in to ask if you have a maid yet."

"A maid?"

"Yes, everyone is expected to have home help. It's cheap, and it provides work the local Africans badly need. If you don't take someone on, you'll be pestered to death until you do. They keep tabs on all new arrivals and my maid, Edina, has asked me to approach you." She smiled. "You'll appreciate it when the weather gets hot, and you don't feel like lifting a finger."

Firstly, I was relieved to hear that Elizabeth ate, since she looked emaciated. Secondly, coming from an egalitarian culture, I did not feel a bit comfortable about having a maid running round after me. As Elizabeth watched me, waiting for an answer, I quickly decided I'd best go with the flow, even if it smacked of imperial elitism. What she'd said about providing work sealed it.

"No, I don't have a maid yet, but–"

"Oh, excellent!" Elizabeth clasped her hands together. "We can share Edina. She'll be thrilled with the extra money. She can come to you three days, me three days, alternating between us. I pay her ten kwachas a month, which is the standard rate, so if you pay the same, she will have doubled her salary."

"A kwacha's like a dollar, right?"

"Yes. The coins are ngwees. One hundred to the kwacha."

She backed towards the door. "I'll tell Edina to call on you to introduce herself and discuss her duties with you. Her English isn't great, but we get by, and she's very reliable."

I'd barely farewelled Elizabeth when the steady stream of visitors continued with the arrival of Nora Mullins.

"Ready to pop into town?" she asked.

"I sure am. Just grab my bag and passport."

To my great relief my money had arrived at the Standard Bank, although I'd lost about $300.00 I could ill afford on the transaction. I opened an account and withdrew some cash, deciding to leave for the moment Mary's recommendation that I transfer to Barclays. I also asked them to make up a cheque book for me.

I was very surprised to see a uniformed security guard patrolling at the bank's entrance, toting a submachine gun.

"Is that usual?" I asked Nora, "or has he been called up to guard my millions?"

Nora chuckled. "It's usual. The army are a strong presence, too. If they ever stop you at a checkpoint, be very cooperative."

Walking back to the car, I was surprised when two young African men strolled past us holding hands. "Is *that* usual?" I asked Nora.

"It's just a part of the culture. Doesn't mean they're gay. They're probably friends, or maybe related. You won't see men and women holding hands, though."

So much to learn.

"We'll go to the supermarket now and you can do a shop."

The next few days passed quickly as I was invited to most of the remaining teachers' houses for meals, being newly arrived, the only Kiwi in town, and hence flavor of the month. Apart from Elizabeth, there were no other singles, although I was assured there were quite a few working at various schools around the township or involved in other areas of expertise.

One Irish couple, Kay and Tony Long, had me over for dinner and then insisted on taking me to the Intercontinental Hotel down by the Falls. It was known in the local lingo as Mosi-o-Tunya, 'the smoke that thunders', which is how the Africans described the Falls to David Livingstone, who then named them after his queen. Most expats referred to the hotel as 'the Mosi'.

"The smoke that thunders".
Spray from the Falls rising above the bush line during the wet season.

Two enormous soapstone lions couchant flanked the front doors, flanked in turn by flaring torches. Inside, the building was opulently furnished in what I would tongue-in-cheek describe as 'African baroque', featuring spectacular masks, giant carvings, wall-mounted heads of animals like buffalo and antelope, alcoves with beautiful native pottery, and a rattan awning with hurricane lamps above the polished wooden bar… just in case you missed the point that you were in Africa. Most of the furniture was made of bamboo, and shimmering draperies in colors of red, gold and turquoise abounded, reinforcing the exotic ambience. The overall effect was stunning.

After a drink in the straw-hut themed Jungle Bar, we went into the dining room where guests and visitors were eating, drinking, and dancing to the resident Congolese band, who were all wearing white tuxedos and red bowties. Tony pointed out (female) characters of local interest, like two striking colored girls, Lorna and Patty, who he claimed were "the town's good time girls, seeking rich white expat husbands". (Well, Patty eventually bagged an Italian working at the Fiat factory, who took her home with him. I don't know what became of Lorna).

Tony was particularly fixated on an attractive young British woman married to a sour-faced Italian who, according to the rumor mill, as relayed by Tony, physically abused her. He crossed the dancefloor to converse at length with her in her booth while her husband glowered. Meanwhile, Tony's plain, expressionless wife endured all this adulation of other women stoically. There was a palpable, brittle hostility between the pair that made me feel uncomfortable. The highlight of the evening was when a tall, slender Frenchman clad in skintight black clothing asked Patty to dance ("He always does," Tony assured me) and the pair lit up the dancefloor with a sinuous display.

However, I found myself unable to relax and enjoy the evening because the Longs had a little girl of about thirteen months, and I'd been shocked when they'd locked her in the house alone, albeit asleep, and proceeded out for the evening.

"What if the baby wakes up?" I asked.

"Oh, feck it, she'll be fine for a few hours. We do it all the time," was her father's response, as he tossed back another drink.

Her mother seemed equally unconcerned, but I felt uneasy all evening and was relieved when we finally returned to the compound, not just for the baby's sake but because Tony was well oiled, and his erratic driving had reflected this.

"The feck of a night watchman locksh the gatesh around midnight," he growled as we drove in. I glanced at my watch. The baby had been left alone for over four hours. I made a mental note to give the Longs and their clearly desperately unhappy union a wide berth. My analysis was confirmed by Mary who told me later, on the quiet, that the Longs' marriage had been one of coercion in true Irish Catholic tradition because of unplanned pregnancy, and the poor little child was the innocent victim of their mutual loathing for each other. Tony taught math at St Mary's while Kay worked in town, so the baby was with her kindly African nanny, Vivian, until noon most days. After that she was relegated to her own devices by her uncaring parents, and I often saw her tiny blonde-haired form parked outside by the back door for hours on end, slumped in her stroller, wretchedly sucking her little fist without so much as a whimper. She'd clearly learned during her nighttime abandonments that crying brought no comfort.

On the weekend, the Mullins family took me down to the Falls, officially the world's largest, for my first viewing. Because it was the dry season, only a series of thin, disconnected cataracts trickled over the 350 feet high rock face, but it was still a grand sight. Near the Falls was a curio market where the local carvers displayed their skills. They were master craftsmen, and I acquired many beautiful pieces during my time in Africa, not just in Zambia but elsewhere on my safaris. You were, of course, expected to bargain strenuously, and it took me a while to get the hang of that.

Also close to the Falls was the Livingstone Cultural Centre, where you could laze away an afternoon seated in the shade with a cold drink while being treated to colorful displays of traditional dancing, drumming and singing.

Finally, we visited Livingstone's game reserve. This could not be called a 'game park' in the true African sense of the words, because it was too small and surrounded by high fencing, hence the term 'reserve' instead. Nevertheless, it covered an expansive area and embraced a good variety of wildlife which included rhinos, zebra, antelopes, giraffes and some big cats – lions, leopards, and cheetahs – in a caged off area. The cheetahs were very tame and rushed the wire for petting and head rubs. It made me sad to see the cats confined. The reserve admin did try to keep an elephant at one stage, but no doubt lonely for her herd, she kept breaking through the fence and they had to give up.

The Falls during the dry season.

Sunday morning, I got a lift to attend Mass at St Theresa's Cathedral in town, where I ended up wedged between an impressively buxom black lady and a restless child whom she insisted on chastising by leaning across me to administer slaps and hissed 'tut-tuts'. I had the breath squeezed out of me several times and was much relieved when the service ended! It hadn't entirely been a crushing experience, though, as I'd enjoyed the beautiful singing and seeing the men, women and children in their colorful Sunday finery. I felt drab by comparison. Outside church, I was introduced to the celebrant, Father Jude, a towering Irish Cistercian priest who, I was later informed, had, as a youth, represented

Expat Blues

Ireland in boxing at the Olympic Games. One of his opponents had been a young Cassius Clay. I remember glancing down at his bare feet, clad in their sturdy leather sandals, and marveling over the longest toes I'd ever seen on a person, especially the two big ones.

On Sunday night, I met the Gibbons when they invited me for dinner. John, who wore snappy safari suits and leather sandals, was Head of English at St Mary's and therefore my HOD. Nell, his wife, who was heavily pregnant with their first child, worked in town in the office of the Mazda dealership. A quietly spoken, refined couple, the Gibbons employed a dignified, elderly houseman who cooked their evening meal before donning his tattered sports coat and bicycle clips for the journey home. Bicycles were a popular mode of transport in Africa and the local shops had hundreds of them for sale, all identical – black, shiny and old fashioned in style – and all made in China.

Before the evening ended, Nell arranged to pick me up after school on Monday and drive me into her place of work so that I could have a look at the available vehicles. They were Japanese imports, regularly driven up in convoy from Beira in Mozambique, and they'd just received a new batch. I told her I'd try to see the school's bursar in the morning of the same day to organize the promised loan. I needed another K800 before I could purchase a new car. What I really lusted after was one of the new Toyota Land Cruisers I'd seen for sale at another dealership, but one of those cost K3,000, which, while it may seem ridiculously cheap now, was way out of my league then.

I thanked the Gibbons for their hospitality and picked my way through the darkness back to my flat, which as luck would have it was directly opposite their house.

Nell called after me, "You must get a—"

"Torch!" I finished. "I'll buy one tomorrow!"

As I painstakingly tucked my mosquito net around my mattress that night, I could think of nothing except the following day and my first encounter with the school routine. I'd visited the site in a quiet moment to get my bearings and had spent hours preparing what I hoped would be interesting lessons. Nevertheless, I had a restless night as one always does prior to the first day on a new job. The drums started up again and coupled with the racket from the insects plus an overactive imagination conjuring all sorts of hideous nocturnal denizens eager to get at me, it was not an environment conducive to sleep.

Chapter Six: School

The next morning, I was up early, allowing myself plenty of time to get to school. I wanted to make a good impression on my first day. I knew Sister Frances would almost certainly have her eye on me, as would Sister Carmel and all the other teachers. I hadn't met any of the Indian teachers, yet, apart from Rahnee and David Paul, who lived in our compound with their young daughter. Rahnee taught science at St Mary's, while David worked elsewhere. I'd met them in passing only. The bulk of the Indian teachers, all Christians, lived in another school compound on the far side of the convent.

Taking a deep breath, I gathered up my books and papers, locked my door, and headed out across the compound, through the double chain link gates towards the school building, which was no more than a few hundred yards away. As I approached the school, it struck me again how Spanish in design it appeared, but later on, when I'd been in Africa a while, I realized it was not Spanish but influenced by the Dutch colonial style. Maybe that style had Spanish influence, though, since Spain had ruled the Netherlands for nearly two hundred years.

The building was shaped like a capital E with the middle phalange missing, white stucco with red roof and sills and a delicately curved gable rising in the middle above a red brick archway. A smooth concrete verandah, its sloping roof supported on rectangular columns ran along all three interior sides. As was common with so many African buildings, a contrasting border – this one deep red – ran along the base of the exterior walls. The classrooms, which all opened out onto the verandah, had windows on both sides, overlooking wasteland and bush on the exterior side, and overlooking the verandah and school front garden on the interior side. A neat gravel path bordered by low shrubs ran from the road that separated the school from the convent up to the main verandah steps, which in turn lead up to a pair of heavy wrought iron security doors below the gabled section that housed the administrative area and Carmel's office. The staffroom was situated to the right of these doors. A large statue of the Virgin Mary stood on a pedestal in the middle of the path, which divided around her before blending again. There were many trees in the grounds, including a magnificent jacaranda that loomed over one end of the verandah and exploded into fiery red blossoms every year during the hot season.

A block of extra classrooms with a library and science lab had been added, positioned parallel along one side of the main building and constructed of the same white stucco with red features. All the external walls of the buildings had a uniform muddy stain running alongside them, about two feet above ground level and doubtless caused by the seasonal heavy rains throwing up splatter from the ochre-red soils. Along the front edges of the verandah were a series of attractive wrought iron planters rising to about waist level, painted white and overflowing with colorful flowers. Overall, it was a very pleasant school environment.

I let myself into the staffroom, where I was apparently the first to arrive. This area was quite small and simply furnished. In the corner opposite the door was a large open cupboard divided up into pigeonholes named for individual teachers, and a closer inspection revealed that my name had already been added. Next to the cupboard, a set of shelves held a modest collection of reference and resource books for the staff. There was a red vinyl sofa with four matching chairs grouped around a coffee table in the center of the room, and at the far end an old dining table with a cluster of bentwood chairs surrounding it served as a teachers' workspace. Attached to the wall at one end of the table were a series of hanging plastic pockets surmounted by the word 'Mail'. Each pocket had a series of letters of the alphabet painted on it and I looked wistfully at the top one marked 'A – D'. It was empty. I'd written to my family, placing my letter with the sisters' post since I couldn't easily get to town and the post office, but I knew it would be at least a month before I received a reply. This was not the age of computers, the internet, or cellphones; all we had was 'snail mail'. None of the teachers' houses had telephones. The nearest ones were at the convent or the school office.

With a sigh, I sat down at the worktable and began to revise my timetable and teaching notes. The teachers started to drift in, and introductions were exchanged with those I hadn't yet met. The female Indian teachers all wore beautiful, brightly colored saris and lots of gleaming gold jewelry. Through the windows, I could see the girls in their impeccable white blouses and blue pleated skirts, trooping across to the school to prepare for classes. A group of them sprang aside to make room for Sister Carmel, picking her way along the gravel path in her trademark high heels.

Sister Frances looked in the door, gave me a peremptory nod, and disappeared. I was timetabled to begin teaching period two, junior history, the United Nations. Each period was forty minutes long, four before interval, four after. Interval itself was thirty minutes, which I thought particularly civilized. The girls needed the time to get over to the boarding school dining room, have their morning tea, and wash up their dishes before returning to classes.

As the school day got underway, heralded by vigorous bell ringing, I enjoyed listening to the hymns the girls sang to accompany their form time prayers. Beautifully harmonized versions of Rock Of Ages, What A Friend We Have In Jesus and Ave Maria drifted across the sunny, early morning environs. Another glorious, cloudless day with not a breath of wind. I really loved the climate – thus far, anyway.

At the end of each period, a senior girl appeared and rang the brass bell that resided for the purpose on a little white table near the main entrance. Period one passed quickly, and the bell announced the beginning of my working career in Africa. I found the classroom easily enough since I'd done a quick recce of the school and its layout the previous Friday, following afternoon study, when I'd been lucky enough to bump into Carmel who'd given me a conducted tour. The students stayed in the classroom designated for their level – doors all clearly labelled – and the teachers moved around – the opposite of the system I'd been accustomed to at home, but identical to the one I'd been educated in. Taking a deep breath, I opened the door and stepped inside. Immediately, what felt like a vast number of black female adolescents rose as one to their feet and stood rigidly impassive, staring at me in stony silence. Quite unnerved by this display rivalling the military precision of a 'ten-hut!', I nevertheless advanced with what I hoped was an air of relaxed confidence to the middle of the room before turning to face them.

"Good morning, girls," I said brightly.

"Good morning, meestress", they intoned in perfect unison.

'Mistress!' I wasn't prepared for that one. "Please sit down," I instructed, and with the same almost robotic discipline they subsided quietly into their seats without so much as a rustle. I was amused to see that all the desks were of the old-fashioned heavy wooden type with hinged flip-up seats, hinged lids, and ink well cavities in the top right-hand corner. The convent school back in New Zealand where I'd been educated over a thirteen-year period had classrooms full of similar desks at primary level. No doubt these desks I was looking at had been donated to the Missions by foreign Catholic schools as they upgraded their own students' desks.

There must have been close to forty students in the class, all around 14 – 15 years of age. They were beautifully presented specimens of young African womanhood in their simple but attractive school uniforms. Most wore open-toed sandals or flip-flops on their feet and most wore their dense, frizzy hair cropped short, with many sporting intricately woven cornrow braids in various patterns. Some even had their hair drawn out in spikes around their heads, like some depictions of Topsy from Uncle Tom's Cabin, while others had hair fashioned into elaborate coronets or tiaras.

I put my books down on the teacher's desk, centrally placed on a dais in front of the blackboard and picked up a piece of chalk resting in a groove in the ledge.

"This is my name," I said, and wrote the words 'Miss Anderson' in large letters on the board. Underneath my name I wrote 'New Zealand' and explained, "This is my country. This is where I come from." I made a conscious effort to speak slowly and clearly.

Not a flicker. Their expressionless faces stared back at me. "It's a very small country," I added lamely. I drew a big circle and then on it a crude but recognizable free-hand African continent and wrote 'Zambia' in the middle of the southern section. Next, I drew

Australia, to provide a bit of context, and just south-east of it the two tiny islands of New Zealand. I labelled everything carefully for extra clarity and drew a picture of a little airplane following a curved trajectory to the middle of Africa before turning back to face the class. "Do you want to ask me any questions?" When there was no response, I strolled nonchalantly across the front of the classroom towards the opposite windows and forty pairs of large brown eyes swiveled to follow my movement. I about-faced to stroll back again, and the forty pairs of eyes swiveled in reverse. This was pretty disconcerting. I felt increasingly concerned.

They hate me. It's instant dislike.

I swallowed hard, picked up the class roll I'd been given and called the names in alphabetical order, trying to pronounce each one as carefully as possible. As I read a name, the girl in question leaped to her feet and replied "Yes, meestress." But not one corrected my pronunciation, even though I was certain I'd made gaffes. Most of them had English Christian names and African surnames. Some had quite odd names, like 'Nursemercy', 'Junior', 'Precious', Innocent' and 'Lovey'. Something had got lost in translation, I surmised. Biblical names were popular, too, like 'Esther', 'Rachel', 'Rebecca'. Having noted previously how the classrooms were arranged, I'd made several copies of a seating template, and now I carefully recorded each girl's first name in a separate square representing her desk. When I first began teaching back in New Zealand, I'd found this was the easiest way to familiarize myself with the students' names. Once I'd filled in all the names, I wrote their level and alphabetical designation at the top of the page: Form 4B.

"Okay," I' said once roll call was over and I'd erased my ill-received geography lesson from the blackboard, "today we are going to learn about the United Nations." I wrote the topic on the board, along with its acronym, circled it, and drew spokes radiating from the circle – simple brainstorming and mind mapping. Well, that was the plan.

"Now, hands up, who can tell me anything they know, anything at all about the United Nations?" Dead silence. You could have heard the proverbial pin drop, but even more disturbing was the rigidity of their body posture – not a muscle twitched, not an eyelid blinked. It was like addressing a class of zombies and utterly alien to anything I'd experienced in my brief teaching career. Needless to add, I filled in the mind map myself, burbling away all the while!

The pattern for the rest of the lesson, indeed the rest of the day had been set. I talked to myself and then listed relevant points on the blackboard. Every time I asked a question it was met with stony silence. If, working from my seating plan, I singled out a student to interrogate, I got the same result – impassive face and liquid dark eyes lowered quickly. *Maybe it's my accent. How much of this is actually going in?* I didn't know anything about TESOL at that point in my life. When I told them to copy down the summary notes, they quietly opened their exercise books and wrote in silence with painstaking neatness and concentration. As soon as the bell rang to end the period, they all leaped to their feet again chanting in perfect unison, "Good morning, meestress, thank you, meestress." It was stressless, but it wasn't my idea of teaching, which, after two years in the profession, I wasn't even confident was my métier. I still hankered after the notion of being a foreign war correspondent, dodging bullets as I reported back from the front line in helmet and Kevlar vest. 'Great romancer', I could hear my parents saying.

Morning tea was the highlight of the day. One of the African sisters who worked in the convent kitchen appeared punctually at break every morning bearing a large tray with a steaming enamel teapot, milk, sugar, teacups, saucers and teaspoons. But it was the cakes that impressed me. Every morning, without fail, we were presented with a plate of freshly baked cupcakes. Feather light – I think they contained lots of cornflour – yellow and buttery, they were plain but delicious and I always looked forward to them. That they never varied was their strength. Better was to come, though. If a pupil or pupils had earned some accolade – sporting, cultural, or academic – or if it was just to celebrate some special occasion, we were given a choice of tea or alcohol, usually bottles of sherry and Cinzano. This meant that the four periods after morning tea were often conducted in a bibulous haze, and it was not uncommon to see a class and their teacher dozing contentedly in the late morning

Expat Blues

heat, the girls taking full advantage of their tutor's lassitude. Sister Carmel worked hard to keep her staff happy and maintain morale, and we all appreciated her for it.

I managed to fit in a visit to the bursar, Sister Aloysius, and when the final bell rang, I walked back to the compound with Peter and Brendan. They asked how things had gone, but I gave little away. I decided I would talk to Sister Carmel and see what she had to say. Later, I learned that everyone had been impressed with how I'd handled myself on my first day! Really?

After lunch, Nell came over and asked if I was ready to go and see about the car. Feeling very excited, I assured her I had the money and showed her the cheque Sister Aloysius had given me for K800.00, the maximum loan permitted. Coupled with the savings I had transferred from New Zealand, I hoped I had enough to buy a car. Nell thought I would just scrape in. First, she took me to the Standard Bank to deposit the loan from St Mary's and pick up my cheque book I'd ordered. Then she drove me to the Mazda dealership where she worked, which was run by Europeans, and introduced me to her boss, who was a typical car salesman, gobby and condescending. Six months before I arrived, he claimed, a new Mazda 1300 cost K1,500, but now they were selling for K1,600 – ridiculously cheap by today's standards, of course. I had just enough cash to cover the cost and I'd still have to arrange insurance. Once I got my first monthly paycheck, I'd have some money, but our salaries were meagre because of our 'missionary' status, so there was some belt-tightening ahead. We lived in our houses rent-free and were not charged for electricity we used either. Those were the contract terms. Neither were there any telephone bills to pay as none of us had one. With my monthly pay of K200.00, I had to feed and clothe myself and pay for my living costs like petrol, entertainment etc. After the car loan repayment at K50.00 per month, I would be left with K150.00 to live on for that period. With the optimism of youth, I was certain I could survive. I had to. I couldn't ask my family for any help, financial or otherwise. My father had made that very clear. I *had* to have a car. There was a bus service in Livingstone, but it was shunned by expats. The buses had been ordered from Czechoslovakia and someone forgot to mention that the country used left side of the road driving. All the buses arrived set up for right hand side driving and were subsequently quite lethal and often involved in collisions. If I drove up on a bus signaling that it was pulling out, I always fell back and let it go because I knew the driver couldn't see me approaching his right side! I also learned quickly to ignore left- and right-hand signals as the African driver usually went in the opposite direction indicated by the flashing light! "Don't know reft from light," was the standard joke. (Explanation later in narrative).

Anyway, I digress. Within an hour all the paperwork was done, and I was the proud owner of a brand-new gleaming white Mazda 1300 two-door saloon. It was very different from the first car I'd owned back in New Zealand, a little secondhand Ford Prefect, and I'd never dreamed that I'd ever own a brand-new car. I made a feeble attempt to beat the price down a little, but the salesman wouldn't budge so I abandoned that. His only concession was that he'd put some petrol in it for me. Nell didn't speak up for me, but to be fair she couldn't oppose her boss. (She did defend me later on, though, when I discovered the car's new battery had been swapped out with a dud. Her boss grudgingly reinstated the new one). Even at the price, cars were clearly much cheaper in Zambia than in New Zealand. I wrote out the cheque and because it would take a couple of days to clear at the bank, I had to leave my brand spanking new baby where she was for pick-up later in the week, probably Thursday. Nell would keep me informed. I couldn't wait!

On the way home, Nell told me that I would need to buy third party insurance. She explained that full insurance was exorbitant so all the expats, unless they had lucrative contracts, settled for third party. In addition, she instructed, I'd need a Zambian driver's license. She warned me that because corruption was rife, I could expect to be failed the first time I sat the test. The fee would be pocketed by the tester who would then reschedule, pass me on the repeat, but only record the one test for audit purposes. Nell advised me to go along with the swindle as protest served no purpose other than to raise one's stress levels. Most Zambian civil servants were extremely poorly paid but usually had large extended families to support. Unemployment for Africans was high, and it was a cultural expectation that anyone fortunate enough to have paid work was expected to support any and all extended family members who gravitated his/her way, as well as his/her own immediate kin. On an average monthly wage of K30.00 this was a huge ask. The families all lived on sacks of mealie-meal at about K5.00 each with little variety of diet. Two meals a day was the norm, if you were lucky, and your nshima ('pap' in South African parlance) might come with some delele (okra) or chibwabwa (pumpkin leaves) on it, or it may not. In comparison, white expat workers were seen as rich and privileged, which many were.

Sure enough, when I did my driving test, I was failed first time on a technicality (not indicating a turn early enough, which was blatantly untrue) but was passed on the second attempt. I admit I did make a token protest. Getting the insurance, thankfully, was straightforward. Zambian bureaucracy, I quickly learned, could be very frustrating.

After I'd picked up my car, a manual transmission, of course, I drove around for a while to familiarize myself with its controls, did some shopping, and returned home. As I passed by the school, I could see the girls at afternoon study. The whole school had two study periods a day. Lunch and the hour or two afterwards were seen as a rest or siesta time and many people did have a snooze. I never could. Shops, businesses, offices closed, and a somnolent torpor settled over the town until everything reopened later in the afternoon. The girls had a break and carried out their boarding-side chores before attending first study from 3.00 p.m. until 4.30 p.m. In the evenings, after dinner, they had a second study period from 7.00 p.m. until 8.30 p.m. After that, it was time for supper and bed.

The girls were so motivated and self-disciplined that it was possible for only one teacher to supervise 400 girls (minus the Indian students who were all locals) for the entire study period. Monitors sat in with junior classes, but the seniors, young women of 18, 19 years, some older, were left to themselves. This meant we were rostered on for an afternoon or evening study only about once a fortnight. I enjoyed them as they were so peaceful. In between strolling the verandahs, I caught up on marking or planning, read a book, wrote letters, or just blobbed. Once evening study ended it was still early enough to head out for a drink and some socializing if you wanted to.

Sister Carmel was always around, keeping an eye on things, popping up out of the darkness unannounced or catching up on work in her office. If a teacher slipped up in any way, for example omitting to turn up for study or missing a deadline, he or she would invariably find a firm but tactful handwritten reprimand in his/her pigeonhole the following day. Sister Carmel was a superb diplomat and fiercely supportive of her staff. In return, she expected professionalism, loyalty and hard work.

At that time in Zambia, only 2% of primary school children went on to secondary education based on their test results, like the British 11+, I guess. The rest just dropped out. Many never attended school at all. To have the chance of a high school education was seen as an immense privilege and to be accepted for St Mary's was even more so as it had a reputation for being one of the best schools in the country. A lot of our third formers came from rural villages or shanty towns and had to be taught how to use a handbasin, shower, flush toilet and how to manage monthly periods with store-bought sanitary pads. They slept in proper beds and had three meals a day, often with stewed meat or fried kapenta (small, dried fish) on their nshima, real luxuries. They loved their school, respected their teachers, and many cried bitterly when it was time to leave.

We prepared the girls for two prestigious qualifications linked to the country's British colonial past: the GCE examination at third form level and the Cambridge examination at form five. The school frequently achieved 100% pass rates in these exams and teachers were expected to maintain them. Not all the schools, for example government co-eds, were so pleasant to teach in, but St Mary's had a well-deserved reputation for excellence, most of it the result of Sister Carmel's firm hand on the helm. She sometimes came across as quite harsh and overly strict with the girls, who were terrified of her, but she also had an in-depth knowledge of how African female teenagers worked and they certainly had a lot of respect for her. The previous principal had apparently had problems with mutinous students, resulting in an unfortunate incident when she was assaulted, but Carmel had restored the school's reputation. Now that Zambia was an independent black state, racial tensions had probably been somewhat mollified, I surmised. The government had a popular 'Zambianization' policy to gradually phase out white expats and replace them with Africans. Hence, Sister Frances was being groomed to take over from Carmel.

One of my fondest memories of Sister Carmel is when she would conduct spot checks on the lengths of the girls' uniform skirts. I learned fairly quickly that in Africa the female breast has none of the erotic aura it enjoys in Western culture. To African men breasts were old hat, but what got them really excited were a female's legs. Possibly, this was the result of the long-held custom which proscribed that a woman's legs should always be modestly covered, and the wrap around sarong called a 'chitenge' was the accustomed garb for a woman to ensure her legs were hidden from lustful male gaze. Malawi, I remembered, enforced this in law with heavy fines for offence, but Zambia was not so strict. One of my more humiliating experiences in Zambia occurred when, not yet having internalized the above cultural norms, I went into town in a pair of cut-off denim shorts and caused a near riot amongst the young bucks lounging about the shop fronts. I literally had to sprint for my car, face burning, and any notion of shopping abandoned.

At St Mary's the girls were allowed to wear their pleated blue skirts no more than one inch above the knee and Carmel was adamant that when kneeling, the hem of said skirt should brush the ground. The senior girls, beginning to assert their young womanhood were the worst offenders when it came to surreptitiously raising their hemlines and Carmel was fully aware of this. She would randomly swoop on a class and order several of them out onto the verandah. While they knelt obediently on the hard concrete, she would check each skirt with a long wooden ruler she kept for the purpose and any girl whose uniform didn't comply would be immediately dispatched boarding-side to unpick and lower the offending hem. Attempts to lean forward slightly or tug the skirt down from the waist to disguise non-compliance were futile. Carmel was onto every trick. The girls never protested once they were busted, but this didn't stop them trying again. Most of them were blessed with a statuesque build and long shapely legs, which they enjoyed flaunting shamelessly, the same way a western girl might wear a push-up bra, I guess. I loved to watch the way they walked, hips undulating, skirts flared over bottoms that curved provocatively away from ramrod straight backs. The swaying gait was so natural to them, but in some countries, they'd probably be arrested for it!

However, the absence of eroticism associated with the female breast involved some cultural adjustment, especially for the male teachers. Even as a woman, I found it quite perturbing at times the way African women breastfed their babies in public, for example in church or in the check-out queue at the supermarket. One day, I saw a woman perched on the edge of the gutter in the town's main street, nonchalantly suckling her child as traffic sped past. Going to the local cinema (or 'bioscope' as it was called all over southern Africa) was an initial culture shock, too. Not only was it acceptable to smoke while viewing, ashtrays jutting from the backs of the seats in front for the purpose, but African couples brought their unweaned babies along as a matter of course. As soon as a child whimpered it was put to the breast. This meant a film was commonly viewed through a haze of cigarette smoke while the dialogue competed with a muted chorus of steady sucking noises, accompanied by burps, belches and the wafting odor of a filled nappy.

At school, there were different problems associated with this cultural phenomenon. I vividly recall one occasion when Sister Carmel assigned a group of girls to dig over the front garden of the school as punishment for some misdemeanor. Each girl was given a grubbing hoe and the task of chopping through the tough elephant grass which had sprouted up following the early rains. The punishment detail quickly organized themselves into a line that stretched the length of the assigned area and set about their work, for an African woman truly knows how to work. Lifting and swinging in perfectly synchronized rhythm, they advanced across the garden, and, as they always did when involved in any group or communal activity, they sang exuberantly, their beautifully harmonized voices floating out across the school grounds. It was a hot, sultry morning, typical of the early rainy season, and the girls soon worked up a sweat. With unselfconscious pragmatism, they divested themselves of their white school blouses, and as was fairly usual, none of them had bothered with undergarments. Why would you when your breasts were as firm as a Greek statue's?

It wasn't long, of course, before the situation was reported to Carmel by a red-faced male teacher who had looked up from his desk to be horribly embarrassed by the nubile vision in the school's front garden. Carmel shot out of her office and once re-attired the girls were sulkily banished boarding-side to await her wrath when school finished at lunchtime.

For myself, I thought they had looked, and sounded, magnificent.

As the temperatures rose from August onwards, the final classes of the morning became a trying time for teachers and students alike. The sun beat down on the school's corrugated iron roofing like a hammer on an anvil, and there were no ceiling fans in the classrooms to alleviate the oppressive heat; air-con was not widely available. Windows on both sides were thrown open to the maximum, as were the doors, but there was no cooling breeze to waft in either. Everything and everyone baked in the stillness of the shimmering heat. I vividly remember writing on the blackboard with rivulets of sweat trickling down my back. By the final period of the morning, a general torpor enveloped the entire school and many students dozed peacefully with their heads on their desktops. Drooping themselves, their teachers generally indulged them. This was the danger time for another practice that horribly embarrassed the male teachers, all of whom were married men. Many of the girls unbuttoned and opened their school blouses trying to get some relief. As a woman teacher, this practice didn't bother me all that much, although we'd been given strict instructions not to tolerate it. I always did a grin when I witnessed a male teacher enter a classroom, only to exit again at high speed, flushed and indignant – not because of the heat – before returning with a grim-looking Carmel in tow. I sympathized with the girls because being black-skinned their bodies absorbed the heat more than ours did and they subsequently suffered more. Everybody sighed with relief when the final bell rang, and we could traipse off in search of a shady spot and a cold drink.

My other abiding memory of Sister Carmel McGill, although I treasure many, was seeing her marching resolutely along the road as I drove to or from Maramba. She frequently had business with the local office of the MOE, but she didn't drive and had no interest in learning. Refusing all offers of assistance from her fellow nuns – the convent owned several vehicles – she would set off to Livingstone township, tottering along in her improbably high heeled sandals, brown leather briefcase swinging from her hand. She never got very far before someone pulled over to offer her a lift as she was a well-known, well-respected local fixture. Apart from getting rides with teachers like me whenever we spotted her, she had no qualms about being hauled into the back of a dangerously overloaded, battered pick-up truck crammed full of beaming Africans and their children and always accepted a ride with typical grace and gratitude, seemingly oblivious to the anxiety she provoked in her colleagues, nuns and expat staff alike, with her itinerant stubbornness. The nuns knew she never had to walk very far, but they worried about her safety. Zambia had an appalling road death toll. A bend taken too fast, or a violent swerve, meant the unrestrained human cargo in the back of a crammed full pickup were hurled out onto the road with fatal results. Even in the cab there were no restraints. Seatbelts in cars hadn't been invented yet. If you were in a collision, you could expect to fly.

By the end of my first week at school I felt pretty despondent. Discipline wasn't a problem. The girls were attentive, polite and followed every instruction to the letter. If I asked them to hand in their books for marking, they brought them to me individually, each girl going down on her knees at my feet to present her work. After the final period of the morning, they'd squabble over who could carry my books across to my house. As soon as they spotted me in the mornings, I'd be rushed for the privilege of doing the reverse. When I checked homework, it was completed to a high standard always, without exception. They just seemed very guarded and unresponsive. I was worried that they didn't like me for some reason, so I decided to talk to someone about it and thought Sister Frances would be a good choice as she had the advantage of being African herself, and the girls loved her. As luck would have it, she was in her office when I visited, and put aside her paperwork to welcome me in with unaffected warmth. At Sister's invitation, I drew up a chair and she listened attentively while I unburdened myself, slow smile forming as she nodded her understanding.

"This is quite normal," she assured me. "To begin with, the girls will be shy and reserved with a new teacher until they get accustomed to you. They are just sizing you up, getting used to your ways and accent." She leaned forwards a little, speaking softly. "I promise you, they do like you and we are all impressed here at school, too."

I felt much relieved and thanked her for her kind words and encouragement.

"It's hard for them, you know," she added. "All their lessons are in English. They have to be since we have more than one tribal language here amongst the girls. They have to get used to Irish, British and Indian accents and now yours as well. We believe that only about forty percent of what is said in the classroom is actually comprehensible to them."

As I murmured my understanding, she drew herself upright, hands clasped in front of her on the desk and said, "Now, I'm pleased you came to me, but also for a different reason because I have a proposition to put to you. It's only two weeks until term holidays. Have you made any plans?"

I shrugged. "I haven't really thought about it."

"Well, one of our third form students, Grace Ndopu, has won a competition organized by the local Wildlife Association. All the secondary schools in Livingstone took part, with junior students writing an essay on the topic of conserving Zambia's wildlife, and Grace came first, which is a huge honor for her – and the school, of course. Her prize is three days in Kafue National Park, five including travel, but she needs a chaperone. I was supposed to go, but I have other commitments and I wondered if you'd like to accompany her. It's all expenses paid and is timed for the third week of the holidays. Grace will go home and then return in time for the trip. There would be no cost for you. Bob Dowsett, a British ornithologist at the Livingstone Museum, organized the competition and is hosting the safari. He's a very nice man."

I could hardly believe my luck! I'd been here no time and already I was being given the opportunity to go on a real African safari! I knew from Sister Carmel's brochure that Zambia had some of the best game parks in Africa, so this was a truly amazing bit of good fortune. How often had I fantasized about going to Africa and doing a safari? It was the fulfilment of a dream.

"I – I'd love to go," I stammered, barely able to hide my excitement.

Sister Frances looked pleased. "Thank you, Erin. I have been offered the opportunity to attend what I believe will be a very worthwhile seminar in the Copperbelt during the holidays, and the dates clashed."

Later, those words would return to haunt me most horribly.

Frances said she'd write down the dates and the specifics of the meeting arrangements and give them to me in due course. I couldn't wait to tell my family back in New Zealand.

I had barely absorbed Sister Frances' exciting news, when Carmel approached me to reveal more.

"The girls have organized a farewell concert for Sister Jessica tonight and we'd like you to come along," she said. "You haven't been officially welcomed to the school yet and the girls would like to combine that with Jessica's farewell."

I told her I'd love to attend.

"It's in the boarders' dining room," she added. "There won't be any study and the girls will come for you at seven o'clock, to make sure you don't get lost."

I returned home feeling quite buoyant. Two nice surprises in one day.

Promptly at seven, there was a gentle knock on the door, and I opened it to find two senior girls standing shyly on the stoop. They escorted me to the convent, shining their torches ahead of my feet to ensure I could see where I was going. *Damn! I still hadn't got a torch!* At the convent, the girls ushered me into the boarders' dining room, which had been rearranged for the evening's event, tables pushed to the side, chairs arranged in rows near the top of the room. All the nuns seemed to be there, but I couldn't see any expat staff. The girls led me to the front row and a seat alongside Sister Jessica, who gave me a sad little smile. Clearly, we were the guests of honor.

I hadn't had much to do with Jessica. She seemed to have a light workload and was seldom seen at school. A young nun, her health had suffered badly since coming to Africa and she had lost a lot of weight, becoming gaunt and frail in the extreme. No explanation had been given that I was aware of, although gossip I'd heard included words like 'breakdown' and 'fierce homesickness' or, more mysteriously 'Africa malady'. Anyway, it was decided that she must be sent back to Ireland before she deteriorated further, and arrangements had been made for her to convalesce in the Kenyan highlands for a few weeks before travelling on home. Hopefully, by the time she was reunited with her family she would look and feel better. Jessica was a well-liked teacher, so the girls had asked if they could give her a good sendoff. Perhaps Carmel hoped to defuse the sadness of the occasion by combining it with my welcome. If the girls were happy to welcome me to St Mary's, then they must truly have warmed to me. That thought cheered me immensely.

That evening was my first real introduction to the girls' talents. I'd heard them singing at school, of course, and always marveled at the way they could effortlessly organize themselves into a superbly harmonized group, but this night they really turned it on. Wearing their most colorful traditional clothes, they danced sang and played the drums in a mesmerizing display, clearly enjoying every moment of their performance as much as we did. Sister Carmel made a brief speech farewelling Jessica and welcoming me and then we had a simple supper of tea or fizzy drink with cake from the convent kitchen. The same two girls walked me back to the teachers' compound and waited until I was safely inside my house. When I thanked them, two sets of dazzling white teeth flashed in the darkness.

I was beginning to feel a part of the place, but I had a long way to go.

Chapter Seven: Maids, Borders, and Blue

Nowadays, when you take up a contract teaching overseas, you invariably do a preliminary orientation course administered by your employers to ensure your smooth transition into what is a foreign country and, often, an alien culture. I, on the other hand, was tossed in the deep end straight off following my arrival in Africa and had to rely on myself or what I was told by the old, or not so old, guard, who, I would later learn, often liked to have malicious fun at the greenhorn's expense. The first three months were hard, although I largely concealed that fact from everyone I dealt with. I've always been a head down, get on with it sort of person, but I struggled badly for a while.

The homesickness was the worst. And it always hit me first thing in the morning, when I got up to prepare for school. I couldn't bear to use the 'Auschwitz' shower as I'd named it, so I always ran a bath, and it was while I wallowed in the bath that I frequently felt overwhelmed with gnawing longing for home, tormented by random little images that flitted across my mind: my mum peeling vegetables at the kitchen sink, the willows by the Avon river that ran through the city, the old red tram car trundling through the streets, a particular building, a familiar beach, the cherry tree in our backyard bursting with fragrant spring blossoms. The Germans call it heimat; the Welsh call it hiraeth. It's a feeling impossible to define. Just as well I had no money and no family support, because I would probably have done a runner otherwise. I don't think anyone who has not experienced homesickness can fully appreciate the intensity of this unique feeling of desolation. And it dogged me for months before it eased. I've never been a quitter, anyway, so I guess the resilience I was forced to build up was further character strengthening.

I was still disappointed with my 'house' and still wary of the big flat wall spiders, (although I'd named some of them in what must have been some sort of desperate attempt to have company. Septimus, for example, had a leg missing. Butch was the biggest in the clan. A smaller spider with an overall pale body I christened Spot). The cockroaches were controlled through diligent observance of basic hygiene, and there were products you could buy to discourage them, for example a fluid with which you could 'paint' your shelves and food storage areas. Even so, they could always be relied upon to pop up in the oddest of places. I had one memorable moment in the bath when I was brutally jerked from my melancholic morning reverie by the unnerving sight of a pair of feathery feelers suddenly thrusting through the metal overflow grille at the end of the tub! Some vigorous lashes with the face cloth and they withdrew, leaving me to scramble out of the water before they could reappear. I don't recall house flies being too much of a problem, but, just the same, I had to be constantly vigilant where the local insect life was concerned.

However, I loved the native geckos that patrolled the walls and ceilings on their sticky feet, single-minded little assassins making soft chittering noises as they hunted. Despite their diligence I'd sustained my share of mosquito bites, but my tough antipodean skin proved pretty impervious, and they didn't itch, swell or fester on me the way they did on the fair-skinned northerners. I'd started taking my recommended Daraprim every day as a prophylactic against malaria and had my salt tablets ready and waiting for the hot season. Always take them on a full stomach, I'd been warned, otherwise you'll be retching your guts up. Made sense. Salt is an emetic.

The resident termites were happily expanding their little metropolis in the wall behind the old red chair, and I left them to it.

Ants were a different story. When walking in the soft red soil, as when crossing to school, you sometimes couldn't avoid standing on a big black shiny stink ant and then the most acridly pungent smell would bloom upwards to sear your nostrils. Not pleasant. Tiny house ants were a continuous nuisance, and I quickly learned not to leave uncovered food lying about to turn into a black heaving mass of the little critters. I also kept the sugar and the sugar bowl in the fridge as I'd been advised, and any food not in the fridge had to be kept in tight containers, not just to foil the ants but the cockroaches, too. Even now, all these years later, I have an obsession about secure food storage (Tupperware for miles!).

Expat Blues

It was Carmel who told me about the old African folklore regarding ants, especially for expats. It went thus: Phase one; you could always pick a new expat, because if they found ants in their food, they threw out the food along with the tiny scavengers. In the second phase, they picked out the ants and then ate the food. Phase three was the old hand in Africa who, finding ants in the food, ate the lot anyway, ants and all. I got to phase two but never, I'm happy to say, to phase three, which I hope was apocryphal.

I was also starting to make friends and, now that I could get around in my car, had met a few of the other single teachers scattered around Livingstone. At this time, I had befriended a young married Irish couple in the compound, Pat and Bernie Coughlan (no relation to Elizabeth) from Cork, who were the same age as me. They were quite daftly funny and good company, so we knocked around together as they were the only married couple in our compound not tied by young children and hence free to enjoy a good time without encumbrance. Pat taught civics at the school and Bernie worked as a nurse in the local hospital, to which she commuted on a baby motorcycle, much to the amusement of the locals. They also happened to have a beautiful golden Labrador, Kitoga, who had just produced a litter of nine gorgeous puppies and, being an avid animal lover, I was frequently over there cuddling and playing with them. I was especially fond of the smallest, shyest one that looked nothing like his uniformly golden siblings, being black and white and more bull terrier in appearance than Labrador, a legacy of his dad, I guess. A couple of the pups were black and white, but he was definitely the misfit, the outsider, a sensitive little chap that always had to be coaxed out of the back of the mud brick kennel Pat had made for mother and litter. One evening, as I was watching Pat making raised drills so he could start planting a vegetable garden, he put me on the spot by asking me if I'd like the plain little pup. It was time, he said, for all the pups to be homed.

Tired Mum. Blue is far right.

I asked Pat for some time to think about it. Back in New Zealand, I'd had a dog, a black and white Lab/Collie cross that I loved dearly, and it had broken my heart having to leave her. I didn't want to go through that again or put an animal through it either. I'd hoped I could leave Maggie, as I named her, at my parents' home while I was overseas because my younger brother loved her, too, but my father wouldn't hear of it and so I'd given her to a Southland farming family with young children who promised to take good care of her. What really hurt was that, not long after I arrived in Africa, Dad got an entirely unsuitable dog, a neurotic little Maltese terrier, that proved a lot more trouble than Maggie would have been.

I told Pat that if I did take the pup, I'd want to wait until the holidays, only a couple of weeks away, so that I could spend time with him. Pat agreed and admitted that he'd been able to find homes for all the pups except the homely little black and white fellow. I think he guessed I had a soft spot for misfits and outsiders.

In the meantime, I had some domestic issues to sort out. Shortly after my conversation with Elizabeth re maids, a softly spoken young African woman had arrived on the stoop one morning to tell me in faltering English that she was looking for work. She said her name was 'Erita' and casting my mind back to the conversation with my colleague, that sounded about right: three syllables and starting with 'E'. Assuming she was the lass Elizabeth had told me about, I welcomed her in, showed her where all the cleaning equipment was and left her to get on with it. She'd barely set to when another young African woman appeared in the doorway, politely introduced herself as 'Edina' and announced that she'd come to commence work. At that moment, Erita walked into the living room clasping a broom, on her way to sweeping the stoop. They both froze, eyeballing each other and then the new arrival launched into a furious tirade in the local tongue, prompting Erita to respond in kind, while I looked on, bewildered by this unexpected turn of events. Things were getting increasingly heated when Elizabeth hurried in and after calming everyone down, explained to me that my newly appointed maid was not the girl I'd agreed to share with her, her own maid, Edina, but an opportunist who'd cunningly pipped her candidate at the post! I was mortified.

Once we'd all had some tea, during which Elizabeth had demonstrated a flair for tactful diplomacy, it was agreed that an understandable mistake had been made, one of confused identity, and Edina sportingly agreed that Erita could keep her job with me, since she, Edina, at least had some work while Erita was unemployed. Erita, it transpired, was also pregnant and desperately needed some money. When she had the baby, it was agreed, Edina would take over for her during her maternity leave. I apologized once more for any upset I'd caused, and everyone dispersed, no harm done, peace restored.

Later that evening, as we enjoyed one of our many scrabble games, Elizabeth and I had a good laugh over it all. She was due to go home at the end of the year and was another one for whom Africa had not been an ideal environment. Like Jessica, she'd become very thin and frail-looking, not helped by the fact that she was a bundle of nerves and smoked incessantly. Semi reclusive anyway, we didn't see much of her over at school as her typing room was convent side, and she went home to smoke in private at morning teatime, only coming to the staffroom for meetings. She once mentioned that there were people on the staff that she 'couldn't stand' but didn't elaborate. It turned out that Elizabeth had been a nun for many years and would not have left her vocation if she'd been allowed to indulge her craving for cigarettes. This struck me as patently unfair, since the priests smoked, drank, partied and pretty much did as they liked. My faith in the Catholic clergy had already taken a beating over the years. Africa was to finish it off.

Erita proved a delightful addition to the household. She scorched my clothes with the iron, (no putsi fly larvae stood a chance of surviving her searing onslaughts!) helped herself to my bread, jam, milk and leftovers, put my laundered clothes away still damp (to be fair, it was hard to wring them out properly without a machine), and was always ecstatic to receive the chicken feet that, to my initial horror, came thrust by default into the cavity of every supermarket fowl purchased. She'd reacted with dismay when she saw me toss them in the rubbish bin, promptly snatching them out again, and so thereafter every chicken foot had Erita's name on it! Apparently, once slowly braised in some kind of sauce, they became soft and gelatinous, delicious 'relish' for the nshima.

Best of all, I loved to watch her energy saving mode of floor polishing. Once she'd liberally daubed the ochre-colored polish all over the floors, she'd slip the hand straps on the big bristle brushes over her bare feet and skate wildly around the house until we had gleaming surfaces. I found it prudent, in order to avoid collision, to plant myself in one secure place while this frenetic ritual was being conducted, so used this time to catch up with some school prep or letter writing, well tucked in at the dining table as she whizzed happily around me and the furniture like a small whirling dervish. When she'd finished, she always made me a nice cup of tea to soothe my nerves. I told my family about her in my letters and to my total surprise they sent a package of baby clothes, and a colorful silk scarf for Erita herself. When I gave these gifts to her, explaining as best as I could their provenance, she went deathly quiet, accepted them with an air of solemn reverence, and wandered off as in a trance, clearly completely overwhelmed. I paid her two kwachas more than the standard maids' rate of ten a month and told her it was our secret. I didn't want to provoke any labor disputes!

Expat Blues

It was also during these early days of my African adventure that I became acquainted with the vagaries and unpredictable nature of African border posts. When I first arrived in Zambia, you could travel reasonably freely between Zambia and Rhodesia – as it was still then known. All that would change in less than five months. Rhodesia's Prime Minister, Ian Smith, had defied Britain's shedding of its African colonies and made a Unilateral Declaration of Independence in 1965 that ensured minority white control of Rhodesia, turning it into a pariah state out of step with post-colonialist doctrine. Rhodesia had been self-governing anyway for over forty years and its white leaders saw the bloody upheavals in the newly independent states of Congo, Ghana and Algeria as dire warnings. They did not want to lose control of one of the best run economies in Africa. The leaders of the two black nationalist parties, ZANU (Shona tribe) and ZAPU (Ndebele, Kalanga tribes), who had started agitating for black majority rule, were expelled by Smith's government and set up their new headquarters in Lusaka to continue their fight. The UN, along with the international community, condemned Rhodesia and its only allies were apartheid South Africa and Portugal which both clung to minority white rule themselves. Dependent on South Africa for economic aid, Botswana and Malawi, both poor, backward nations, remained nominally neutral. South Africa maintained an armed presence in the Caprivi Strip, a geographic salient running from Namibia across to Rhodesia, to show its support for Smith while intimidating Zambia. The Portuguese were also facing increasing liberationist militancy in their colonial possessions of Angola and Mozambique during this period. The black insurrectionists in Mozambique were called Frelimo, while in Angola three guerilla factions formed along tribal lines warred with the Portuguese and with each other.

Terrorist activity in Rhodesia was in its nascent stages, but tensions were growing, especially as Rhodesia knew Zambia was harboring and training black guerillas in bush camps within its borders. The Zambians, of course, referred to them as 'freedom

fighters'. This was a challenging and fascinating (not to mention dangerous) time to be in Africa.

Erin Eldridge

The big attraction in Rhodesia for white expats living in Zambia was the cheap food and alcohol along with a much greater range in most commodities that were often unavailable in Zambia, like cooking oil, fresh vegetables, soap and flour. Sanctions didn't appear to be biting too hard. Victoria Falls township, the Rhodesian counterpart to Livingstone, situated on the southern side of the gorges, had beautiful shops, hotels and restaurants and was a popular tourist destination. However, people claimed the best views of the Falls, which at just on 6,000 feet wide spanned both countries, were to be had on the Zambian side, and when I got to compare, I had to agree. The magnificent statue of David Livingstone gazing over the thundering cataracts was, however, on the Rhodesian side. I remember watching in amazement when an American tourist took a photo of the great explorer; the camera made a sort of whirring noise and disgorged the colored snapshot instantly into his waiting hand. I'd never even heard of polaroid cameras until then!

Statue of David Livingstone, overlooking Victoria Falls.

The Mullins often went over to Victoria Falls and, one Sunday, they asked me if I'd like to join them. Of course, I said I'd love to, and then listened in disbelief as they went through a bewildering array of documents that I'd need to cross both borders, with the Zambian officials being the most exacting. A quick inventory established that I had all the prerequisites except the ID card and

Expat Blues

Tax Clearance Certificate, which I hadn't even heard of. I'd made an appointment with local officialdom to get the ID card, but it was still a couple of weeks away, and Peter promised to help me obtain the tax clearance. He thought we should risk the trip as I had the most important documents like passport, immunization booklet, and work permit. Sometimes, he explained, they asked for everything, but just as often they checked you through on only a couple of items. Currency could be an issue, too, and Peter said they almost always checked that one. You weren't allowed to take kwachas out of Zambia and the Rhodesians wouldn't accept them anyway. Most other currencies were okay. Peter and Nora had some English sterling and I still had nearly all my travelers' cheques, so we were good to go. Livingstone was only twelve kms or so from the border and the Falls, so it would be no big inconvenience if we were turned back.

We duly set out on Sunday morning after Mass, me sharing the back seat with the two little girls and eagerly looking forward to visiting another new country, a controversial one at that. Livingstone and Victoria Falls were separated by the spectacular gorges through which the dramatically compressed Zambesi River thundered, forming a natural border.

The drive out along the Falls Road was a treat in itself, and with Peter doing the driving, I was able to focus on and fully appreciate the nature of the terrain. Trees and bush lined either side of the road and I was especially intrigued by the baobabs, their thick barrel-like trunks swollen with the water they absorbed, and their spindly tangle of branches that made them look as if they were wearing their roots on their heads. The Africans call this unique species 'the tree of life', revering it the same way Pacific peoples venerate the coconut palm and for the same reasons: baobabs are bountiful, providing food, medicines, fibres, and material for tools, like hunting and fishing equipment.

Erin Eldridge

Baobabs. "The tree of life."

I felt nervous when I went up to the counter at the Zambian border post, but it all went smoothly, and I wasn't asked for the items I lacked. To reach the Rhodesian Customs, we then had to cross the iconic Victoria Falls Bridge, an impressive steel parabolic structure spawned by Cecil Rhodes' ambition to build a railway from the Cape to Cairo. 'The trains,' he'd boasted, 'will catch the spray of the Falls as they pass.' Very romantic.

The bridge had been manufactured in Britain and then shipped in sections to Beira on the Mozambique coast before being transported up to the Falls and assembled in fourteen weeks. Amazing. It comprised road, rail and footbridge sections, and was officially opened by Charles Darwin's son, Professor Sir George Darwin, in 1905.

At 128 meters above the surging water, the views as we crossed the bridge were jaw-dropping, if somewhat vertiginous: a vista of green river, glistening black rock faces, and lush foliage. As we approached the Rhodesian end of the bridge, I was surprised to see soldiers in camouflage manning a sandbagged machine gun nest on a raised platform that commanded a view of anyone and anything crossing over the gorge.

"South African soldiers," Peter explained. "They keep a token force here to give moral and military support to the Rhodesian security forces. The Zambian army has a bivouac on their side, on a bluff overlooking the gorges. Now and again, they take potshots at each other."

The soldiers looked like boys.

In contrast to the Zambian border post, the Rhodesian officials were all white and so were their immaculate uniforms.

"Good to see some rine," said the chatty young man I was dealing with. "The formers will be pleased."

'Rine'? 'Formers'? This was my first experience of that peculiar and distinctive accent which predominated in all of southern Africa, especially in South Africa itself, and not just in Boer enclaves. It was commonly called a 'yarpie accent', from the Afrikaans for farmboy – 'japie'. There were also many Afrikaans words that were common slang in this part of the world. Examples: anything defined as good or nice was 'lekker', 'baas' was commonly used for boss/employer, 'kafirs' was the derogatory term for Africans, 'plakkies' were thongs, and 'voetsek' meant fuck off.

At last, all the paperwork was completed, and we cruised on into Victoria Falls. It was a charming little township, beautifully laid out, impressively clean, and with a pleasant, relaxed atmosphere. The supermarket the Mullins chose was well-stocked with plenty of variety on offer and we treated ourselves to goods that were often absent or in short supply in Zambia, like soap, butter, cooking oil, cleaning products, cosmetics and fresh fruit and vegetables. Then it was on to the liquor store. We were careful not to buy too much or exceed limits imposed by both Zambia and Rhodesia, keeping all receipts in case they were requested.

Shopping completed, we had lunch, treated the kids to ice-cream, and then toured some of the curio shops. I bought a couple of things to send home to my family: a copper bowl and an animal hide rug. Outside the Vic Falls Tourist Centre, I spotted two Africans, a youth and a girl, he playing drums and she a traditional xylophone. The girl was wearing a tiny grass skirt and was naked from the waist up. The white tourists congregated around the pair, mainly middle-aged men, were clicking away with their cameras. Seemed like a good time to go home.

We checked and double-checked our purchases to make sure we'd complied with the rules, made a quick pit stop at the impressively clean public toilets, and headed off back to Zambia. The kids promptly fell asleep, and I was feeling weary myself. Putting politics aside, Victoria Falls was every bit as lovely as Peter and Nora had claimed, and I was looking forward to getting back there again as well as exploring more of this country and its dramatic history.

And so, we transitioned from a rebel country still under white colonial rule to a country that had slipped that yoke and was now ruled by Africans. I had a feeling much turmoil was to come.

Victoria Falls bridge and view of the gorges.

The return to Zambia went smoothly, although we had to declare all our purchases at the Rhodesian customs. As relations between the two countries continued to decline, Rhodesian hostility to white expats working in an independent black state increased exponentially and, on a whim, a Rhodesian customs officer might confiscate goods he knew were in short supply in Zambia. There was no offer of compensation, just a cutting remark like, "If you want to work for those black bastards you can go without." This said within earshot of an African menial preparing to serve them their afternoon tea. On one memorable occasion, I saw a woman who was about to have some groceries confiscated scoop them up, bolt outside, and toss them into the gorge. "If I can't have them, you wankers aren't going to get them," she yelled defiantly.

There was one other gauntlet to run at the border posts – large, brazen Chacma baboons who would swipe your goodies in a lightning fast hit-and-run, even diving into your car through a window you'd been foolish enough to leave wound down while you were inside, in search of treats. Sometimes you'd find them sitting on the bonnet of your car when you emerged from customs, and you'd just have to be patient, waiting until they moved on. They had formidable teeth and could attack without warning. There was a notoriously cranky one that only had one arm. Everybody gave him a wide berth!

But for today, it was all peaceful. I'd enjoyed my first foray into the rebel state and hoped I could go again. Not all my border crossings were destined to be so uneventful.

It was also around this time that I met the hunting spiders that Brendan and Peter had described in such lurid detail. To my horror, I learned that on this occasion they had not actually been exaggerating. The spiders only appeared briefly each year, around the beginning of the hot season in August/September, but it felt like an interminable nightmare and even now I shudder as I recall these fearsome arachnids. Maramba was semi-rural, and the teachers' compound was close to the bush line, so we got a lot of wildlife, including snakes, toads and large lizards, along with a wide variety of insects, like moths and mantids. I encountered a big tawny lizard in my bathroom one morning and bravely made a dive for it to carry it outside. I'd always thought it was an old wives' tale, but he promptly jettisoned his tail into my grasping hand and fled. The tail segment, with a tiny red pearl of blood on its detached end, continued to wriggle on my palm until I dropped it with a shriek and likewise fled. When Erita arrived, she chuckled as I recounted what had happened and quickly took control. The errant reptile was outed and both tail segment and stunted owner were unceremoniously tossed outside.

One night, as I sat in the living room marking some English exercise books, I heard a slight scrabbling noise coming from the direction of my front door, which opened directly onto my small stoop. I stood up to get a better view and watched in horror as an enormous spider expertly squeezed itself through the gap between the floor and door bottom and, after pausing for a moment in the full glare of the interior light, shot with blurring speed across the floor, straight towards me. I let out a yell, leaping first onto the chair and then onto the table itself, scattering the kids' books. Heart pounding, I took a moment to regain my control before dropping to my knees and peering cautiously over the edge of the table. And there it was. It had stopped at the entrance leading to my narrow hallway and I had a bird's eye view of it in all its repulsive entirety. It must have been ten centimeters long or more, and a lot of its length was taken up by a pair of wicked looking mandibles curving out of its head. The greyish-pink body was bloated with the insects it had consumed before entering my house, attracted by the bar of light that gleamed through the gap at the bottom of the door. And then it was gone, moving with lightning speed into the gloom of the corridor and deeper into my house.

People told all sorts of stories about the big hunters. Some said their bite was poisonous, others said it wasn't, but it could make you very sick. There was a popular belief that if you cornered one it would attack you, and they moved so fast! I knew I could never share space with these critters the way I did with the big flat dozy wall spiders.

With mounting horror, I realized my bedroom door was open. What if it hid in there and attacked me while I was sleeping? Those jaws looked as if they could slice through a mosquito net like a razor. (Vivid imagination beginning to run riot at this point of verging on hysteria).

Expat Blues

Summoning all my courage, I climbed down off the table and tiptoed into the corridor. I reached the light switch and flicked it on, scanning desperately. No sign of it in the hallway. At that point I decided I needed a weapon, so, after a quick check before diving in there, I grabbed the broom from the utility cupboard. With the kind of stealth that the SAS are trained in, I crept into the kitchen where I'd left the light on. Cautiously, I peered around and under things. No sign of the beast. It had to be in the bedroom. Fortunately, the light switch was right beside the door, so I flicked it on and slid soundlessly into the room, broom poised ready for combat. Immediately, the spider shot out from under the bed, and I will never know if it was deliberate or random, but with mandibles raised menacingly it sped straight towards me. With another wild shriek, I slammed the broom down and missed it. Temporarily nonplussed, it skidded to a halt, backed up slightly and then charged at me again. This time I got it fair and square and learned the brutal truth of something I recalled Brendan had said: 'They're all guts.'

I had to go and make a steadying cup of tea before I could face cleaning up the mess.

Once I'd done that, I pressed towels firmly along the bottoms of both outside doors and made sure when I went to bed that my mosquito net was tucked so tightly around my mattress it was fairly twanging.

The hunters only came at night, adding to their sinister reputation, and the towels didn't necessarily stop their home invasions. One morning, I woke to the horrifying sight of an enormous one clinging to the outside of the mosquito net, suspended just above my face! Another night, I returned home from an outing to find two of them nestled in the bath, looking particularly gruesome against the stark white porcelain. In both instances, capture and disposal was a harrowing affair I prefer not to dwell on, and I was beginning to fear for my sanity when their nocturnal rampages ended as suddenly as they had begun. Hunting spider season was, thankfully, over.

Erin Eldridge

I had completed my first term at St Mary's (partial term, that is) and was looking forward to four weeks of holidays. My classes were going well, I had made friends, and I could now sleep through the nocturnal insect racket and frequent drumming, no problem. It probably helped that I'd learned the drumming usually related to coming-of-age rituals for the youth of the village, and nothing sinister at all. I had my new pup and my much-anticipated trip to Kafue Game Park to look forward to. My homesickness had abated somewhat.

Just before the term finished, I was carrying out my rostered turn at supervising nighttime study, strolling the verandahs and pausing to glance through the windows at the girls with their heads bent over their books, when I heard steps on the gravel driveway and turned to see Sister Carmel emerge from the darkness. An indefatigable worker, she often turned up unannounced at study time to check that all was going well and to have an informal chat. She disapproved of teachers lounging in the staffroom and liked to see you on patrol, so I got a warm smile.

"Everything all right?"

"Everything's fine, Sister."

We stood side by side on the verandah, gazing out into the inky blackness of the African night, star-strewn sky overhead, the only sound the familiar insect ensemble. I felt Carmel had something more she wanted to say.

"You know, Miss Anderson, I'm very impressed with the way you've settled in here so quickly. We all are."

"Oh, thanks," I blurted out, as the thought of how well I must have concealed my wretched homesickness flashed through my mind. "I really love it here. It's what I've always dreamed of, coming to Africa, teaching African kids. I used to tell the nuns at my old school that I was going to help the black babies one day."

Carmel chuckled, then turned those frank blue eyes on me. "You know, we've never had a New Zealander here before. It's quite remarkable really, the whole thing."

Puzzled, I was about to ask her what she meant, but she pre-empted me and continued.

"Every year, the principals of the mission schools go to Lusaka to a conference at the Catholic Secretariat, and each of us is given a list of teachers who've applied to come to Zambia, with a brief resume for each applicant. I browsed through the list and your name was on it. I couldn't decide who I wanted right then, or if I wanted anyone at all, so I told Father O'Riordan I'd let him know and returned home. Well, that night I couldn't sleep a wink, tossed and turned, and your name kept scrolling endlessly through my head. In the morning, I rang Father and said, "You'd better send me that New Zealander. And so here you are."

I didn't know what to say. I felt tingly all over.

"Do you believe in fate, Erin?" Carmel asked softly.

"I – I don't really know. Or maybe I do, now!"

Carmel chuckled. "Well, as I said, it's grand the way you've settled in. Lots don't, you know. Many a one we've had to send home early, sometimes only a few weeks after they've arrived. Have you got home help yet, a maid, a cook?"

"Just a maid. I don't need a cook." I could barely afford the maid.

Carmel nodded, glancing at her watch. "Well, I'll leave you to it. I'm pleased to see you have a torch at last. Always carry it at night and shine it well ahead of you. Snakes often sleep on the warm, smooth paths and could strike if you stand on them. Stomp your feet a bit, too. They'll feel the vibrations and get out of your way. Was there anything else?"

"Oh, no, really, I'm fine. I've found some of the creepy-crawlies a bit tricky, but I guess everyone does when they're new."

"I quite understand. I've been in Africa for over forty years, and I've never got used to them. It will get easier though. Just give it time and take sensible precautions, like using your mosquito netting, keeping your window screens down when the windows are open, check shoes and clothing for unwelcome guests, don't leave food exposed." Carmel's face became serious. "I haven't really taken the time to give you any sort of an orientation, and I apologize for that."

"Please, don't worry, Sister. I know how busy you are."

"No, no, I should have." She led me to a bench between the admin and staffroom doorways, and we sat down together.

"Let me see, what advice can I give you?" She placed a finger on her chin, looking off into the distance. "Well, being young, you'll almost certainly do some travelling while you're here. Most of the time it's safe, but please don't go near the Congo – Zaire, as it's called now. It's wildly dangerous and corrupt. The soldiers will steal your car, take all your money. Travelling within Zambia can be dangerous, too. Did you know it has the world's worst road toll? Only four million people and roughly four thousand are killed in road accidents every year. A number of factors contribute to this: bad roads, no regular maintenance of vehicles or warrant checks, overloading, driving without a license, and so on. And never believe a Zambian driver's signals. Bide your time 'til you know which way he's going. You'll almost certainly have an accident while you're here," she added bluntly. "Just pray it's not a bad one."

She stood up. "Good night. Please don't hesitate to come to me if you need help with anything. My door is always open. I hope you enjoy the holidays. Frances told me you'd agreed to chaperone Grace to the game park. Thank you for doing that."

"Honestly, I was thrilled to be asked. It will be a privilege."

Carmel smiled and tottered off into the night in her high heels. As I resumed my patrol of the classrooms, I pondered her amazing account of how I'd ended up here, and I felt deeply moved as well as truly humbled. Who was I, with all the significance of an ant in a furnace, to question the workings of the Universe? As always, the Bard said it best; there really was a divinity that shaped our ends. Hopefully, there wouldn't be too much rough hewing.

School finished, the girls left in a flurry of cars, buses, or to catch trains, and an unaccustomed emptiness and silence settled over the school and convent. The Coughlans decided it was time for me to take on ownership of my pup, whom I'd christened Blue because of his odd little air of melancholy. On the Saturday after school finished, they duly delivered the pudgy wee ten-week-old animal to my house. I'd bought him some sturdy enameled feed and water bowls and made him a bed out of an old cardboard box. We had a cup of tea while we watched the little chap exploring his new environs, and then Pat and Bernie left us to it. I'd kept a chop bone from a recent dinner, and I now offered it to the pup as a gesture of good will, anticipating the mateship I hoped we'd enjoy. He tossed it about, nibbled it a bit, and then sat back on his haunches staring at me. He really was no beauty. He was short-haired, a sort of mottled black with a white chest and throat, white paws, comical flop ears, and small, almost piggy, brown eyes. His long black tail had a white tip and he looked more bull terrier than anything else, bearing no resemblance whatsoever to his beautiful platinum blonde mother. If I thought his moment of intense scrutiny directed my way signaled the moment of bonding, I was quickly disabused when he thrust his blunt little muzzle skywards and commenced to howl like a banshee. I tried everything: cuddling, petting, offering food, dangling the bone temptingly – nothing alleviated his miserable yowling.

Eventually, he fell asleep in a wretched little heap beside the door, and, anxious not to disturb him, I tiptoed out to the kitchen to prepare my evening meal. He slept for an hour or so, awoke, looked at me with undisguised horror and recommenced his pitiful crying.

That continued pretty much all night. I'd placed him in his box beside my bed, one arm dangling over him to offer consoling pats along with comforting noises, but this only soothed him briefly before the whimpering began again. By dawn, sleepless and irritable, I scooped him up and shoved him out into the compound, but not before he christened Erita's beautifully polished floors with a large pee puddle. Kitoga, his mother, having heard his wailings, was hovering anxiously on the stoop and his delight when he saw her would have been heartwarming if I hadn't been so knackered. He waddled joyfully over to her, lunging for one of her big swinging nipples with a ferocity that made me wince. Kitoga promptly decided there was nothing wrong with him and turned speedily for home trying to flick him off by alternately lifting and shaking each back leg, while he skidded determinedly along, clamped to her teat. I shut the door and went back to bed.

Later that morning, Pat strolled over, cigarette characteristically dangling from his lower lip, carrying one small pup in his arms.

"He hates me. It's hopeless," I greeted him.

Pat plonked Blue down on the floor and removed his cigarette, flicking ash away. "Well, see here, now, Erin. His poor mam's fecked out. He's yer feckin' pup now, so he is, and that's the way of it. Give him a day or two and he'll be clinging to ye like shite to a blanket."

With this poetic prediction, he sauntered off and it was just me and Blue again. He sat on his fat little haunches, gazing at me solemnly. Then he yawned hugely, flopped over, and went to sleep, his little belly noticeably swollen. Full of mother's milk, no doubt.

"Yeah, it's okay for you," I muttered peevishly, my eyeballs feeling hot and gritty from lack of sleep. But he did look cute, curled up like a little black cashew nut, and I couldn't help smiling.

As the days passed, and I spent a lot of time with the pup, he made it clear that I had indeed supplanted his mother in his affections. He seldom sought her out now and hung around me devotedly. I bought a collar and leash and took him for short walks and rides in the car, which he made clear from the first he didn't enjoy. I suspected motion sickness. On our first sortie he flung himself out of the open window! Luckily, I was going slowly, and he rolled to the edge of the stormwater drain, whence I quickly retrieved him, without falling in. One day, I took him down to the Zambesi River, near the Falls, for a picnic and let him fossick about while I sat and watched him, munching on my sandwich. He got very excited and started running madly around me in ever-widening circles until, to my horror, he plunged off the bank into the swiftly flowing water. I leaped to my feet and raced along the river's edge, one eye on my bobbing pup and the other on the dodgy terrain. I managed to plunge in and scoop him up in the nick of time before he was carried well out, headed for the Falls. We were both very quiet for a long time.

Blue house trained easily and slept obediently in his cardboard box at night, waddling into my room when he needed to be let out to relieve himself. I had him vaccinated against rabies and other ills, wormed him, and fed him on the best food I could afford. His favorite treat was an egg flip: milk, eggs and sugar whipped up together, sometimes with bits of bread added. His coat began to gleam. Erita loved him on sight, and he enjoyed following her around while she cleaned. When she did her skating routine, he chased her yapping boisterously. It was a comfort to me to know the little guy would have Erita around to keep an eye on him three out of the five days I'd be away at school.

Unfortunately, I had no idea what a curse the ticks were for animals in Africa, and I soon noticed what appeared to be odd little lumps under Blue's normally smooth coat. An investigation revealed repulsive grey bloated creatures firmly locked into the dog's flesh. The ticks were minute brown insects, barely visible, until they burrowed into the dog's fur. Once aboard, they embedded their jaws in the animal's flesh and quickly ballooned up into hideous bluish-grey blobs, engorged with the dog's own blood. They also got into Blue's ears, where they hung like clusters of mutant grapes. When fully sated, they'd drop off and crawl up the inside walls of the house, which always freaked me out. If you squashed a few, it looked like a murder scene! I loathed them and the discomfort they caused hapless animals. People said you had to burn them off with a cigarette or else you risked leaving their embedded jaws behind, which could cause fatal tick fever. I didn't smoke, so I carefully used tweezers and flushed the engorged monsters down the loo. Blue would sit patiently beside the toilet bowl, only making the odd little whimper, as if he understood I was trying to help him. When they were all removed, I swabbed the affected areas with disinfectant. Removing ticks became a dreaded daily routine and was also the principal reason that many expats were reluctant to keep dogs. Eventually, the local chemist got a shipment of tick collars which, to my delight and Blue's comfort, completely solved the problem. I built up a good-sized stash of the collars in case they suddenly became unavailable, as so many items did in Zambia. Whenever I was in Rhodesia, where the collars were plentiful, I bought more. The ticks were most active as winter ended and temperatures rose, and then, thankfully, they tapered off.

After the inauspicious start with the chop bone, Blue developed a deep fondness for the Barotse beef bones I bought him from the local butcher's, especially the juicy marrow. He would proudly waddle outside with his treat clasped firmly in his jaws, find a shady spot in the compound, settle down with the bone between his forepaws, and proceed to give it a right dealing to. This led to the Crows' Wars, which was one of the funniest things I've ever witnessed. Two big African crows, reminiscent of a couple of swaggering, black-jacketed louts looking for a rumble, would plonk down on one of the roof tops right on cue whenever Blue was enjoying a bone. After a bit of a confab conducted in raucous squawks, they'd launch into their familiar routine which never failed, and which I couldn't resist watching. It went like this: one crow glided down and stood just out of Blue's reach, drawing attention to himself with a loud squawk. The pup studied the bird for a bit before returning to his much more enticing treat. The crow lurched closer and closer before sidling up quickly and feigning a lunge for the bone. This outrageously brazen behavior never failed to incense the pup and he scrambled to his feet to pursue the crow, which now with faultless timing, flapped off around the nearest house, keeping tantalizingly just above ground level but safely out of reach. As soon as bird and dog disappeared, the other crow swooped down, seized the bone and returned with it to his perch on the roof, where he was promptly joined by his accomplice for a shared feast. At this point Blue would come rocketing back around the house and slide to a halt on the spot where his tasty morsel had been. The look of bewilderment on his little face was touching, but also achingly funny. This scenario played out many times until Blue grew older and wiser, and the crow brothers never scored another bone.

Chapter Eight: On Safari, Tragic Loss, Life Goes On

In the third week of the holidays, I was scheduled to accompany our prize-winning essayist, Grace, on safari to Kafue National Park in northeastern Zambia. Frances had introduced me to Grace before the holidays and confirmed that she would arrive on an early morning train on the morning of our departure. Sister had asked me to meet Grace at the convent about 8 a.m. and take her back to my place to await the arrival of Bob Dowsett, who'd been briefed that I would be Grace's chaperone and given directions to my house.

I wandered down to the convent at the prescribed time and waited around for quite a while, but there was no sign of Grace, so I left word for her to come down to the compound, where I'd keep an eye out for her, and returned home. I was just having breakfast at the dining table when a green four-door land rover pulled up outside my front window in a noisy crunch of gravel and a tall, fair-haired man with glasses, probably mid-thirties, got out and knocked on my front door. Dressed in a khaki safari jacket, matching shorts and sturdy jungle boots he certainly looked the business. He thrust out a hand and introduced himself as 'Bob Dowsett'. I invited him in, explained that I'd been unable to find Grace and offered him a cup of tea.

"Well, I hope she turns up," he said somewhat irritably, flinging himself into one of the armchairs and gesturing towards the window. "I've got a land rover full of food sitting out there and," he glanced at his watch, "we should be leaving now. Are you ready?"

I nodded. I'd packed a light travel bag I'd been able to borrow, dropped Blue off at the Coughlans, who'd sportingly offered to pup-sit, and just had to hand them over my house and car keys for safekeeping.

"We may have to go without Grace," said Bob despondently, draining his tea.

I looked at him in surprise. This was supposed to be Grace's prize trip for winning the essay competition.

"Perhaps we could take someone else?" Bob looked at me hopefully.

I was about to reply that I thought that might be difficult in the middle of the holidays, when I happened to glance through the window, across the land rover's bonnet, as I gathered up the tea things, and there was Grace, standing under the mopane tree opposite the house, lifting a tentative hand to wave to me. Africans were often too shy to approach and would wait some distance away until you noticed them. I hoped she hadn't been there too long, fretting about being late.

"She's here!" I plonked the tray down and ran to the door. "Grace, come!"

She hurried over and stood on the stoop, contritely wringing her hands.

"I'm sorry, miss, sir, but the train was late."

"No problem," said Bob kindly. "You're here, that's the main thing, and we're not too badly delayed. Have you got your things?"

Grace pointed to where her bag sat on the bench under the tree. "Yes, sir."

"Splendid!" Bob fairly rocketed out of the armchair. "We just have to pick up my assistant, Abner, and we're off!"

Abner turned out to be a diminutive Zambian with impeccable manners, a dazzling smile and bright little shoe-button eyes.

"Eyes like a hawk, has Abner," boomed Bob, as we pulled out onto the highway to begin our adventure. "If there's a beast trying to lurk about, Abner will spot it, won't you Abner? Eyes like a hawk."

"If you say so, baas." Abner hunched his shoulders self-effacingly and treated us to one of his heartwarming smiles.

Expat Blues

We headed out on the road to Lusaka before turning left and taking the route leading north-west to Kafue, leaving the tar seal for dirt roads. I use the term 'tar seal' loosely; the road to Lusaka consisted of a narrow strip of macadam down the middle with broader strips of shingle road either side. Most odd. Bob said the journey was roughly 400kms and would take about five to six hours. It was hot and vehicles had no air-con back then, so we had to roll the windows down to try and keep cool, and Abner opened the sunroof as well. Of course, that meant being invaded by dust and insects, of which the big tsetse flies, that could carry the dreaded sleeping sickness parasite, were the worst. Their bite, against which clothing provided no barrier, was really painful. Bob sportingly shared his insect repellent around and that, along with vigilance and a will to swat vigorously, helped to ease the problem.

I suspected that Bob was a confirmed bachelor who wasn't entirely comfortable in the presence of women, especially a young one, but once I got him talking about familiar things, he relaxed and proved a mine of knowledge. I gave him a brief summary of my background and he reciprocated with his. He'd come to Africa to escape the 'horrible weather' in Britain, he explained, and served seven years as a game warden in Kenya before taking up his post at Livingstone Museum where he was resident ornithologist. Birds, he claimed, were his real passion, and Zambia had an abundance of them. Meanwhile, Grace and Abner, seated modestly well apart, chatted away in the back seat.

I confided to Bob how I had always dreamed of coming to Africa and going on safari in a land rover. He chuckled.

"I had the same romantic ideas until I actually had to drive around in one. They have really heavy suspensions so they're not very comfortable on rough, uneven roads, of which Africa has plenty. You can even develop a condition called 'land rover back' over time."

Yes, she was a jolty old ride, but I still thought she was beautiful, her obvious strength and solidity very reassuring.

I asked Bob about the animals we could expect to see in Kafue, and he was typically muted in his response.

"I doubt we'll see rhino as they're being poached mercilessly. We'll be lucky to see the big cats, too, but we should see a good variety of antelope, including lechwes, hippos, crocs, elephant, buffalo and, hopefully, lots of birds."

"Is poaching a bad problem?"

"Yes, it is, that's why we've got the wildlife awareness program going with the school kids like Grace. We're trying to educate them to appreciate their wildlife, not just to see it as a food source or something to be exploited. The government needs to do more, too. They sell shooting licenses to hunters for big game like elephants." He shook his head. "We need to train armed anti-poaching squads as well if we want these animals to be around still in fifty to a hundred years."

Bob listened indulgently as I trotted out what I knew of African wildlife, most of it derived from Hollywood, and then politely dismantled most of my ideas. I didn't mind. I was learning lots and lapped it all up. When I said I thought hyenas were very unattractive animals, he raised an eyebrow.

"'Unattractive'? What's that got to do with anything? They're vital to the balance of nature, the garbage men of the plains that do a great clean-up job." He smiled. "And they have cute round furry ears."

We made a couple of comfort stops at places where the sanitary facilities were primitive but adequate and continued our journey, Bob promising we'd have lunch when we reached the sanctuary, which raised our faltering morale. It was raised further when we finally arrived at the entrance to Kafue, but plummeted somewhat when Bob pointed out that the place was roughly the size of Wales at 22,400 square kilometers, so we still had quite a distance to go within the park itself before we reached our camp. He encouraged us to get animal spotting, and Abner took up position with his head through the sunroof, binoculars glued to his eyes. Bob was delighted when we spotted a fish eagle, the national emblem of Zambia, perched in the top branches of a tree with a slender green snake dangling from its beak. Obviously, the species did not live on fish alone. A little further on, Abner quietly informed us that there was a cheetah not far off the road with a kill. Bob stopped the

Expat Blues

land rover and we all got out and followed him silently into the bush. Sure enough, Hawkeye Abner had spotted a young cheetah, on its own, which had recently killed a small antelope called a dik-dik. The angry cat backed away from the human intruders, hissing and snarling, raising its hackles, but bravely standing its ground and refusing to abandon its precious kill. Abner brought the dik-dik's carcass over so we could look at it and Bob and I took some photos before dinner was returned to the outraged cheetah. None of this was pretty, but it was nature in the raw and a stunning start to our safari.

When Bob parked the land rover alongside a swathe of grass beside the river and announced lunch, we were all more than ready for the break. I'd only had a piece of toast for breakfast and didn't know whether Grace had eaten anything before her train journey. I guessed she was ravenous like me.

Bob and Abner spread a tarp near the water and set out the food and drink. The river cut into the bank at this point, creating a calm, deep pool and I was astonished to see it was inhabited by a huddle of hippos, heads barely visible above the water level, and not far from them a flotilla of crocodiles, lying motionless like a sinisterly deceptive collection of logs. They weren't on top of us or anything like that, but they weren't far away either. I looked quizzically at Bob, and he smiled.

"It's fine, we're all perfectly safe. Hard-boiled egg?"

And so, we ate our picnic lunch in the company of crocs and hippos. That's something you don't do every day!

"They don't attack each other?" I asked, around a mouthful of egg and deliciously soft buttered bread, which Bob said had been made by his own cook/houseboy, who was an excellent baker. He shook his head.

"No. One's a herbivore, and the carnivore, although deadly, isn't stupid enough to take on a hippo, though a stray or sick calf is fair game. They co-exist happily most of the time, but if it does come to a fight between two adults, the hippo will win, no question. Help yourself to cordial. We'll have a cup of tea when we reach camp."

Eventually, one big hippo, who'd been watching us, flicking his comical little trumpet ears and snorting through his wide nostrils, detached himself from his pod and advanced slowly towards us. Bob got to his feet.

"Okay, time to go."

We all pitched in to tidy things away quickly and Bob threw our eggshells into the water in front of the advancing behemoth, perhaps to distract the animal. I'll never know. I did know that they could charge with amazing speed for their bulk, all 3 tons or more of it fully grown. I assumed Bob had a rifle somewhere in the land rover, but out of sight.

As we drove away, Bob told me the story of how a tourism entrepreneur in Livingstone had started up sunset cruises on the Zambesi, with a braii dinner and champagne thrown in. One evening, as he stopped beside one of the river's many islands and ushered his guests ashore for the cook-up, a huge hippo charged out of the brush and bit one of the tourists clean in half!

"End of sunset cruises," said Bob laconically.

We reached our camp mid-afternoon, hot, tired, and achy from the bone-jarring drive, so it was a welcome sight. I hadn't known what to expect, but this was undoubtedly a picturesque oasis in the bush. Our base for the next few days comprised a cluster of white-washed, circular rondavels with conical thatched roofs, the traditional native house found all over southern Africa, and first impressions were of a neatly laid out and beautifully maintained campsite. There was an outdoor, open-sided thatched dining room, a lapa, centrally placed among the rondavels, and across the clearing to the left, at a discreet distance from the guests' accommodation, two service rondavels where the staff worked and slept. Three of them wearing immaculate white shirts and pants with red sashes at the waist and matching red fezzes now came hurrying out to greet us. After introductions, accompanied by the traditional handshaking, nodding and smiling, two of them unloaded the food from the land rover with well-oiled efficiency, while the third showed us to our accommodation. Inside, our appointed rondavel was clean, spacious and cozily furnished.

Looking up, I marveled at the exposed roof braces made from tree branches, silently hoping not too many denizens lurked among the thatch.

Open-air dining room where we ate our meals, Kafue Game Park.

There were two bedrooms, each with its own bathroom and two single beds. I was sharing one room with Grace and Bob and Abner shared the other. Grace was understandably shy about sharing a bedroom with a teacher, so I tried to put her at ease with some jokes, like, "Throw something at me if I snore, Grace.". She was only 13 but very mature and dignified with a sweet, gentle demeanor. We'd barely unpacked our things, which were few as we both travelled light, when Bob called out "Tea's up!" like the good Brit he was, and we went outside to join the boys.

I was gagging for a cup of tea and a bit taken aback when Bob splashed a dollop of lime cordial into each cup as he poured.

"Trust me, this will be both refreshing and stop the liquid oozing out through your pores as soon as you drink it. Old bush lore."

I was dubious, but it did in fact taste quite nice and was indeed refreshing as he claimed. I never did make a habit of it, though. Bit of a purist with my tea.

I gazed around. "We seem to be the only people here, but it's school holidays."

Bob grunted. "Hard to fathom, I know. It's such a superb game park, too. Bit out of the way, but even so you'd think it would get more patronage than it does." He shrugged. "Oh well, means we have everyone's undivided attention, I guess. Drink up and then we're off. We can get in some game viewing before dinner."

We saw many animals before dusk arrived, and Grace started to come out of her shell, showing genuine excitement when we spotted antelope, buffalo, or thirsty elephants heading down to the river in their matriarchal herds. She kept making that lovely 'eeeee' sound that Africans make when they're impressed, and I saw Bob grin with satisfaction. He proved adept at putting her at ease, including her in the conversations, and drawing her out to express her own thoughts and ideas about wildlife conservation, as she had done in her prizewinning essay. Grace giggled when Bob said he loved taking the St Mary's girls on local field trips because they sang so beautifully all the way there and back again.

We drove back to camp, weary but elated, taking turns to list all the wildlife we'd spotted so far. There were so many different species of antelope, but I'd already learned to distinguish waterbuck, bushbuck, kudu, roan and impala. I loved the warthogs best, the way they trotted off in their little family units, mum shepherding the kids and protective dad bringing up the rear, tail standing up ramrod straight like a warning flag, pausing hid jaunty strut from time to time to turn and give us a challenging glare. Bob said they made great parents.

As dusk drew in, I was left humbled by that most iconic of all African images – beautiful, ancient acacia trees with their slender branches and flat evergreen tops silhouetted against the stunning African sunset.

Expat Blues

Acacia sunset.

A delicious dinner eaten under the stars, the only sounds the chirping of insects and the hissing of the tilly lamps, was a perfect ending to an amazing day. As we got ready to retire for the night, Bob said with a twinkle in his eye, "Been a long day, so I'll give you a bit of a sleep-in tomorrow. Wakeup call is 5.30."

Grace and I groaned simultaneously. "You're kidding, right?"

He wasn't.

Our time in Kafue passed all too quickly. I loved heading out in the land rover every day, never knowing what game we might find. Kafue boasted a diverse terrain comprising tree savannahs, shallow wetlands and numerous watercourses, so the variety of game reflected the varied terrain and we never returned to camp disappointed. The one animal we hadn't spotted that I was dying to see was the lion, and our time was running out.

In the evenings, I loved to sit by the river, watching the cormorants on the opposite bank standing motionless with their wings spread to dry in the fading sunshine. Another family had arrived, a couple with two young kids. They'd taken a boat out on the river and returned to camp badly shaken and all talking at once about a nasty encounter they'd had with an aggressive hippo. After they'd gone to their rondavel to recover, Bob muttered, "Boating around hippos...madness, especially with kids. In all my years as a game warden that's the only animal I had to kill in self-defense." He strode off to have words with the camp employees.

Then it was time to leave. I was looking forward to getting home and seeing my pup again, but I was also sad I'd missed out on lions. Bob told us all to keep our eyes peeled. There was still hope. We rounded a bend and saw a cluster of cars pulled over to the side of the road ahead. Bob was instantly on high alert.

"Something's happening up ahead."

We pulled in behind the end vehicle, jumped out, and hurried towards the small group of people standing silently in the bush some yards away. Bob put a finger to his lips, and we crept along as quietly as we could. As we drew abreast of one man clutching a pair of binoculars, he turned towards us and whispered the magic word. "Lions! We spotted the vultures in the trees and guessed there must be a kill."

A short distance away in a small clearing was a remarkable sight. A dead antelope, partially devoured, lay on the ground with a mass of vultures swarming and flapping over the carcass. But there was no sign of any lions.

"Two lionesses," whispered the man again. "We've spooked them, and they ran into the bushes over there." He pointed. "We're hoping they'll come out again."

"Not a chance," said Bob firmly. "All these people around? They won't come back to the kill."

Barely were his words out when we all gasped as a huge lioness erupted from the bushes and charged towards the carcass, rearing up on her hind legs to swat at the hastily departing vultures that scrambled away in a roar of beating wings. Rivals dispatched, the lioness dropped down beside her kill, licked her lips with satisfaction, and stared at us. As if that hadn't been dramatic enough, the second lioness now emerged from the bush to saunter to the carcass at a more sedate pace, and following in her wake were three cubs! While the cameras clicked madly, they all settled

Expat Blues

down to resume their dinner, ignoring us. Bob scratched his head, not best pleased at being so thoroughly proved wrong.

"I can't believe it. They just don't return to a disturbed kill as a rule, especially when they're with cubs."

I smiled to myself. Hungry tums will always win the day.

We watched the incredible scene for as long as we could and then everyone drifted back to their vehicles. As I clambered into the land rover, I knew I'd remember that encounter until the day I died. I got to see my lions…and how!

On the way back to Livingstone, Bob asked me if I'd consider starting up a club at St Mary's to promote education among the girls about Zambia's rich bounty of wildlife.

"A Wildlife Club?" I quipped. "Our motto will be 'preserve wildlife, throw a party every night'."

Seeing Bob roll his eyes reminded me that not everyone shared my wacky sense of humor. I cleared my throat.

"Actually, I am down to take a Friday club of some sort next term. They let me off last term because I was new and settling in. I'll have to run it past the boss, but I'm sure she'll approve. What sort of things should I do?"

"Animal identification and characteristics, films, slides, books, field trips, that kind of thing. I can help you out with a lot of it."

"I'll happily do it, to show my gratitude for the privilege of this wonderful safari if nothing else."

Bob beamed. "Great, thank you. I just remembered something else, too. Our local Wildlife Association President and his wife are hosting the annual braaivleis for members in a couple of weeks and I can't attend, but maybe you'd like to go, meet some of the folk involved? Most of them are expats, but we're working hard to attract more Zambian members."

"Sure, I'd be glad to."

"Thanks again. After we get back, I'll come out to Maramba with some resources for your club and give you the details then."

I turned to Grace, drooping sleepily in the back. "Will you join my Wildlife Club, Grace?"

"Yes, meestress. I am Science Club, but I can change."

"There!" I said to Bob. "Got a member already."

"Lekker!"

Blue was as happy to see me as I was to see him. The Coughlans were likewise happy to be rid of him. Apparently, they'd been impressed with his house training since they had not come across any piddles – until an unpleasant odor emanating from the furniture prompted the discovery that he'd been surreptitiously peeing on the couch squabs! Glancing over at their house, I could see all the stripped cushion covers flapping on the washing line.

"Well, did you pop him outside regularly? He is just a pup."

"He's a feckin' eejit, so he is."

The last week of the holidays passed quickly, and I was looking forward to the new term, especially as I no longer had to take religious education and had a lighter timetable. I was also looking forward to catching up with Sister Frances, who was due back Saturday or Sunday, to tell her all about the safari with Grace. When I drove past the convent over the weekend, I could see the girls arriving to settle back in for the third and final term of the year.

Once we'd all assembled in the staff room on the first Monday morning of the new term, Sister Carmel came in, closed the door behind her, and broke the terrible news to us that Sister Frances and a nun based in Lusaka, who had accompanied her to the conference, had been involved in a horrific head-on collision on the main north-south highway (popularly called 'Death Alley') as they were returning from the Copperbelt. Both were in Lusaka hospital with shocking injuries, and a few of the St Mary's sisters had already left to be at Frances' bedside. She added that the girls had not yet been told, and that she would break the news to them when they assembled for lunch at morning's end. As regards the continued smooth running of the school, she would remain and John Kay John, a well-liked Indian teacher, would serve as Deputy Principal. In the meantime, we were to act normally and say nothing, not even to each other, while we were on school premises. She asked us all to pray as hard as we could. Then she left.

The girls were all happy to be back and they made me feel they were pleased to see me, too, which was nice. I felt guilty witnessing their carefree adolescent chattiness and excitement as they caught up with each other while knowing what I did about one of their most beloved teachers.

The morning went smoothly, and then we expats returned to the compound for lunch, discussing the dreadful news as we walked. We all felt for Carmel who would right now be breaking that news to the girls as they assembled in the dining room.

I was dreading the next day, knowing the girls had been told about Frances and wondering how they'd cope. They revered Sister Frances. She was a precious asset and role model, a stabilizing and respected influence at the school. However, everything was calm and normal, the girls clearly subdued, but settling into their daily routine without any problems. A pall of sadness hung over everyone. Rumor had it that Carmel had downplayed Frances' status and given the girls hope for her recovery. Another rumor circulated, too, that a nun who had visited Frances in hospital said her condition was dire and that 'her bones were sticking out all over her body'. I couldn't even begin to imagine what that implied, let alone erase the ghastly image from my mind.

Wednesday morning, I was up by six as school commenced half an hour earlier now that the hot season was upon us. I'd fed Blue, enjoyed a lukewarm bath, eaten my breakfast and was standing, still half asleep, in front of the bathroom wash basin in my dressing gown, when I heard it. I'd always thought the expression 'hairs standing up on the back of your neck' was just that, a fanciful saying, but now I learned the truth of it as one by one the hairs on the back of my neck rose involuntarily, a cold tremor ran down my spine and I went completely rigid. The high-pitched unearthly sound, steadily increasing in volume, was the girls ululating, all 400 of them, and I knew exactly what it meant – Frances was gone. I jumped as someone pounded on the door and I opened it to see Brendan standing white-faced and agitated on the stoop.

"Frances died last night. Carmel's just told the girls, as you can hear. She wants us all over there as quickly as possible."

Brendan strode off and I threw on my clothes to follow him with all haste. By the time I reached the school, it was mayhem. Girls were milling about aimlessly, flinging themselves around recklessly, others lying in desolate heaps or draped over classroom furniture, and all the time the bloodcurdling wailing of grief went on and on, as mourning tradition demanded. Some girls clawed at their faces, necks and arms drawing blood. Others beat their fists bloody against the walls. All were sobbing uncontrollably. Lessons were, of course, abandoned and Sister Carmel, assisted by staff and others who'd come to help, like priests from the St Mary's parish church, struggled to impose some semblance of control and prevent self-harm. Day students were turned around and sent back home as they arrived. It took a long time, and was immensely draining on us all, but gradually we managed to channel the outpouring of grief into something resembling order. On Carmel's instructions, we carried chairs from the school outside onto the grounds and each adult placed him or herself amongst a cluster of students, talking to them calmly, soothing them, saying prayers with them, comforting them. The ululation became more muted. The girls subsided into sorrowful little heaps, holding onto each other.

An impromptu Mass for Frances was organized, and we shepherded the girls down to the church where the grieving continued unabated. They even refused to stop their lamentations to sing the hymns. I clearly remember one child, standing with her face pressed into a corner, arms spread against the wall above her head, not moving for the entire service.

This went on for two days, until Sister Carmel put a firm end to it, her personal cachet sufficient for the girls to respect this, and we all returned to class. I'd had to put my own grief on hold, and when I got home from school on Friday, after one of the worst weeks of my life, I flung myself on the bed and wept bitterly. Blue clambered up beside me and lay quietly with his small warm body pressed against mine. The knowledge that if Frances had accompanied Grace to Kafue instead of me then she'd still be alive haunted me for a long time.

Sister Beatrice, from a Lusaka convent and the only passenger in the vehicle, also died. Sister Frances' funeral, held in her home village, was attended by hundreds, including the President of Zambia himself.

†

Terrible things happen, but life must go on – or as C S Lewis put it, not because it *must* but just because it *does*. We had exams coming up, GCE and Cambridge, so that had to be the focus now, especially as we had high pass rates to maintain. Academically, this would be my first big test.

Apart from exam prep, there was plenty to distract us from our sorrow. Our first young African teacher arrived, Lucy Masiye. She wore brightly colored short dresses with flaring medieval sleeves and was a big hit with the girls, to whom she taught civics. Then a young woman from Belfast, Catherine Hegarty, arrived as an addition to the English department, moving into the flat previously occupied by the Mullins, whose new house was finally completed. She had red hair and freckles, a wicked sense of humor, and likewise wore her dresses very short. I was delighted to have another single expat teacher in the compound, but Catherine scandalized everyone by promptly taking up with an expat Indian man employed with the Zambian Airforce, which had a base in Livingstone, and we rarely saw her except at school. With her red hair and freckles, not to mention broad Belfast accent unleashed from the corner of her mouth, the girls disliked her on sight and would hiss loudly when she walked past the classrooms. John Gibbons, our head of Department, had finished his contract and was preparing to move on to a more lucrative one, accompanied by his wife, Nell, and recently born baby daughter, teaching English in Saudi Arabia. Carmel told me that I was her new Head of English. I was stunned, but there was no refusing her.

John gave me some precious training before he left, but I was pretty much thrown in the deep end. For my first assignment as new HOD, my principal, who herself liked to avoid personal conflict at all costs, told me to persuade Catherine to go home! Our contracts designated us as 'lay missionaries' (all sorts of jokes about that, of course) and we were supposed to uphold decent moral standards, but everyone knew, Carmel explained, that Catherine was conducting an affair with an Indian air force officer, a divorcee who had two small boys. As if that weren't bad enough, the male Indian teachers on the staff had formed an indignant posse that had come to Carmel's office demanding she do something about the way the young Irishwoman bent over the morning tea table so that her short dresses rode up exposing her bunched knickers and half her buttocks!

I told Carmel I felt most unhappy about performing this task, but she insisted, so I duly summoned Catherine for a chat in my small office at the back of the library. I decided the best way to tackle the unpleasant assignment was to just come out with it. Catherine stared at me in disbelief, and then burst into tears. Once she calmed down, we discussed her options, and the outcome was that she flatly refused to go home. Her relationship with Jimmy Patel, who was, as it turned out, Anglo-Indian with a weakness for Irish women, was serious and she refused to either give him up or leave him. Going home, back to the savage Northern Ireland Troubles she'd escaped from, would be devastating. I felt immense sympathy for her. Finally, I had to deal with the embarrassing business of her flashing her knickers at morning teatime and upsetting the Indian teachers on the staff. She promised to be more circumspect, and we concluded our meeting.

I nervously reported back to Sister Carmel, who was none too pleased by my lack of success – except with the knickers item – and I went home that day experiencing a toxic mix of emotions: anger and humiliation at being put in such a position, guilt over my failure, compassion for Catherine. As it turned out, she stayed, the matter was never mentioned again, and she and Jimmy, who became my firm friends, eventually married.

With Carmel's blessing, I duly set up my Wildlife Club with approximately twenty students, who included Grace, and set about educating them to love and respect their native fauna. The girls elected a club president, a popular student called Gertrude Sakubita, and we were ready to launch. First up, Grace and I told the members about our trip to Kafue and I showed them my slides, which Bob had supplemented with much better shots taken using his telephoto lens, something I lacked. I got each girl an exercise book and we started by drawing and recording data about the more well-known species.

I attended the braaivleis hosted by the local Wildlife Association's President, as requested by Bob, and found it an illuminating experience. The president and his wife were an elderly British couple who'd settled in Zambia during the days of empire, established a business and stayed on after independence. They were both dressed up to the nines, even for a casual barbecue, and all the food was cooked and served by African boys clad in white uniforms with red cummerbunds and matching fezzes, much like the African staff at Kafue. I recognized the president's wife immediately. She'd been pointed out to me in the township one day as an eccentric hangover from colonial times. Aways immaculately dressed, she cruised around in a battered Ford Anglia permanently welded into second gear, long elegant cigarette holder clamped between her teeth. Her florid-faced husband, who favored cigars, was a cheerful old lecher with wandering hands, but also a cordial and generous host. His wife was gracious to her guests but directed her staff with embarrassing hauteur and rudeness. A sad footnote was that some months into my contract I learned that her husband had blown his brains out with a shotgun in his garden, and their children, who lived in Australia, had flown over for the funeral before taking their mother back with them. Apparently, the image of white privilege was a hollow façade; they were in fact penniless, desperately clinging to the trappings of a lifestyle that was no longer relevant and which in the new Zambia they could no longer finance.

The president and his wife were not the only anachronisms I encountered. I sometimes had a drink at the old colonial Livingstone Hotel and frequently enjoyed a chat with another British eccentric, a charming elderly man, whose name I can't recall, who always dressed in a white suit with a red bowtie, carried a gold-topped cane, and was accompanied everywhere by his devoted companion, a chowchow dog. We'd sit out on the stoop, me with a beer, him sipping from a glass of Campari. He showed me how the dog had a black tongue, one of only two animals on the planet with this feature. The other one, he said, was the polar bear. Pathetically dislocated in time and place, he likewise disappeared, along with his dog.

My dealings with expat life in Livingstone continued to have its ups and downs. Although no longer so homesick, I frequently felt lonely, and was grateful to have my dear old mutt. He was growing fast and although he often had Erita for company, he missed me when I went to school. One of Erita's tasks was to keep him in the compound, but he quickly learned to evade her vigilance.

One morning, as I was taking a senior class for English, he suddenly appeared, framed in the open window, paws planted on the sill. I supposed he'd tracked me down by my voice. As soon as he saw me, he did this thing with his ears that never failed to crack me up; he corkscrewed them with an almost audible twang, such was his delight to see Mum. The girls laughed and I let him in, introducing him as my dog, Blue. Zambians had an endearing habit of mixing up the letters l and r. "Brue!" they chorused, and thus he remained to them thereafter. After touring each aisle and enjoying some pats, Blue settled down under my desk and was soon snoring. Snoring wasn't the only thing he did, and the girls quickly informed me of their disapproval.

"Meestress, Brue is farting!"

At morning teatime, Blue accompanied me to the staffroom ambling along with his distinctive walk that reminded me of an old whore lazily swinging her hips. Once I'd procured my tea and cake, he settled himself by my chair and gazed around at the bemused staff looking very pleased with himself, especially when I shared my cake with him. Then he did what all dogs enjoy doing in company – cocked one leg over his shoulder and commenced licking his genitals. After that, he had a good scratch, grunting contentedly. I could hear the mutters of disgust building from some quarters. Following morning tea, he accompanied me to my next class and snored off under my desk again. Sometimes, as the mood took him, he returned to the compound to check on Erita and the other domestics.

Of course, there were immediate complaints to Carmel by a predictable squad of staff members, and I always loved her for her response. She told those curmudgeonly anti-animal people that if I wanted to have my dog at school it was fine with her. She couldn't see that it did any harm and clearly Blue, whom she'd met when I brought him to study with me, was a well-behaved dog. Which he was – most of the time.

On one occasion we were all in an afternoon staff meeting when there was a thump at the door. The room went silent with expectation. Then we all watched fascinated as the door handle began to descend with horror movie slowness. When it reached its nadir, the door burst open and Blue bounced in. He made a beeline for me, tail wagging furiously, and cleared every cup and saucer off the coffee table! I was mortified. Carmel made light of the dramatic canine intrusion and we quickly cleared away the mess and carried on. Blue sprawled happily beside my chair and commenced snoring – and farting.

I accepted an offer to teach English at night school to make a bit of extra money for the end of year holidays. I was keen to explore more of Rhodesia and a cousin in the Marist Brothers back home had given me the addresses of Marist houses in Bulawayo and Salisbury, assuring me I'd easily get free accommodation there if I dropped his name, since he'd stayed in both houses during his recent sabbatical.

I taught an adult English class at the local primary school, conveniently located a short walk from the compound, two nights a week. They were a good group, a mix of men and women who were all keen as mustard. When the supervisor gave me the class roll, I became somewhat nonplussed as I scrolled down the names. Some of our students at St Mary's had unusual names, but these were on another level. Zambians often chose names for their children without really understanding connotation or context, but because they liked the sound of the word. As a result, in my night school class I had a Wireless, a Cabbage, and most disconcerting of all, a Hitler. Hitler Iputu. He was a lovely, friendly guy, always nicely turned out in stylish pants, open-necked shirt and tailored jacket. He also loved to answer questions and was always first up with his hand.

"Yes, Hitler?"

Every time I said it, I had to press my fingernails into the palms of my hands to stop myself breaking into hysterical laughter.

Blue, who mostly wandered about freely now, but never strayed far, soon sussed out where I went when I disappeared of an evening. I was in the middle of the lesson one night when I heard a noise at the door and looked over to see the familiar slow-motion lowering of the door handle. Sure enough, Blue bounced in and after briefly pinning me to the blackboard with his meaty paws, did the rounds of the classroom, tail wagging, greeting everyone. The students were mostly receptive, but then he disgraced himself. Lessons went from 7 p.m. to 9 p.m. with a ten-minute break at 8 p.m. Each classroom was provided with a big plastic bucket full of cold water and a dipper so the students could refresh themselves. Teachers could go to the staffroom for a cup of tea. Returning to the front of the room where the bucket was placed, Blue plunged his muzzle into the water and lapped greedily and noisily. The students were outraged. Red-faced, I quickly collared Blue and organized a replacement bucket.

On the way home after lessons, I told him how he had embarrassed me. He strolled along, swinging his rump and yawning hugely. I could never stay mad with him for long.

However, there is one escapade Blue starred in that still makes me smile when I think of it. The incident of the kidnapped chicken.

I was in the middle of teaching a class one morning when I heard a light rap on the door. I called, "Come in," but nobody did. The light rap was repeated. I opened the door and was surprised to see Erita standing there, clearly upset, wringing her hands.

"Madum, come quickly. Brue bad."

I placed the class monitor at my desk, told the girls to continue with their assignment, and sprinted after Erita, who already had a good head start on me despite being by now heavily pregnant. As we neared the compound, I could hear a lot of shouting and yahooing growing steadily louder, and when I charged through the open gates, close on Erita's heels, I was met with a unique sight. Clearly enjoying himself, Blue was loping around the compound, weaving in and out of the houses, keeping just ahead of an angry mob that included house boys, house girls, and people I'd never seen before. At the forefront was an enormous African lady wearing a voluminous kaftan, a colorful turban, and brandishing a machete, all the while screaming invective in her own language. I rapidly deduced that the cause of both her fury and determined retrieval was the chicken that Blue had clamped in his jaws, squawking pitifully as it flopped helplessly around.

I'd been giving Blue some obedience training – shake hands, sit, stay, come and so on – and now I drew myself up to full height and bellowed, "Blue! Come here!"

He stopped dead, and so did his trailing conga of irate Africans, all heads turning towards me. Cork-screwing his ears, Blue lolloped over to me, the hapless chicken bobbing in his jaws. "Sit!" I roared. He knew he was in trouble. The corkscrews slowly unwound, and he lowered his rump to the ground, regarding me plaintively. "Drop it!" I hadn't actually taught him that command, but he complied, and I snatched up the poor fowl as its owner advanced on me, machete raised. A quick inspection revealed that the chicken was unharmed, just a tad mauled, dog slobber more than anything, and badly traumatized. I thrust it towards her, and she snatched it, tucking it under one meaty arm. I naively thought that was the end of it, but she continued to berate me, waving the machete about menacingly. Clearly rather weary now, Blue slumped to the ground with a grunt and watched the proceedings with much interest, as did the entourage.

"Erita," I whispered out of the corner of my mouth. "What's going on?"

"She not happy, madum."

"I can see that, but the chicken's safe now, right? No harm done".

Erita sighed. "Madum, Brue has stolen this chicken five times."

I stared at her dumfounded. "*Five times*! The same chicken?" Clearly, my dog had a warped sense of fun rather than a killer instinct. "Where from?"

Erita pointed in the direction of the nearby village, the source of most of the nocturnal drumming. "We always took it back."

"Why didn't you tell me? Oh, never mind. Is the lady still angry?"

A redundant question. She was snorting like an enraged bull and eyeballing Blue with thinly disguised malice, fingers flexing and unflexing along the handle of the machete.

"Yes, madum." Erita lowered her voice to a whisper. "She say she want some money."

The machete-wielding lady wanted compensation. Fair enough. I doubted if her poor traumatized chook would ever lay again. "Tell her to wait."

I was shortly back with a five-kwacha bill, which I handed to the woman. She snatched it, looked at it disdainfully, curled her lip muttering something I was probably better off not understanding, and stalked off, the very picture of affronted dignity. The posse likewise drifted away.

I led Blue by the collar to my stoop where I kept a chain looped through the decorative concrete latticework at the end of the building. I rarely used the chain, but on this occasion needs must. Once I'd secured him, I went inside and fetched the hearth brush that resided by the fireplace. Erita said "Eeeee!" and fled to the kitchen. Returning to the stoop, I stood over my dog, whom I'd never raised so much as a finger to, and said, "This is going to hurt me way more than it hurts you." Then I delivered three hefty whacks to his well-padded rump. He looked at me with hurt disbelief, yelped, and flung himself into the corner. I had to do it.

Expat Blues

Clearly, he'd exhausted goodwill and if he kept abducting the chicken, I knew they'd put a spear through him. That's exactly what had happened to an Indian teacher's beautiful German Shepherd. Erita brought him a bowl of water and stroked his head.

Blue suitably chastised, I returned to school and explained my temporary absence to a deeply amused Carmel, who always knew exactly what was going on at any given moment. My recount of the saga of the serially abducted chicken provided entertainment at tea break, and the rest of my morning passed without incident.

When Blue saw me approaching after school finished, he leaped to his feet and lunged to the limit of his chain, whining his happiness. I released him and we had a big cuddle. Animals are so forgiving. I still felt pretty rotten, though, so I took him into town after lunch and bought him an ice cream, which he enjoyed immensely.

"That five kwachas is coming out of your feed, by the way," I told him sternly as he slurped. He paused to give me a doggy grin; we both knew I didn't mean it.

Blue never touched another chicken – live one, that is – but about a week after the Chook Chase Challenge, as it became known in compound annals, he swiped half a cooked chicken I was planning to have for dinner off the bench while I was momentarily distracted, scooting off outside with it before I could stop him. I guess he had the last laugh – and revenge.

Chapter Nine: Work and Play, A Brush With Witchcraft, A Close-Run Thing.

When I wasn't working or spending time with Blue, I did my best to negotiate the minefield that was expat social life in Livingstone. Most of this centered on the club scene. There were several clubs, hangovers from the colonial culture, and which one you hung out at was an indication of your social status. Not all expats were created equal. For example, if you were employed as an engineer or a bureaucrat you would be on a pretty lucrative contract with flash car (BMW or Mercedes) thrown in, spacious bungalow, servants – who often lived in separate quarters on site – and socialized accordingly. If you were a poorly paid teacher like me, you generally hung out with lots of other teachers in a more shabby environment. The available clubs included the Airport Club, MOTH Club, Boat Club, Golf Club and Sports Club. The Airport Club and the Boat Club were favored by the well-heeled. The Golf Club was exclusive to the seriously elite. Nearly all the teachers joined the Sports Club, which offered cheap subscriptions, but you could frequent the other clubs if a member invited you as a guest or if there was an inter-club competition. So, I joined the Sports Club, a complex which included a parking area, a single storey white stucco building which housed the main clubhouse featuring French doors opening onto a covered stoop, a bar, squash courts, showers and toilets. As well there was a playing field out front for football games, an overgrown basketball court, and a stagnant swimming pool that nobody used. None of the members cared a hoot about doing sports. The principal recreation at the club was drinking. Liquor was cheap and the expat drinking culture was a tradition well established. It was in Africa that I really learned how to drink. Cigarettes were cheap, too, about twenty-seven ngwe (cents) for a slim little box of twenty Stuyvesant, so almost everybody smoked as well.

Besides drinking, there were regular movies, usually shown on a Friday night by projecting the film onto the white-washed end wall of the building, with patrons seated on rows of chairs taken outside for the occasion. During the rainy season we squashed inside and used an interior wall. There were whist drives, a curry lunch with rice and salads every Saturday, regular raffles, and a pokie machine which frequently disgorged a nice jackpot. If you won, you were expected to shout drinks for everyone present in the bar. Easy come, easy go. Snacks like potato crisps, nuts and jerky were available, and at one end of the bar there was a regularly topped-up jar of pickled eggs which were a bit of an acquired taste but went down well with a cold beer.

Usually, we had a braaivleis and party to celebrate events like New Year and Valentine's Day, and I recall one memorable bash named the Prostitutes' and Tramps' Ball. Football matches drew big crowds, like a very intense game between the Italians (they had a big presence in Livingstone, both training the air force and running a Fiat assembly factory) and the Irish, where a fair bit of blood was shed – not really what you expect in a football game. The club barman was a polite, inscrutable African Muslim named Isaac. God alone knows what he thought of all the antics, or the fact there were no African members, though coloreds and Indians were welcomed.

Racially, Africa was a complicated place, and this fact was always at the forefront of your consciousness, whether you wanted it or not.

Indians made up the commercial class in the town, owning most of the shops and businesses, which were often family enterprises, like the town's casino and taxi company. They tended to socialize amongst themselves, gathering at their community center to watch Indian movies, and celebrating Hindu festivals. Africans were largely unemployed, and many lived in a squalid shanty town on the outskirts of Livingstone which had sprung up as a result of urban drift, now a common phenomenon in post-colonial Africa. Many Africans deserted their traditional rural subsistence way of life seeking wealth and opportunity in the cities and towns, but most found only poverty and hardship. Shebeens, unlicensed makeshift pubs sprang up selling the traditional munkoyo brew made from maize and sorghum, fueling violence and keeping the crime rate high. There was an 'urban legend' that at least one murder occurred every night in the shanty town. Another legend held that when the beer started to run low, they urinated it back into the barrel to be drunk again, resulting in numerous deaths.

Then there were the coloreds, which throughout the continent of Africa meant people of mixed black and white heritage and was not necessarily a derogatory term. This category was further broken down into 'African coloreds', who were paler-skinned than full-blooded Africans but still had some African features e.g., frizzy hair, and 'European coloreds' who were a lighter coffee-color and might feature blue eyes, straight black hair, or even fair hair. Indians and coloreds were generally welcomed at the clubs, but Africans were noticeably absent. There were unspoken taboos everyone was expected to respect, unless they courted social death.

Just as my contract was ending, 'Zambianization' was getting into its stride, and we had at least one African club member I can recall. Abe had a local government position, a dog called Rover, and drove a BMW. Locals referred to such people as 'honorary whites'.

When I first started patronizing the Sports Club, there was a colored family who regularly turned up, consisting of mother, father, young son aged about fourteen, and his paternal uncle. They ran a hardscrabble farm of sorts down by the Zambesi River. One evening they arrived full of a riveting story involving the son and a crocodile. The boy, the father and the uncle had been hauling in a fishing net at dusk when a huge crocodile had reared up and seized the boy. The father and uncle had grabbed the boy before the croc could pull him under for the death roll, and a titanic wrestling match had ensued, with the miraculous outcome being that the boy had been rescued from the croc's jaws and certain death. This remarkable tale was somewhat skeptically received, but at his father's prodding, the boy obligingly raised his shirt to reveal an amazing pattern of scars across his torso, front and back, that conformed exactly to the teeth and jaw shape of a crocodile. I peered closely just as everyone did, and there could be no doubting the truth of the amazing survival story. Crocodiles don't rip and tear, they clamp before pulling prey under to drown, so it all made sense. By some miracle and after a prolonged battle the two men had managed to prise the croc's jaws apart. The family was feted with free drinks for the rest of the evening. Sadly, they were all eventually barred after the wife was seen on many subsequent occasions to be bearing the unmistakable signs of domestic abuse.

Expat Blues

There was one other category: white Zambians, Europeans who'd been born in the country and had lived there all their lives or who had taken residency, like the Wildlife Club President and his wife mentioned earlier. These were a distinctive, edgy breed of folk who always gave me the feeling that they had to battle a sense of alienated inferiority on a regular basis and were frequently borderline troppo, as the popular expression went, covering everything from outright insanity to just mild eccentricity. They seemed to live on a knife edge.

Complicated indeed. But, for all that, I only saw two instances of overt racism while I was in Africa, and one occurred at the Sports Club. The other happened in a game park, and I'll touch on that later in the narrative. The incident at the Sports Club involved a drunken South African, Louis Botha, a local white farmer who'd moved from South Africa to Zambia with his family, and whom popular rumor claimed was poor and struggling. He'd often turn up at the club on a weekend with his big, rawboned, unsmiling wife and three little kids, who'd remain sitting stoically in the car while he tanked up at the bar alone. On this particular occasion, he'd become a bit aggressive with some patrons as he got steadily lubricated, and finally Isaac, our barman, refused to serve him any more alcohol. Somebody called out, "Go home, Louis, and make sure your wife drives!"

The big Boer quickly turned ugly, and singled out Isaac to vent his nastiness on, mocking his appearance and describing him as a 'funny little black man' who had no right to tell him, as a white man, what to do. Somebody fetched his wife, who marched in, collared him and hauled him out to the car. Isaac, who had stood on his side of the bar staring unflinchingly past Botha during his tirade, picked up his cloth and wiped down the counter as if nothing had happened. There were a lot of people in the bar that afternoon, including a few well-built men, but no one, myself included, had really made any effort to defend Isaac, and I felt bad about that. Botha was subsequently barred.

In the racial pantheon that was post-colonial Africa, there was one category that was particularly tragic. This was the African albino. They had all the classic African features: the tight, cotton wool hair, thick lips and broad noses, but their skin was milky white, their hair blond, their eyes pink. Often, they were murdered at birth, especially in remote places, and if they survived, they eked out lives of desperate, impoverished ostracism unless they were lucky enough to be taken in by one of the mission stations. Africans were deeply superstitious people who believed in witchcraft; twins and triplets were also seen as cursed and frequently murdered as newborns by being buried alive.

There was considerable racial tension amongst the white tribes in Livingstone, too, and I was pleased that, as a Kiwi, I was excluded from the friction. The expat population of Livingstone was largely British and Irish, which could be problematic. Back in Northern Ireland, 'The Troubles' were in full swing. In January 1972, just six months before I arrived in Zambia, British soldiers had shot and killed fourteen unarmed Irish civilians during an anti-internment demonstration in Derry, a tragic atrocity known as 'Bloody Sunday'. The British Embassy in Dublin was burned to the ground. The hatred, bred over centuries of brutal British occupation of Ireland, was raw and sometimes spilled over. At one St Patrick's Day celebration in Livingstone, a dinner dance at the old colonial hotel, the British present refused to stand for the Irish national anthem and a right old full-on donnybrook was only narrowly avoided, largely due to the quick intervention and diplomacy of the clergy present. Wounded patriotic pride and free-flowing alcohol do not a good combination make, and the atmosphere remained hair-trigger combustible for the rest of the evening, the ever-vigilant clergy damping down hotspots as they flared. Thankfully, the night concluded without bloodshed, but to quote the Duke of Wellington after Waterloo, it was a close-run thing.

There was one little dandy of an Irishman, John Clare, who delighted in parading around in a black beret and camo blouse (acknowledged 'uniform' of the IRA) while singing drunken renditions of The Ballad of James Connolly (Irish rebel hero executed by the British) whenever and wherever he could, going down on one knee with particularly explosive passion while rendering the line, 'God's curse on you, England, you blackhearted villain!'. One big Belfast Protestant whom I remember only as

Mike, would turn puce, itching to throttle the chanteur, but it would have looked bad because he was so big and John Clare so small. However, Big Mike exacted revenge and caused equal upset for the Catholic Irish with lusty renditions of the Ulster Protestant anthem, The Sash My Father Wore. Different vibes for different tribes. Old enmities were not softened by a change in setting.

DNA testing later in my life showed that I am 45% Irish, but I didn't know that back then, and anyway I just tried to be color blind and non-tribal and get along with everyone. I have to say though, I did enjoy an affinity with the Irish craic, especially the music and songs, even the political ones. There was one Irishman, Teddy Lodge, who had a fine voice and who'd bring his guitar to the club when he was in town, sit at the bar and sing all night, inviting a few others to contribute songs as well. Pat Coughlan, for example, always sang a lovely rendition of The Cliffs of Moher. These nights were most enjoyable and well attended by the British, too. Everyone just sipped their drinks quietly and took pleasure in the music. Teddy knew how to perform an eclectic repertoire that pleased his entire audience and avoided bloodshed.

I didn't emerge from this racially heightened world entirely unscathed, though. One afternoon, as I was driving on the narrow dirt road that led past the 'council houses', headed towards the main road and into town, I noticed a group of three teenaged African boys walking along the verge towards me. As I got closer, I smiled. The boy in front worked his jaw furiously and landed a huge gob of spittle on my windscreen, followed by the shouted words, "Go home, white bitch!"

It took me some days to get over that.

I mostly enjoyed the socializing that centered on the club and discovered that I also really enjoyed playing darts. I bought my own set of 'arrows' and gained something of a reputation for being a top scorer, which got me onto the club team. I also played a lot of squash, and at one stage was briefly top of the club ladder (for women, that is) before I was toppled in a challenge. This game worked up a good sweat and kept me fit. That fitness was somewhat offset by the expat drinking culture, with which I happily connived. I'm not sure how I got home some nights. Sometimes, I was very late as the club didn't really have set hours, and the compound gates would be locked. I'd toot softly, so as not to wake people, and flash my lights hoping to alert the night watchman to come and open them, and this sometimes worked but often didn't, probably because he was tucked up fast asleep somewhere. When it became obvious that he wasn't coming, I had no choice but to lock up the car and scale the gates, trying to avoid nasty injuries from straddling the barbed wire crest, and hoping I dropped down safely on the other side; no mean feat when you're far from sober. When daylight revealed one's car on the wrong side of the gates, everyone knew who'd been a dirty stop-out.

Livingstone had a fine outdoor municipal pool, too, and I swam there often. Entry was the equivalent of nine cents and as soon as I pulled into the carpark on a hot afternoon, I'd be besieged by a group of grubby little African urchins all clamoring with outstretched hands for some money to get in for a swim. I could never refuse them, so I dispensed coins and then we'd all troop in together under the gorgon gaze of the lady receptionist. The African lifeguard was a strapping fellow who was always deeply annoyed by the prospect of snotty little kids invading and befouling his pristine pool. To my perennial amusement, watching from the water or stretched on my towel, sunbathing on the grass berm, he'd line them all up military style, make them strip, and scrub them raw with a large bristle brush and equally large block of tallow soap at the tap next to the pool. During this ritual he'd frequently glance over and glare at me for complicating his job. Once the little kids were sanitized, they were allowed to put their shorts or knickers back on (no – because usually filthy – dresses or tops allowed) and plunge in, all shrieking happily. They were really bloody annoying if you were attempting laps, splashing about wildly or jumping in on top of you, but I always loved to witness their sheer delight. There was a bountiful mango tree growing just outside the fence, and when they were done swimming, they'd shinny up it in a boisterous swarm to grab an afternoon snack.

Meanwhile, back in the compound life was a fairly predictable routine. I'd hoped Catherine would provide some company, as a fellow single, but she was always off with Jimmy when she wasn't working. I still spent a fair bit of time with the Coughlans, but I was becoming increasingly disenchanted with them. Some baseline unsavory people, when they know you're on your own, have nobody to look out for you, will become users who take advantage, and they fell into this category. For example, faced with a good offer they couldn't resist, they'd sold their car and had a period of waiting before they could take possession of their new one from a soon-to-depart expat. During the hiatus, they made it clear that I could become their personal chauffeur in my car. Every day, after lunch, they'd arrive on the stoop with requests to be driven here there and everywhere on whatever pretext. I wouldn't have minded if they'd shared the petrol costs since I was on a tight budget, but not once did they offer to fill the tank, and I, like a mug, didn't protest. One Sunday, they asked me to take them into Rhodesia and I duly complied. Again, they gave me nothing towards petrol, but on the way home Pat suggested we stop at the charming vintage Falls Hotel down by the river for a steak sandwich, which he claimed were really good value at 75 ngwes, and therefore an understandable favorite with him and Bernie. After we'd eaten, Pat went up to the service desk and paid for our meals. I thought, oh well, at least he bought me supper. Then we carried on home.

The next morning, as I was getting ready for school, Pat knocked on the door, breezed in with outstretched palm and said in his inimitable, thin-lipped Cork accent, "Ye owe me 75 ngwes for yer steak sandwich last night. Ye forgot to pay me."

I was speechless. I gave him the wretched money and he left. I felt empty inside for the rest of the day. I felt used. Surely the worst kind of people will capitalize on the loneliness of another.

Thank God they picked up their new car shortly thereafter and I saw little of them, which suited me fine. When they came to the club, they'd always choose costly drinks if someone else was paying, but then find an excuse to leave abruptly when it was their turn to shout a round. This did not endear them to people. The consensus was that Cork people were tight. No kidding!

My daily routine by now was pretty predictable. I rose early to let Blue out for his doggy devoirs (I always made sure he was safely inside at night. There were many nocturnal hazards for a young dog), fed him, had a bath, dressed, ate breakfast and headed over to school. When school finished around noon, I returned home, ate lunch, did marking, took study if I was rostered, and hosted my Wildlife Club on a Friday afternoon. I sometimes gave senior students extra tuition as well. Often, I'd drive into town to find something nice for dinner, post letters, go for a swim, or maybe check out what was showing at the bioscope. I also enjoyed exploring the little backstreet shops, which were something of a pack-rat's treasure trove. That was where I found a fine pair of hand painted enamel bowls for Blue, along with a leather collar and leash. Everything in the little shops was very cheap. In the evenings, I fed Blue and then cooked myself some dinner. I remember the first time I bought a supermarket chicken, planning to roast it. When I got it home and removed the plastic wrapping (and the feet tucked inside the bird) an awful pong wafted up to pucker my nostrils and I almost gagged. Smarting over the waste, I was carrying the chicken to the big rubbish drum we all shared in the middle of the compound, near the septic tank, just as Nora was dumping some trash. She looked at my stinky chicken that I was holding at arm's length.

"Smell bad?"

"Sure does. I have to chuck it."

She whipped the chicken from my hands and commanded, "Follow me."

Bewildered, I traipsed after her into her kitchen. She rinsed the chicken under running water in the sink, patted it dry with a tea towel, then took a bowl from the cupboard, filled it with water, added a good dollop of vinegar and immersed the chicken completely.

"There," she said, handing me the bowl, "let it soak for about an hour or longer and the smell will be gone. They all come pongy from the supermarket, and everyone does this. Cook it well, you'll be fine."

Expat Blues

She was right on both counts, so from then on that was how I dealt with African chickens, and I never got sick.

One evening, the Indian family in our compound, Rahnee and David Paul, invited me for a curry. I was really looking forward to it as I loved a good curry, and this would be the genuine article. My mother made curry when we were growing up, at first only for our father when we were little, but when we were older, we all shared it. Of course, Mum made it the way all Kiwis did, with raj style curry powder blend. I'd enjoyed Nora's curry on my very first night in Livingstone, but Rahnee's curry was like nothing I'd ever tasted before; fragrant, flavorful, packing some heat – it blew my taste buds away! When I asked her what was in it, she reeled off a list of spices I'd never heard of, and delighted with my sincere enthusiasm for her cooking, offered to get me some from Indian grocers in town and show me how to make her Ceylonese chicken curry. She was as good as her word, and thus began my lifelong love affair with authentic Indian curries. If I don't have a curry at least once a week, I get withdrawal symptoms and I have one entire cupboard dedicated to my array of spices.

I worried about Rahnee, who also showed me how to fry and grind spices. I worried because she often presented at school with what looked like nasty bruises on her upper arms. When I mentioned it to one or two people, my concerns aroused a negligible response. There seemed to be an unexpressed look-the-other-way policy amongst the expats, the same attitude shown to the Longs' shocking neglect of their child.

The government imported quantities of often bizarre specialty foodstuffs to keep the expats happy, but what we really needed was much simpler fare. For example, obtaining fresh fruit and vegetables in Livingstone was tricky and there were long periods of drought. Agriculture was rudimentary still; subsistence farming the norm with the slash and burn method still widely practiced. Maize (eaten as nshima or the coarser version, samp – like Southern USA grits) was the staple crop, grown once a year, and if the rains were not optimal, too severe or too meagre, the crop could fail, causing starvation for the coming year as Africans could not afford expensive imported foods – like English trout, which I once incredulously spotted piled high in the supermarket freezer!

The Irish got twitchy about potato shortages, the Indians about scarcity of onions, and everyone moaned about cooking oil sometimes being hard to get. (I'd had to get used to using cooking oil, which was still largely absent from New Zealand cuisine. Like all the women of her generation, Mum favored lard or 'dripping', as she called it, for frying and roasting). In search of vegetables, all the expats drove out to a single market garden on the outskirts of town prosaically called 'The Farm' to snap up whatever was on offer. Sometimes there was a good choice, other times pickings were slim, and fresh fruit was virtually impossible to procure. I had to learn to cook vegetables previously unknown to me, like aubergines and okra, which not knowing any better, I boiled into a tasteless mush and a slimy mush respectively! I remember one time I bought a bunch of green chilis, not knowing what they were but imagining they would be like the sweet peppers we'd had at home, just a skinnier version. I chopped several of them into my curry and almost blew my head off! Gradually, I learned how to cope with alien foods and shortages. I always took a daily vitamin supplement, along with my anti-malarial Daraprim.

The last term of 1972, leading up to Christmas, was both a trying and eventful one. The weather at this time of year was hot and sultry, so we started and finished half an hour early. By 7.30a.m. I'd feel the sweat pouring down my back in rivulets during a lesson and the girls were lifeless.

One morning, as I pulled back the living room curtains after a hot, restless night, I was surprised to see a car with two nuns from the convent inside shoot past the window and brake to a halt outside the Coughlan's house. One nun stayed at the wheel while the other dashed inside and quickly returned with Bernie in tow, clad in her dressing gown. The pair dived into the car which backed up, turned and sped away in a flurry of dust. We didn't have to wait long for an explanation of this odd incident. By the time I got over to school, most of the staff were already seated quietly in the staff room and John Kay ushered me in to join them, murmuring that Carmel would be along shortly. She duly arrived, grim-faced, a hush descending as we all watched her expectantly. She took a deep breath before informing us that one of the girls had given birth to a baby in the dorm, in the early hours of the morning. By the time the sisters were alerted, the girl had bled heavily, hence the need to fetch Bernie in such dramatic fashion. Both baby and mother were now in Livingstone Hospital doing well, thanks be to God. She said all the students knew and were angry because they felt the teenager in question had brought shame on the school. Carmel asked us not to gossip about the unfortunate events outside St Mary's and hurried off, leaving us to prepare for classes. Later, it transpired that the convent was, understandably, terribly embarrassed that nobody had noticed the girl's pregnancy. She was, however, a large girl and had disguised her condition well. Her education was terminated, of course, and she was sent back to her village with her baby boy, but every baby was welcomed in Africa so there was no fear of her not being supported or of the child not being cared for because of some social stigma. They would be just fine. What was sad was that the girl's chance at education was finished. The government was immoveable on this rule. When our nubile girls went home for the holidays, they were prey for randy young village bucks used to getting their way in a heavily patriarchal society. Even if identified, the fathers of course were never held to account. I remember a girl in my form class, Elizabeth, an exquisitely beautiful child with outstanding intelligence and a promising future who inexplicably disappeared mid-term. When I questioned the students, they shyly and reluctantly disclosed that she had left because of pregnancy. I was heartbroken.

The next event of note was something that happened to me, personally. I'd noticed. for a while that a girl in my fourth form English class was behaving strangely, and that the other girls were shunning her, even hissing whenever she came near. I reported my concerns to Carmel, and she told me to keep an eye on the child and let her know immediately if things got worse. We both thought it might be just a case of teenage bullying. The girls did fall out with each other, like normal teens everywhere. One morning, I'd had to break up a dreadful cat fight between two senior girls taking place on the verandah, just as I arrived at school. By the time I got them apart, they'd torn bloody chunks out of each other's necks with their fingernails.

But this child behaving strangely was different. Her eyes had become heavy-lidded, her face expressionless, her movements unnatural and robotic. The other students' hostility towards her was clearly escalating, although I never witnessed any physical or verbal abuse. I tried to talk to the poor girl, but she was steadfastly remote and non-communicative. I assumed she was reluctant to dob anyone in, according to that unwritten code kids have.

As it happened, the president of my Wildlife Club, Gertrude, was in the same class, so I took her aside one morning and asked her what was going on between the child and her classmates. Gertrude was reluctant to talk at first, but we had a bond and she finally disclosed that the girl was a victim of witchcraft. She was cursed, possessed by a demon, and the other students were mortally afraid of her. Hiding my shock, I thanked Gertrude and relayed the information to Carmel, who expressed her skepticism, blaming African superstition, and told me to keep monitoring the situation. Other teachers had reported to her with their concerns also, but she was sure there was nothing seriously amiss.

It was in my English class that things finally came to a head. The possessed girl, if that's truly what she was, was sitting on her own at the back of the classroom surrounded by empty desks, and I noticed that several of the students had bunched up awkwardly sharing seats with other girls to avoid being near her. I chose not to make an issue of this and commenced my lesson. The instruction segment finished with, I set the girls a written task and sat down at the teacher's desk feeling decidedly uneasy. The atmosphere in the room was electric, the girls muttering to themselves and constantly glancing over at the affected child.

Then, abruptly, she stood up. There was a collective gasp before the familiar 'eeeeee' sound began, but low and ominous. I tensed. The possessed girl's bulging, bloodshot eyes were focused unblinkingly on me. I swallowed hard. Then she moved, from the desk to the aisle, and began advancing towards me, the glowing coals of her eyes never once leaving my face. But what haunts me to this day, since I consider myself a rational person, is that she wasn't walking. I swear she was *floating*. I rose to my feet. I heard a girl cry out, "Run, meestress!" but I couldn't have moved if I'd wanted to. I was rooted to the spot.

Expat Blues

"Jesus, Mary and Joseph, protect me," I whispered.

By the time she came abreast of my desk, my heart was hammering in my chest, and I couldn't tear my gaze away from those burning eyes. Then, she abruptly veered right and drifted out of the open door and away. I collapsed onto my chair, and the girls exhaled a collective groan of relief. After I'd pulled myself together and restored order, I sent Gertrude to fetch Carmel. None of us ever saw the possessed girl again and the nuns, especially Carmel, were tightlipped about her fate. I have pondered it long and hard and am none the wiser. But there is no doubt in my mind that unholy forces were at work there, forces nobody wants to meddle with. The memory of those burning, ghoulish eyes, of her floating towards me, still makes me shudder. I consider myself an open-minded person and I accept that there are, to paraphrase the Bard, 'more things in heaven and Earth than are dreamt of in my philosophy'. I'm convinced that, on that morning, I'd had a glimpse into the heart of darkness. It remains my hope that the poor, benighted child recovered, that her demons were driven out, whether by traditional or Christian exorcism I'll never know.

On a happier note, I was asked if I'd take on the senior debating team and was more than happy to do so. This was a great way to get to know the girls better and we enjoyed a string of successes in challenges with other schools. Each win meant a boozy congratulatory morning tea, for me at least. My team members got more conventional treats appropriate to their age. One debate I really enjoyed had equal rights for women as its theme and of course we took the affirmative. This provided an opportunity for revealing discussions with the girls about a woman's lot in post-independence Zambian culture. They were all ambitious, wanting a good education, jobs and careers rather than just becoming a man's chattel, saddled with babies and endless hard work. They had a tough road ahead of them, as from what I'd observed, their culture still largely enforced traditional roles for women. Even in my culture, feminism as a force hadn't really got underway yet. It was still in its nascent stages. Anyway, I encouraged my team members to shoot for the stars, assuring them that 'girls can do anything'!

One image sticks in my mind that provided a perfect illustration of the lot of the African woman. I was in town one afternoon when I saw an African family that had just disembarked from the train and were strolling down the main thoroughfare. The husband, a tall, well-dressed man wielding an ornate walking stick, strode out ahead of the little procession, erect and dignified. Bringing up the rear (women traditionally walked behind their husbands) was his wife. She was hugely pregnant and also carried a toddler slung on her back in the customary carrying shawl, tied across her breasts. Another young child clutched her free hand and with the other she steadied a tower of three suitcases on her head. How I wished I'd had my camera. Whenever I drove into town past the brightly colored little houses in the Maramba complex, I'd see the women toiling away in their shambas, minding little children as well, while their men sat on chairs in the shade, typically peering into hand mirrors as they plucked hairs from their chins.

Sometimes, on my travels, I'd see little girls down by a river, struggling to manhandle and wash the big black cauldrons or heavy long-handled pots that food had been cooked in. Add to that the danger of lurking crocodiles that took hundreds every year. My heart always went out to them. They were the ones who were burdened with babysitting younger siblings and doing menial tasks. From a young age in their villages, they were trained to know their place and their allotted roles. When they married, the groom paid the bride's family in cattle, a dowry known as lobola. Once married, they were subservient to their husbands, who might take a second, younger wife when the original lost her youth and vigor. It was a harsh old life.

The term was certainly a mix of good and bad for everyone. Suddenly we had a 'flu epidemic on our hands and the girls went down like flies. Classrooms were virtually emptied, so Carmel made the call to close the school for two days, with teachers being seconded to help out where they could in the boarding side's dorms full of sick kids. I never caught the illness, and I can't recall any of the other teachers catching it, though I think a few nuns did. Anyway, it ran its course and things soon returned to normal.

Expat Blues

It was also during this term that I became involved in some social work. The convent's complement of nuns only included one or two who taught (Carmel always took at least one senior class), the rest fulfilling other roles, like quartermaster, bursar, running the boarding side, taking charge of the kitchen etc. Sister Adrian was the community social worker representing the Society of St Vincent de Paul. She was a lovely person, short, stocky, slightly slovenly and distinguished by the fact that she sported a full beard which she shaved every day, leaving a blueish shadow around her jawline. I always tried hard not to stare. She approached me and asked me if I'd like to accompany her on one of her visits to the local shanty town, where she regularly distributed food, medicine and other commodities to the most desperate cases. I agreed, although I was a tad suspicious about her motives. Years spent being taught by nuns meant I had pretty sound antennae for their machinations, one of which was always trying to recruit new members to their order. I was aware that they had a young Irish girl around my age currently staying at the convent, June, who'd come to Livingstone for several months to experience the missionary way of life and decide if she truly wanted to become a Franciscan nun. I had a sneaking suspicion they might be teeing me up for a similar fate!

I walked down to the convent to meet Sister Adrian on a Saturday morning, and we drove out to the slum, which turned out to be far worse than anything I could ever imagine. I got out of the car and had to take a moment to process the stench, the confusion of ramshackle dwellings and the throngs of ragged adults and mudlark children, some of whom were scantily dressed, others running about stark naked. The stench came from the open pit toilets, their overflowing contents meandering in stinking rivulets amongst the densely clustered dwellings. I watched in horror as a group of little kids amused themselves sailing tiny 'boats' they'd made from plastic garbage along these runnels of filth. Thin, wary dogs, bearing signs of longterm inbreeding, skulked amongst reeking piles of rubbish.

Pulling myself together, I made myself useful by taking charge of Sister's crammed basket, following her into this realm of horrors, which she navigated with an ease born of deep familiarity, greeting and being greeted as she went. She'd been visiting here for a while and knew exactly who needed help most. The bulk of her regular clients were elderly, both men and women. You didn't ever see many elderly Africans in Zambia because, sadly, life expectancy was low, around late forties, early fifties. Sister also had the advantage of speaking fluent Lozi.

One of the things that struck me was the inventiveness of the housing materials. Cardboard was common, and of course I could imagine what happened to that when the rains came. Rusting corrugated iron was much in evidence, too, and there was one tiny hut built creatively out of split and flattened Coca-Cola cans. These crude and basic little shelters were called pondoks. Taps with running water were few and far between, all of them surrounded by clusters of jostling women armed with all manner of containers. Women cooked in black cast iron kettles over open fires and the air was acrid with smoke. Every day was a grim struggle for survival for these people, amongst the heat, stench and disease, with little hope or prospect of improvement. This was urbanization at its worst. Some people dwelling in the shanty town did in fact have jobs, which meant they then had to support not only themselves but any family members who came to join them, all on a pitifully low wage. No one had any chance of ever getting ahead. And yet the place had a raw sense of community, of the stubborn doggedness of suffering humanity that was as old as time.

We stopped in front of an elderly man squatting under a strip of polyurethane supported on two rickety poles at one end, the other ends perforated and tied with string to the roof of a hut against which he rested his back. A few little items of domestic trivia nestled beside him – a plate, cup, spoon, small cooking pot. Everything he possessed in this world. Smiling broadly, he scrambled to his feet, delighted to see Adrian, and she introduced him to me according to polite custom. Introductions were a formal ritual in Zambia and taken very seriously. First you bowed towards the person, with the greeting 'Muzihile' while the other person responded 'Ennisha' which might be repeated a couple of times. Then you gripped each other's hands, both of them, and slowly pumped up and down. I dipped my head and opened with 'Muzihile'; the old man responded, and then he thrust out his hands. I blinked. The digits on both hands were mere stumps of unnatural uniformity. He was a leper. For a split second I hesitated, and then I clasped what remained of his hands, he beamed, we pumped slowly. Sister Adrian smiled and nodded. We gave the old man a bag of mealie meal, a packet of biscuits, and most prized of all, salt, sugar and soap. How on earth does he manage, I wondered, with his fingers so diminished. Sister asked him how his headaches were, and he shook his head sadly.

"I am paining, I am paining."

I knew Africans suffered badly from headaches. Our girls were often afflicted, especially in the heat. Traditionally, the tribal medicine man would make horizontal incisions near the eyebrows and let the patient bleed, reminiscent of medieval phlebotomy, the rationale, I guess, being to relieve pressure and thereby pain. Lots of my students showed evidence of these threadlike, tiered scars on their temples.

Sister gave the old man packets of pain killers, and Daraprim for malaria. He accepted everything with both 'hands', humbly thanking her over and over.

As we moved on, Sister said, "You won't catch leprosy, so don't worry. You did well."

I thought, *Would have been great if you'd forewarned me*! And made a mental note to scrub like a surgeon when I got home, just the same! I have a hand washing fetish anyway, ever since I suffered from impetigo/school sores on my face as a child and was told it was my own fault for being a dirty little girl who didn't wash her hands. The arrowhead on that insult pierced right to the heart bone and remained embedded.

"He has a hut, at least," I observed, assuming the old man was just enjoying some outside time, watching the world go by.

Adrian shook her head. "No. The occupants let him use their wall to attach his plastic, but that's his home, just that narrow strip of polyurethane."

I was silent. What could I say? *The rains!*

"He is shunned," she added simply.

One thing that lifted my spirits was seeing some of the little kids, boys mainly, running about with a popular toy peculiar to this part of Africa and which never ceased to intrigue me. The toy in question was a square box made completely from sculpted wire with four little wheels attached, and all of them were identical – spindly, insubstantial clones, virtual parodies of what you imagined a 'cart' should be. An 'operator's handle' protruded from the back allowing the owner to push the bizarre little vehicle along, enjoying boisterous races with other children. I have no idea who made them, but they were unique, and I knew of expats who went out of their way to buy them for their own children, or to take home as a souvenir.

Little boy with wire trolley.

I went to the slum with Sister Adrian several times before she was recalled to Ireland for health reasons, and nobody took up her mantle. I could not afford to buy the many things the people needed, and neither could I risk, as a young white woman, going into the shanty town alone. Sister Adrian had carried an aura of protection with her that included me, but I had no such status. So, I did not go again.

I saw so much poverty and suffering while I was in Africa and, coming from a country of comparative material wealth and comfort, it completely recalibrated my world view. Dealing with the beggars I found especially painful, and I had to strike a balance between my compassionate nature and my own survival needs. I tended to offer food rather than money, which was likely to be squandered at the nearest shebeen. So many Africans eked out lives characterized by wretchedness and want, bereft of hope or any chance of betterment.

To this day, I have a horror of wasting even the tiniest morsel of food.

June, the young aspirant, visited me regularly and became a friend. She was always bouncy, cheerful and full of life and I missed her when she left. June returned to Ireland and soon thereafter entered the convent to train as a nun.

Tragedy and joy often go hand in hand. I received one of my father's cryptic telegrams informing me that my sister had given birth to a third child. It read, 'Cheryl a boy.' She now had three sons – which was the joy. Shortly thereafter, we were all galvanized by the shocking news coming out of the Olympic Games in Munich, Germany – the murders by Palestinian terrorists of eleven Israeli athletes. Once again, Jews were dying on German soil.

★

As it happened, I ended the school year on a bum note – and I'm not being figurative. There were two things I loved to get the girls to do – laugh and sing. First, laughing. We didn't necessarily share the same sense of humor. Sometimes I'd say something I thought was funny and they'd look at me blankly. Other times, I'd say something that to me was a perfectly ordinary statement and they'd laugh their socks off. It was the *way* they laughed that was unique. As if there were some invisible, pre-arranged signal, they'd all start laughing at once, in perfect unison, at the same pitch. This would last for a few seconds and then someone would go "Yee-ha!" and the laughter would cease, like abruptly turning off a tap. It never failed to delight me.

Next, the singing. Any excuse, and I'd get them to sing for me. They loved to sing, I loved to listen. One morning, as the Yuletide season approached, my junior class asked me to teach them a Christmas carol. I decided on Jingle Bells, wrote the lyrics on the blackboard and then sang it for them. The only problem was that I'm tone deaf, not a musical bone in my body, whereas they had perfect pitch. They looked a bit puzzled and then obediently sang back to me this truly awful flat, off-key rendition of Jingle Bells. The whole school heard, and I never lived that one down. Carmel laughed 'til she cried.

Before I'd become disenchanted with the Coughlans, I'd mentioned to them that I was keen to go to Rhodesia for Christmas and that I had contacts who might provide free accommodation. They latched onto this like bidi-bids on your woolen socks and expressed great enthusiasm to join me. I'd be taking my car, of course, wouldn't I? No point taking two. I'd sighed and agreed. Better to have company and another driver (Bernie didn't drive) I told myself. I put it out there that we'd need to share costs like petrol, then, and they nodded in the affirmative. I didn't like my chances.

So, I wrote my letters to the Marist brothers, and they responded promptly with assurances of accommodation for three in both Bulawayo and Salisbury, the two places I wanted to explore. The Coughlans were delighted, and we settled on a departure date about one week before Christmas, after exams finished and the schools had broken up for the year. To make some extra money, I joined a group of expat teachers at one of the government high schools in Livingstone to mark examination papers. Preparations were underway for my next adventure.

First, I had to go to the bank and organize money for my trip. I had decided to hang on to the few remaining travelers' cheques I'd brought from home because I had it in the back of my mind to do a really big safari northwards at some point, so I went to the bank and filled out a form for a new set of cheques, writing in my intended destination as 'Rhodesia'. I was aware that relations between Zambia and Rhodesia were nosediving rapidly – when I'd applied for my ID card, the Zambian official had ticked me off for having 'too many' Rhodesian stamps on my passport – but you could still cross the border, even though you got a cold reception from both sides. I was therefore stunned when I picked up the cheques and discovered 'Not negotiable in Rhodesia' stamped on the back of every single one. Furious, I remonstrated with the bank, but they refused to budge, so I cancelled the cheques and my bank account before storming out. Thereafter, I banked with Barclays, as Mary had recommended. When I was telling people at the Sports Club what had happened, an Indian friend told me not to worry, he'd get me some Rhodesian dollars. He was as good as his word, and, to my relief, a couple of days later I had the money to finance my holiday, R$120. Sounds a small amount, but back then it was more than enough to have a good time in Rhodesia where everything was dirt cheap. Pat and Bernie had some British pounds and had managed to get some US dollars as well, mainly through Pat hanging around the border post and buying them from tourists coming through. This was highly illegal, and he was lucky not to be caught. It was virtually impossible to buy foreign currency for travelling purposes from banks in Zambia, while the kwacha was spurned everywhere outside the country.

I made my final arrangements and this time I left Blue with the Mullins, who promised to take good care of him. Since the chicken incident he'd been a pretty quiet boy. I often took him to the Club with me, and he made friends with everyone, especially any kids.

The distance from Livingstone to Bulawayo was 450kms on a beautiful straight road, about a five-hour drive, so we planned to leave around 11 a.m., allowing time for the border formalities plus any stops, and arrive in Bulawayo around dinnertime.

Some of the happiest memories of my time in Africa are getting behind the wheel of my car and heading off into the unknown, keen to embrace whatever adventures and new experiences came my way. The hum of the engine, the tyres drumming on the dead straight road, the bush stretching to the horizon on either side, always filled me with a heady sense of anticipation, and always brought to mind the quote from Lauren van der Post's book that I'd read before coming to Africa:

It's the not-yet in the now, the taste of the fruit that does not yet exist, hanging the blossom on the bough.

I was young, free of responsibilities, believed I was bulletproof. Life was good. Of course, I still had niggling reservations about my fellow travelers, but, no matter, I was prepared to make the best of things.

So, we set off on a fine morning, headed for the Falls border post. I'd checked and re-checked all my documentation and was confident I'd met all the requirements. I'd had no problems thus far. I took the remaining New Zealand travelers' cheques along as backup, hoping I wouldn't have to use them.

The border post was quiet, just one elderly American couple besides us, so we were getting processed quickly. The customs men didn't always ask you to produce your money, but this time they did, and I was selected. I'd just placed my passport on the counter and so I got out my Rhodesian dollars and put them next to it. The customs officer picked up the money and counted it, his face expressionless. Then, still holding the sheaf of notes in one fist, he reached under the counter, drew out a thick white pad of blank dockets, placed it between us and picked up a pen. The book of dockets was upside down to me, but I could easily read the heading in thick black type: 'Seizure Notice'. My blood ran cold.

"What are you doing?"

Without looking up, he replied coolly, "This money is illegal currency. I am taking it."

For a moment I didn't react. I still find it hard to believe what I did next. A voice in my head, an actual voice, said with the clarity of a bell ringing in an alpine meadow, 'Grab it'. So, I did. I snatched that money from the custom officer's hand in one fluid swipe, at the same time as I bellowed, "Pat! Bernie! Run!" Then I bolted for the door, and bless them, the Coughlans, showing commendable reflexes, were right behind me. The two Americans began shrieking and threw themselves to the floor, even though nobody was armed. The border post staff were standing frozen with shock, which gave us the vital few seconds we needed. I raced for the car, parked, as luck would have it. just opposite the door, unlocked it and hurled myself in. Bernie dived into the back, Pat into the passenger seat. The customs men had by now gathered their wits, dashed out from behind the counter and were in hot pursuit. As the leader reached for my door handle, I brought my fist down on the interior lock button, bellowing at Pat to do the same. I shoved the money into my bra, started the car, and took off in a spray of gravel, headed back to town.

"Sorry," I said, "but they were going to seize my money, all of it. I snatched it back."

"They'll be calling the police," said Pat. "Take the back road."

"Good idea." I groaned. "Oh god!"

"What?"

"I left my passport on the counter!"

"Jasus!"

As we flew along the narrow shingle road at a furious speed, Bernie, bouncing around on the back seat, really let me have it. "Slow down! Ye'll kill us all! Ye feckin' mad New Zealander, what were ye *thinking*?"

As she spat out the last word, she also spat out her partial dental plate. It went flying past my left ear, ricocheted off the dashboard, and landed between my upper thighs.

"Now look what ye'f made me do! Pat, find me teef!"

As I stifled an impulse to break into hysterical laughter, my peripheral vision registered Pat reaching a tentative hand towards my groin. "Don't even think about it!" I snarled and the hand was quickly withdrawn. I didn't dare take one of my hands off the steering wheel as the car slewed over gravel and juddered over corrugations.

As I rejoined the main road and slowed down coming into town, I was scanning for waiting police cars, but there were none. I parked, retrieved Bernie's teeth and passed them over my shoulder. She gave them a cursory wipe and put them back in amidst a lot of cross muttering. "This is the end for us. We're all going to be kicked out of the country, probably go to prison. Ye've done it this time."

"Bernie, nothing bad will happen to you. I'm the one who has committed the crime," I replied more calmly than I felt. "Now, anyone got any ideas as to what we should do next? I saw that customs guy writing down my rego as we took off, and they have my passport."

"Jude," said Pat. "We must go to Father Jude, at the church."

Nice, I thought, kind of like seeking sanctuary in the Middle Ages. "Okay, let's do that." I started the engine.

I parked around the back of St Theresa's, well out of sight, and with my disgruntled accomplices in tow knocked on the presbytery door, which was opened by the priest's housekeeper. As luck would have it, Father Jude was in and she ushered us into the lounge, where he and his visitor, Father Vinnie O'Connell, were enjoying tea and cake. Father O'Connell, whom I knew well, was a tall, handsome Holy Ghost father who bore a strong resemblance to the actor Roger Moore. Jude instructed the housekeeper to make a fresh pot of tea and sat us down. He and Father Vinnie listened with riveted interest as I recounted the events that had caused the three of us to become fugitives from the law – well, me, anyway.

Neither priest seemed particularly concerned, which was encouraging. They conferred with each other briefly and then Father Vinnie rose to his feet to announce their decision.

"Pat and Bernie, you stay here. I'm taking Erin to see Jack O'Brien. If anyone can sort this out, he can." He turned to me. "Leave your car here, we'll go in mine."

I nodded, already feeling better. Jack O'Brien was a middle-aged, highly respected expat Irishman who was the local Chief of Police. That job had not yet been Zambianized.

Expat Blues

Both Jack O'Brien and his sociable, impeccably attired wife were at home, a superb bungalow surrounded by lush gardens and maintained by an army of servants. More tea was fetched, and we sat out in the shade on the expansive stoop. I repeated my story to Jack, who listened attentively as he sipped. When I concluded my account, he replaced his cup on its saucer, laid it aside, and folded his hands in his lap.

"Why did you snatch the money from the customs officer?"

I blinked. I would have thought that was pretty obvious.

"It – it was all the money I have in the world."

Jack lifted his hands and brought them down on his knees. "Perfect answer! Now finish your tea, and then you and I are going to visit Gus, the Head of Customs. His office is in the township. He's a good friend of mine and I want you to tell him exactly what you've just told me. As an African, he will relate to it without hesitation. It was all the money you had in the world."

He turned to his wife. "You can entertain Vinnie until I get back, dear."

Mrs. O'Brien simpered in her handsome guest's direction, suggesting this would be no hardship. I thanked Father O'Connell sincerely for his part in my rescue and he wished me well.

Gus was a softly spoken, kindly man who put me at ease immediately and listened with sympathy as I repeated the statement Jack had endorsed while apologizing profusely for my actions. He knew about the incident. His men had telephoned to inform him, but they had also claimed it was Pat who had snatched the money. I denied that vehemently and reiterated that I had acted alone. He accepted that, phoned the border, told his officials that I would return to claim my passport and would leave the Rhodesian money with the Chief of Police. We shook hands, I thanked Gus repeatedly, and then I left with Jack.

When we were in his car, Jack chuckled and said, "The customs fellows didn't want to admit they'd been embarrassed by a woman.

Don't make a habit of it, but well done, just the same. You're a gutsy young woman."

"Thanks. I didn't know Rhodesian dollars were illegal currency. The friend I bought them off mentioned nothing." I told him about the failed attempt to buy travelers' cheques. "That should have warned me. I feel really stupid."

Jack sighed. "Don't blame yourself. Things are getting nasty, on both sides. They're changing the rules almost daily. That money would never have been turned in; they'd have shared it amongst themselves and sold it for a mark-up on the black market – no pun intended. Where are the dollars now?"

I patted my chest. "In my bra."

Jack chuckled. "Find another hiding place, just in case. I'm not saying they'll do a strip search or anything, but you never know. Now, what other money have you got – legal tender, that is?"

I told him about my New Zealand travelers' cheques, which I had with me as backup if my dollars ran out, but hoped not to use, and he said to show them those. By the time I finished thanking him for everything, we were back at St Theresa's. Jack waved goodbye, I issued yet more thanks to Father Jude, collected Pat and Bernie, and better late than never, we were on our way.

The Rhodesian dollars went through the border in the bottom of a box of tissues (the beginning of my career as a smuggler). The customs men were sheepish but polite as they stamped and returned my passport, and everything went smoothly on the Rhodesian side, too. I began to relax and enjoy the journey.

A couple of weeks' later, when we returned to Livingstone, shortly before the Rhodesians closed the border, the whole expat community was abuzz with my take-the-money-and-run exploits, and I'd morphed into something of a local legend – for hooliganism. Of course, like Chinese whispers, some versions of what went down bore little resemblance to the truth. For example, it was widely believed that Pat, well known for his fiery temper, had assaulted one of the Zambian customs officers. The expat community loved to embellish their gossip with lurid details.

Expat Blues

As it happened, I wasn't the only one who had problems at the border. John Clare had gone through wearing his trademark IRA get-up of camo and black beret, and the Rhodesians, hypersensitive to anything that smacked of terrorism, had roasted him, stripped him to his undies, searched and thoroughly humiliated him, even relieving him of some of his possessions. Most of the expats, Irish included, felt little sympathy with John.

Bulawayo was a neat, clean colonial town, similar to Livingstone but much bigger. The main thoroughfare through town was massively wide, the legacy of the settler farmers who'd needed plenty of space to turn their bullock carts when they came to town.

The Marist brother with whom I'd corresponded had enclosed a rough map and I found their residence easily enough. The brothers were kind and welcoming and our accommodation spartan but adequate. There was a communal dining room for guests that provided a self-help breakfast of cereal, tea and toast. For other meals we had to fend for ourselves. We unloaded our things and headed back to town to find the famous Greek restaurant that served a mixed grill for one Rhodesian dollar. I kid you not. Steak, sausage, a chop, beans, egg and chips, all for one dollar. Rhodesia – however you felt about their politics, best place ever for a safe, cheap holiday.

That night, I slept like a log.

The next day, we travelled up to the Matopos Hills, a strikingly beautiful area 35kms south of Bulawayo, and a unique place of softly undulating whale-backed dwalas, broken kopjes, huge, rounded boulders and balancing rocks, all created by millions of years of erosion of the granite plateau. First inhabited during the stone age, this UNESCO National Park, established in 1926 as a bequest from Cecil Rhodes, features caves with stunning artwork over 1,300 years old.

The distinctive round boulders of the Matopos Hills.

We climbed the hill called World's View, brightly colored lizards in hues of blue, orange and green darting away from our feet, and sat in awestruck silence drinking in the beauty of the place. Here the fierce Matabele warriors, an offshoot of the Zulus who had fled north under their chief, Mzilikazi, to escape Shaka's tyranny, made their indaba against the British, charging up the hills armed with assegais into the torrent of bullets from the Maxim guns that scythed them down like ripe wheat. The warriors called them 'the mowing guns'. Thousands died. The white settlement of Rhodesia by Rhodes' victorious British South Africa Company went ahead.

A little rhyme I'd read somewhere that summed up imperialist arrogance popped into my head.

Whatever happens

We have got

The Maxim gun

And they have not.

Hardly what you'd call a fair fight, and the reason Bulawayo means 'place of slaughter' in Ndebele. The Africans believe the ghosts of their dead chiefs haunt the Matopos Hills, which they regard as a deeply spiritual, sacred place. Cecil Rhodes loved the hills so much he asked to be buried there and to fulfil his wishes his tomb was painstakingly hewn out of the solid rock. Not far from his resting place is the tomb of his friend and cohort, Leander Starr Jameson, of 'Jameson Raid' fame. Such romantic names. There is also a striking monument to the legendary Shangani Patrol, a party of 34 settler soldiers who, in 1893, were trapped by the rising river of that name and annihilated by around 3,000 Matabele after a courageous last stand, sometimes referred to as Britain's Alamo or Little Big Horn. Mzilikazi is also buried in the Matopos. It was he who named this beautiful place, using a play on the Zulu word for 'bald heads' – matobo – to describe the smooth, rounded boulders.

We lingered for a long time, soaking up the dramatic history of the place along with its stunning scenery, and I took many photos, hoping at the same time I might get back there again before my tour ended.

Grave of Cecil Rhodes, Matopos Hills.

On the way back to town, a beautiful hornbill flew out of nowhere and crashed into my windscreen, dying instantly. It was inexplicable and upsetting, marring an otherwise perfect day.

That night, we returned to the Greek restaurant, and I devoured half a delicious roast chicken with vegetables and gravy, again for a ridiculously cheap price. There was a strong Greek business community in Bulawayo.

Then it was thanks and goodbye to the Bulawayo Marist brothers, and onwards to Salisbury, capital of Rhodesia.

Salisbury (now Harare) was one of those young, newly risen colonial cities that reminded me a lot of towns back home in New Zealand: similar construction materials, architecture, layout and an old-fashioned, conservative English ambience. This was the seat of Ian Smith's rebel white minority government. Police cars still bore the old British imperial insignia on their doors: BSAP (British South African Police). Again, the brothers were welcoming and our accommodation comfortable. We had Christmas dinner at a hotel, explored the shops, went to the movies and a nightclub and made several forays out into rural areas where white owned farms worked by African labor were in abundance. Rhodesia was dubbed 'the breadbasket of Africa' and it certainly radiated a feeling of prosperity and plenty. Even while you were enjoying it, though, you kept having the niggling feeling that it was doomed, that it couldn't last, that the resentment and violence simmering just beneath the surface was about to erupt. And it did. White majority rule would end just six years later in 1979 after a long, bitter 'bush war' and atrocities on both sides that left 20,000 dead.

We had an enjoyable New Year's Eve, joining the locals on the city streets to listen to music and watch the fireworks. A random young man grabbed hold of me, wishing me a great year ahead before planting a kiss on my lips. A kiss goodbye. We headed home, arriving back in Livingstone just before the Rhodesians slammed the border shut with a vengeance on January 9th 1973 after guerillas attacked a white farmer and two soldiers were killed when their jeep hit a mine. No more crossing Cecil Rhodes' Falls bridge over the churning Zambesi gorges. Henceforth, if you wanted to go to Rhodesia, you had to travel 62 kms to Kazungula, cross the Zambesi River by pontoon into Botswana at Kasane and from there travel around 40 minutes on a lonely dirt road into Victoria Falls township, praying you didn't encounter terrorists along the way. I made this journey often.

One morning, while friends and I were enjoying breakfast in our favorite Victoria Falls restaurant owned by a charming Swiss couple, we learned that terrorists had ambushed and killed four white South African soldiers on that very road the day before, and not long after we'd driven over it ourselves. I suddenly had no appetite for breakfast.

Apart from making himself horribly ill by eating congealed fat from a roasting pan Nora had placed outside on the doorstep for some reason, Blue had been a good boy, and we had a joyful reunion. While I was away, Brendan had kindly removed the termites from my wall, replastered and painted it. Inspired to build further on this welcome improvement and to make the place more homely, I arranged my growing collection of carvings on the mantlepiece, hung a striking war shield above it, found a nice tablecloth for my large dining table, and splashed out on a shortwave radio and secondhand record player. Outside, I painted the kerosine tin white and gave the sad, unidentifiable little plant it contained some badly needed nourishment to perk it up. Finally, I tidied up the unravelling black plastic binding on my lonely little outdoor chair.

I'd survived two weeks of the Coughlans without murdering them with my tyre iron and feeding them to the closest pack of lions, although the temptation had been strong on occasions.

The holidays were coming to an end. Time to plan my next adventure – a big one.

Chapter Ten: The Italian Connection, The Mother of all Safaris, A Brush With Death

The first term for 1973 got underway, and by now I felt like an old hand. The exam results were in, and my kids had done well, many of them getting special commendations. I was very pleased and felt I must be doing something right. Sister Carmel was delighted, and my personal cachet took a boost.

Erita took maternity leave to be with her new little daughter and Edina filled in for her. Apparently, there was something of a baby boom in Maramba. The Browne's nanny/housekeeper caused great excitement the first time she brought her newborn twin boys to the compound to show them off. They were heartbreakingly beautiful. When I asked their names, their mother announced proudly, "This one Benson, this one Hedges."

Blue came to school regularly and the girls had by now accepted him as part of the furniture, although they still complained about his farting. I tried to explain that it was a Bull Terrier thing, but I'm not sure the girls understood. One evening, I noticed he was listless and had left half his dinner on the plate, which was unusual for him. Bluey loved his tucker. When I got up the next morning to let him out, he couldn't move off the sofa and refused all food. I noticed that his breathing was a bit labored. I asked Edina to fetch me if she felt concerned and as soon as I had a free period, I hurried home to check on him. He was clearly ill. As soon as school finished, I bundled him into the car and took him to the vet, who had a dodgy reputation. There were doubts he was even qualified. He scraped a patch of fur off Blue's right foreleg with a rusty razor, drawing blood, and then gave him an injection after randomly stabbing around for a vein while the poor dog whimpered pitifully, and I did my best to console him. It was awful. The injection, the 'vet' said dismissively, was all he could do. Blue had pneumonia. The locals went down with this disease like flies as the seasons changed from hot and humid to cooler, and clearly animals could be affected, too.

Realizing we'd get no further help here, I rushed Blue home, laid him back on the couch, and sprinted over to the Coughlans, who were just finishing their lunch. I told them I thought Blue was dying and they followed me back to my house. Bernie examined Blue and confirmed that he had pneumonia.

"He needs antibiotics."

"The vet wouldn't give me any. Just injected him with something."

Pat snorted. "That eejit! It's a death sentence taking an animal to him, so it is."

Bernie straightened up. "Drive me up to the hospital and I can get what he needs."

I felt relief flood through me. Blue would make it. This daft old dog made life bearable, and I couldn't face losing him. One night, with pay day some way off and the bank account empty, we'd shared the remains of a box of cornflakes for dinner. Blue had eaten his portion with gusto, smacked his lips and grinned at me as much as to say, "She'll be right, Mum!" Best mate.

Pat said, "I'll stay with the poor cratur. He's one of our pups, after all." He stroked Blue's head tenderly and, I felt really guilty about my fantasies with the tyre iron.

I tried not to drive too fast to the hospital, wrestling with my sense of urgency; I didn't want Bernie losing her teeth again. While I parked, engine running, she disappeared into the dispensary and re-emerged wearing an innocent expression, hands empty.

"In my bra," she whispered as she got in the car. I grinned. Useful things, bras.

Back home, I dosed Blue up under Bernie's supervision, and we left him to sleep. All afternoon, I sat at the dining table, marking books, planning lessons, drinking endless cups of tea and trying to concentrate while also keeping an eye on my pet, soothing him from time to time with my voice and hands. As evening approached, I gave him more tetracycline as per Bernie's instructions. He still refused food, but he wagged his tail and my heart soared. By bedtime, his breathing was already much improved. Just before lights out, I heard his enamel dinner bowl, which I'd optimistically filled for him, scrape on the kitchen floor, music to my ears.

Blue made a full recovery, although it took him a while to get his energy levels up again. I bought him the best food I could afford, and he gobbled it all down with gusto. He came with me when I dropped a bottle of wine off to Pat and Bernie along with my heartfelt thanks, and he made a big fuss of them both. It wasn't the last time the Coughlans would come to my rescue.

A lifetime of raising pets has taught me that when you help a sick animal, they form an extra strong bond with you. Blue and I were now as close as it's possible for dog and human to be. Animals understand gratitude.

The next event on the social calendar after Christmas and New Year, was Valentine's Day, and the Sports Club hosted a braai and dance, the music provided by Father Jude's talented young African rock band. I trotted out one of the new dresses I'd bought in Rhodesia and went to the party with Mary and Brendan. The poor old Coughlans had the 'flu.

A big crowd attended, and I finally got to meet two of the three newly arrived young Irishwomen who'd taken up teaching positions at St Theresa's Primary School. Kitty and Noeline were both attractive, genuinely friendly people in their twenties, like me, and I felt elated to get acquainted with some potential single female pals at last. I'd already met a few of the single male teachers in Livingstone, like the aforementioned John Clare, and his sidekick, Pat O'Connell, but hadn't really struck up friendships with any of them.

That night, I also met Berto, an Italian expat contracted to work as an engineer for Zambian Railways, and, as it turned out, something of a legend in southern Africa as a big game hunter. He was about 16 years older than me, short and stocky, with hazel eyes and fair hair. Berto came over and introduced himself politely before asking me to dance, immediately impressing me with his lovely manners. He was pleasant company, and I had a great night. At the end of the evening, he invited me to his house the following day as

Expat Blues

he had a few friends coming around for drinks and food. Safety in numbers, I thought, and agreed. He gave me directions and we said goodnight. On the drive home, I endured much teasing from Brendan and Mary.

The next day, Sunday, I drove to the address Berto had given me, and parked my Mazda amongst a cluster of Fiats on the grass apron in front of a very nice bungalow. All the Italian expats in Livingstone drove Fiats, so I could safely guess the nationality of the guest list. Berto welcomed me warmly, pressed a glass of Chianti into my hand, and led me around the assembled throng for introductions. They were all men, all Italian, various ages, all polite and gentlemanly in a slightly chauvinistic way that was charming rather than demeaning. I'd met some of them at the Mosi Friday night disco. They could be amorous and quite forward, but at least they liked women, and coming from a misogynistic culture that venerated male mateship, I found that refreshing.

Berto, as it turned out, was an accomplished cook and, with the assistance of his houseboy, an impressive array of food was soon spread out on the dining table, to which we helped ourselves. I especially enjoyed the chicken, braised to melting tenderness in sage, white wine and garlic – delicious. After we'd eaten, the purpose of the get together was revealed as the table was cleared, the curtains drawn, and a screen erected. Berto was going to show us the slides from his most recent hunting expedition. I settled down in the dress circle chair he'd ushered me to, sipped my glass of wine, and waited expectantly for the show to begin. I had no idea what to expect.

For the best part of an hour, we sat through slide after slide of Berto, flamboyant in slouch hat, safari vest, shorts, and jungle boots, cradling an enormous high-powered rifle at port arms, perched triumphantly atop dead elephants oozing blood from the bullet wounds he'd inflicted. His guests applauded and cheered each photo. As if that weren't bad enough, the last ten minutes or so were devoted to ghoulish, gory photos of local African villagers slicing chunks of meat off the quarry for a big feast. Some of them were pictured sawing their way through the trunk, which Berto explained was 'a delicacy' for them. "Nothing is wasted," he intoned. "They are so thankful for the meat."

I felt physically sick, the delicious chicken I'd consumed steadily rising in my gorge. Of course, the sprawled carcass of the elephant being butchered had two bloody sockets where its tusks had been, and I knew who'd snaffled those. Ivory was the object of the hunt.

As the show ended and the curtains were opened, I jumped up, told a surprised Berto that I'd just remembered another engagement, thanked him for his hospitality and fled. For days afterwards, I couldn't get those hellish images out of my mind.

Berto didn't give up easily. I suppose I should have expected that from a hunter. When, a few days after the slaughter fest, I came home from school at lunchtime, Erita, now returned from pregnancy leave, intercepted me before I was even through the door, excitedly pointing to a beautifully gift-wrapped box on the dining table.

"A man bring!" she said, smiling and nodding. Every African woman had a man. She probably thought it was weird the way I lived alone, with no man and no family.

I opened the parcel, Erita hovering curiously, to reveal a little card which read, *A gift for you, my dear Ereena. What do you want from life? I haven't a clue. I hope we can talk. Berto.* I chortled. Then I opened the box itself and drew out a bottle of Chanel No. 5. Wow. I'd never, ever been given such an expensive gift, especially from someone I hardly knew. I unscrewed the top and sniffed. Heavenly.

"Perfume," I explained to Erita, miming a spraying motion directed under my tilted chin. She nodded her understanding, eyes wide. I dabbed a little on her wrists and she sniffed it cautiously, her face lighting up. I dabbed some on her neck as well. "Your husband will love it."

Erita ducked her head, giggling, gathered up her things – which probably included the leftovers I'd planned to eat for lunch – and hurried off home.

Expat Blues

Communications in Livingstone were tricky. Cellphones and computers hadn't yet been invented, of course. I had no landline in my house; none of us did. It was snail mail, telegrams, or face to face. To acknowledge Berto's gift and thank him for it I would have to drive to his home, and chances were he'd be at work. I decided to wait until I saw him again, which wasn't long in coming. He knew I patronized the Sports Club and he'd started attending regularly himself, so at the end of that week, on the Friday night, we bumped into each other again. I thanked him for the perfume, and he bought me a drink. Before we parted for the evening, he invited me for lunch at his house the following day, Saturday, and I accepted, on the condition I could bring Blue. He replied that Blue was most welcome adding that he loved dogs and had owned one until recently when it died of old age. Apart from his penchant for blowing away pachyderms, I was learning that he was a kind, warm-hearted person who was easy-going pleasant company. And a great cook. And had an endless supply of Chianti. He showed me the room in his house where he stock-piled his ivory, sending home a few tusks at a time as 'gifts' for his family in Venice to avoid import tax. They represented, he said, his nest egg for his old age.

"It's entirely legal. The Zambian government sells the licenses, and elephants everywhere have to be culled from time to time."

That may have been so, but I just felt gutted as I stood looking at the pile of tusks, which symbolized the cruel deaths of at least a dozen beautiful elephants. We came to an agreement that he would keep this aspect of his life exclusively to himself, but there was always an elephant in the room just the same.

So Berto became my boyfriend, which generated lots of gossip of course, and I found him to be a kind, considerate, gentlemanly companion. On our first proper date, he took me to the Mosi for dinner and I made an effort to dress up and look nice. I ordered the prawns piri piri because one, I love prawns, and two, I love spicy food, welcoming a bit of heat, but they were so incredibly fiery I could barely eat them. A concerned Berto kept topping up my water as I spluttered and gasped forcing them down, not wanting the money he was spending to be wasted. The next time we went to the Mosi, I ordered a medium steak, thinking I'd be safe, but it was cooked so rare it was basically raw. Instead of sending it back, I forced it down and felt nauseous for the rest of the day. The best meals we enjoyed were the ones he cooked in traditional Italian style: antipasti first, then pasta, then a main dish. One memorable dish he cooked for me was pigs' trotters. I'd baulked when he told me what was on the menu, but they were one of the most flavorsome things I've ever eaten. He was an expert at seasoning food, a naturally good cook. Berto also introduced me to avocados which proliferated on a tree in his backyard. We ate them with sugar and whipped cream for dessert and I loved them.

Berto had no problems getting hold of quality Italian foodstuffs and wines from his friends and fellow countrymen in the air force and at the Fiat factory as they were well supplied by regular cargo flights from home. They often visited his house while I was there and it cracked me up the way they'd try and speak English for my benefit until someone said something contentious and then it was all on in loud, voluble Italian accompanied by much gesticulation, while I sat there in the dark, shaking my head and laughing.

Sometimes, Berto excused himself and disappeared in his land rover for a while; I suspected he was hunting. He also had mysterious 'business interests' in South Africa, where he had lived long-term before moving up to Zambia, but I never probed him about anything. That was his private concern. He told me he was from Venice, a divorcee with no children, and that he wished to marry again and have bambinos. Oo er!

I'd made other friends besides Berto during this period, principally the three young Irish women teachers at St Theresa's Primary: Kitty Hughes, Noeline McCartan, and Mary Connolly. It was also around this time, early 1973, that I began to hatch my plans for a major safari. My aim was to head north, crossing Zambia into Tanzania and going all the way to Kenya. It was a journey of about 8,000kms, would take about four weeks – the entire holiday break – and we would go there and back in my little tin-pot Japanese car. I must have been insane. I wasn't the only one. When I mooted it to the girls, they were enthusiastic, and Kitty said she had a relative, serving as a priest in Nairobi, who she was sure would put us up for a few nights. Even better, one of the nuns attached to St Theresa's had a brother who was a priest at a remote mission station near Voi, which was the first town after crossing the Kenyan border, and when she heard of our plans, she got to work organizing a stay there for us as well. The Catholic network was proving useful yet again.

Delighted, with our progress, I set to work on finalizing the logistics of this great adventure. I'd bought a Michelin fold out map of Africa before I left New Zealand, and now I used it to plot the journey, recording everything in a little notebook. We sure had some terrain to cover.

When fellow expats got wind of my proposed road trip their verdict was collectively negative: I was a suicidal nutjob. I heard on the grapevine that Sister Carmel was 'deeply concerned', and the consensus was that she would forbid the venture.

One night, just as I was thinking about going to bed, Blue barked at a knock on the front door and I opened it to find Carmel standing there, her expression grim. Uh oh, I thought. This is where she tells me the trip's a no-no. She refused to come in, apologizing for the late hour, then drew herself up to full height, which was still small, and delivered some devastating news.

"Erin, Father O'Riordan has been in touch with me. Apparently, New Zealand is about to host a rugby tour by the South African Springboks. Did you know about it?"

I shrugged. "They're our biggest rivals at the game, but I didn't know a tour was imminent."

There was no TV. I had a radio, but I mainly listened to music, and I never bought the national newspaper. I lived in my wee African bubble and any news from home was relayed via my family's infrequent letters, which were mostly about domestic trivia. I wasn't a rugby aficionado, anyway, and had never been drawn into the Kiwi obsession with sport.

Carmel nodded, biting her lip. "Well, some of your countrymen are protesting on racial grounds because, as I'm sure you know, blacks are excluded from the team. There's been a bit of civil violence and it's possible that your PM, Mr. Kirk, may cancel the tour."

"Gosh," I replied. "That'll upset the rugby fanatics, like my dad." I chuckled.

Sister's face remained serious.

"Erin, you'd better pray that he *does* cancel it, or it will be very bad for you."

"For me?" I was utterly baffled.

"If the tour goes ahead, President Kaunda will kick you and every other New Zealander out of the country. It's called being PIed – Prohibited Immigrant. Even worse, they'll seize all your assets, everything: car, clothes, possessions, money. You'll be left with nothing and put on the next flight home." She paused to let this sink in. "I'm so sorry. We'll be shattered if we lose you."

Well, that was a nice sentiment anyway. It hit me, then, how much I wanted to stay.

"So, it's all up to my PM, then. When will we know?"

"Father thinks in about twenty-four hours. Hope for the best, prepare for the worst."

After she'd gone, I settled Blue down for the night with a last pee and a snack and went to bed. There was no sleep to be had, though.

The following evening, an ecstatic Carmel hurried over to tell me that Norman Kirk had indeed cancelled the tour and I was safe. Thank you, Norman, you saved the butt of one lone Kiwi in the heart of Africa. The diehard rugby fans were incensed, of course, and the Prime Minister's bid to avoid civil strife cost him the next election.

The relief for me was tremendous, and I spontaneously hugged my little principal, while we both did a brief jig on the stoop. She never mentioned my trip, and as soon as she'd left, I got out map and notebook to tackle the plotting of my safari route with renewed zeal. I was up to where we would cross the Tanzanian border, at a remote outpost called Tunduma.

When I finally told Berto my plans, he threw his hands in the air and said, *"Pazza!"* which I thought probably wasn't a compliment or expression of approval. Sometimes Berto's attitude to women reminded me of my mother.

"Are you mad, Ereena?" (He still called me this, no matter how often I corrected him). "Have you any idea what a journey like this will involve, and in a car only fit for getting around town?"

I felt myself bristle. "Well, of course I have. I've been working out a route and we've got some accommodation organized, mostly with priests and nuns. There'll be four of us, and the car–"

"Petrol. How will you get petrol?"

I blinked. "From a petrol station."

Berto threw his hands in the air again. *"Sognatrice!* There won't *be* any, for long, long stretches!"

I nodded. "Okay." I was beginning to feel out of my depth.

"You'll need to take jerry cans, keep them filled up every chance you get. I can give you some, and a funnel."

I brightened. "Thanks, that's great."

"And you will have to carry them all in the boot, at least three. Four is better. So, there's three other girls going? Where will you put your luggage?"

I was deflated again. "Um. Don't know."

Berto groaned, rubbing his hands over his face. *"Dio ci aiuti!* A roof rack. You will have to fit a roof rack, find a waterproof tarpaulin to protect the load, and get some bungee cords. You only have a tiny car, so it's center of gravity will be altered. You will need to be very careful taking bends."

He removed his hands and regarded me with a mixture of sadness and solicitation. "I will probably never see you again."

"Of course you will. Don't be a doomsayer."

Berto picked up one of my hands, looking into my eyes. "When you return, I will have something important to ask you. I think you understand. You can think about this while you are away."

Oo er!

I relayed all this information regarding the logistics of our road trip to the girls who often had me over for a classic Irish dinner on a Saturday or Sunday night: bacon and cabbage. They promised to put out feelers for a roof rack. We would not be dissuaded. We were all of one mind: determined to go. The four of us agreed we must travel light, just one smallish bag each. As it turned out, it was Father John Mary who found and fitted a roof rack for us and supplied us with a tarp and bungee cords. Kitty had successfully organized our accommodation in Kenya. The countdown had begun. Once again, the snag was getting money out of Zambia. I still had my New Zealand issued travelers' cheques, so I was okay, but getting any issued in Zambia for any destination was now impossible. The girls' decided to get money transferred from Ireland to a bank in Mombasa, our first port of call in Kenya. Until they were able to claim that money though, I'd pay for everything, keep all receipts, and then they'd pay me back. The niggling worry was, would the Tanzanian Customs give us entry with just one of us having any funds, even though we would only be in transit? The girls were friendly with a kindly young Irishman working for Zambian Customs, David O'Sullivan, and he offered to radio their Tanzanian counterpart to ensure our smooth transition when we reached the border post at Tunduma. A couple of days passed, and he relayed the good news that we were all clear, good to go, and gave me a written document with official heading as proof of their assurance. The Kenyan border shouldn't be a problem, we concurred, because the girls had documented proof of the funds waiting for them in Mombasa. There was only one thing left to do: I had to get a *carnet de passage*, a kind of export/import license for my car to add to the already bulging bag of documents I carried. Honestly, African borders were a minefield (literally, in some cases!).

Expat Blues

I said goodbye to Blue, whom I was once again leaving in the care of the Coughlans. This would be our longest separation to date, so I hoped he'd cope okay. I explained it all to him because I always felt he understood every word I said, and he'd talk back to me in a way I'd never heard a dog do before or since. When I hugged him, he trembled and made a low guttural sound, pressing his head into me. He really was a very special dog.

The night before our departure, I stayed at the girls' house so we could get a really early start together in the morning. They shared a comfortable six-bedroom bungalow owned by the cathedral parish and known as 'the teachers' house'. We had to clock up huge distances each day for the itinerary to work, driving from dawn to dusk, covering an average of 800-900kms a day. Destination on our first day was Kabwe, in north-eastern Zambia, where we planned to stay the night at the Dominican convent. This meant that, after negotiating the weird half macadam, half shingle, road to Lusaka, dodging road-hogging aggressive lorry drivers that frequently forced you to slew onto the shingle, we had a long drive up the infamous road known as 'Death Alley', where Sister Frances had been killed. Traffic was light, so I slowed as we neared the fatal spot, and you could still make out the scars on the road, even though it was months since the accident. I muttered a prayer to Saint Christopher to please watch over us. I was responsible for three other lives, and it suddenly seemed a crushing responsibility.

The Zambians had a very effective way of reminding you to be a cautious driver, though. The wrecks of cars, trucks, tankers, buses etc. written off in accidents were simply stripped of anything salvageable and the hulks shoved onto the sides of the roads to rust away and remind passing motorists of their mortality. On one occasion, we passed the battered skeleton of a Volkswagen, which was the make of vehicle the girls owned and shared, sitting forlornly on its roof, and my passengers squealed their distress. Volkswagens had a bad rep for rolling, so I was glad we'd taken my car. Besides, who wants a tank load of fuel sitting in front of them in an accident! Bad enough having gallons of the stuff stashed in your rear.

Erin Eldridge

The night spent in The Dominican convent in Kabwe was pleasant enough. We had dinner with the nuns and then slept in one of the deserted, eerily quiet dorms, the girls all being gone for the school holidays. I'd told the Reverend Mother, who'd been very nice to us but had shocked us over dinner with her sniping at her fellow nuns, that we had to be away at the crack of dawn so she kindly arranged for a breakfast hamper of food, like buttered bread and hard-boiled eggs, that we could eat on the journey. By 5.30 a.m., after a quick cup of tea, we were back on the road. Lunch in Mpika was a forgettable goat curry (Kitty actually threw hers out the window) and then onwards to the border at Tunduma, my stomach already churning with nerves.

I was glad I'd listened to Berto's advice regarding the need to carry petrol, as the further east we travelled now, the more infrequent became the gas stations, and we appreciated the security of having the extra petrol on hand. Every time I gassed up, I filled the tank, and any jerry cans we'd emptied, too. The car was effectively a rocket on wheels, but I tried not to think about that.

For accommodation, we stayed in cheap but reasonable guesthouses or bomas, mostly all bunking in together and finding food where we could. I always paid one of the little street urchins to guard the car overnight, with the promise of half now, the rest in the morning if he did a good job, and we had no problems. Wherever we stayed for the night, we always emptied the roof rack and then set it all up with our luggage again at daybreak.

I was doing all the driving, but I liked it that way. I was more used to open road driving than the girls and I didn't get tired, although, they assured me, I did get grumpy on occasions. I slept like a log every night and woke refreshed and ready for the next long haul. I had one bad moment when Mary dropped a lighted cigarette down the back of my seat while I was barreling along at 120kph. I was livid, not just because of the pain and damage to seat and clothing, but more so because she was utterly uncontrite! I could have lost control of the car and killed us all. Henceforth, I banned Mary from sitting in the seat directly behind me.

We idled up to the border post at Tunduma late in the afternoon, not before I halted further back up the road and issued strict instructions to hide all cash. We all had spare notes of varying provenance and denomination and there was never any guarantee that they wouldn't be seized on a whim. We rolled them up into cigarette size and slid them into the plastic clips that partially opened the back quarter windows.

We passed through the Zambian customs at Nakonde speedily enough, and then braced ourselves for the Tanzanians. I located the letter David had written for me, placed it close to hand and breezed into the post, trying to look confident, the girls trailing in my wake. There were only two customs men on duty, and they looked very surprised to suddenly be confronted with four young travel weary white women. The larger of the two took command, his manner haughty and patronizing, but we just kept smiling, filling out the paperwork and obediently producing everything he asked for in the way of documentation, gritting our teeth as we complied with even the most pedantic request. Then he asked us to show our money. I handed him my booklet of travelers' cheques and he flicked through them before handing them back to me. He turned to Mary, Kitty and Noeline extending a hand.

"Your money for Tanzania?"

"They don't have any," I said evenly. "I'm paying for us all."

He turned amused eyes onto me. "What?"

I repeated what I'd just said and handed him David's official letter. "It was all cleared back in Zambia. You – that is, Tunduma Customs – assured this official that we would be allowed in on the basis that I am the only one carrying the cash. We'll only be in transit. I have more than enough for us all."

He read the letter, folded it, and handed it back to me.

"This is no good. I know nothing about this. They," he gestured towards my three crestfallen companions, "cannot have entry with no money."

Bloody borders! Bloody customs men! The girls gasped. I felt a mix of anger and despair. It was now dark outside. Africa had a fleeting twilight. One moment it was light, the next inky black. We were tired, hungry, and in the middle of nowhere. As I opened my mouth to remonstrate with the guy, Kitty insinuated herself between us and then did a remarkable thing. She cocked her head to one side, twirling a strand of hair around a finger, fluttered her eyelashes, smiled sweetly and proceeded to flirt outrageously with our nemesis. She was an attractive girl, classic Irish looks with black curly hair, creamy skin, and blue eyes. He was instantly ensnared. As Kitty purred on about how desperate we were for rest and sustenance, how their money would be waiting for them in a bank (in Kenya, actually!), and how keen we all were to see Tanzania having heard how beautiful it was etc., the customs man visibly puddled like a big cat being petted in all the right places. After telling Kitty he hoped to see her on our way back and maybe even visit her one day, to which proposition she enthusiastically agreed, he decided that he was going to let us in after all, but to preserve his aura of authority he added that we could only leave once he'd checked our luggage. Just one bag would suffice, he reassured us.

As it happened, the one case I wrestled down from the roof rack was Kitty's. She opened it and the bumptious officer made a big display of fossicking about amongst its contents, lifting items of clothing and peering under them. He picked up a small box and turned around, holding it towards her.

"What is this?"

Kitty affected a shy giggle before leaning in a little to whisper, "Those are *ladies'* things. You know, *monthly?*"

The guy dropped the box back in her bag like a hot potato, slammed it shut, and spun around, clearing his throat. I swear I saw a pink tinge under his black skin.

"That is fine. You can go now."

He strode back into the customs building as we scrambled into the car to get away while the going was good. Once we were a safe distance up the road, we exploded into wild laughter that released all the tension, and over dinner in Mbeya, where we found comfortable accommodation for the night, we toasted Kitty, the undisputed heroine of the hour.

Expat Blues

Tanzania was a wild, beautiful country that seemed very undeveloped and sparsely populated. The roads were not as good as those in Zambia, the German colonizers clearly not as adept at roadbuilding as their imperial British counterparts. Lack of maintenance was probably a factor as well. One night, just after darkness fell and as we were nearing the small town where we planned to stop for the night, the car bottomed out badly in a huge pothole I didn't spot in time, and I was sure she must have sustained some damage. While the girls settled into a hostel for the night, I drove to the local garage and got them to check my undercarriage. All was well and I sighed with relief. I didn't even want to imagine what it would be like for us if the car broke down. She was our lifeline, and thus far had performed admirably.

On the road, we saw few cars but lots of big tankers, and numerous burned-out carcasses of the unlucky ones strewn along the verges on either side. One day, I had to brake suddenly as a huge black snake slithered across the road in front of us. Of course, we all had to pile out and grab a photo, which was pretty foolish in the middle of a vast highway. Another time I slowed in disbelief when we encountered a massive bachelor bull elephant standing nonchalantly just a few meters from the road, waving his tent-flap ears idly back and forth.

"Oh my god," shrieked Mary. "He's got five legs!"

"Nope", I responded. "He's just very, very happy in the moment."

"Ohhhh…!"

As realization dawned on Mary, the rest of us fell about howling with laughter.

The 'five-legged' bull elephant.

What we did see a lot of were long columns of trucks full of Chinese workers employed in building the TanZam railway which would give landlocked Zambia access to the port of Dar es Salaam. The trucks were all clones of old World War Two Chevrolets the Americans had given Chiang Kai shek's government to assist with fighting their mutual enemy, Japan. Seems the Communists liked them so much they churned out thousands of their own duplicates. The coolies riding in the backs of the trucks all wore identical work clothes: dark-colored wide-legged pants, matching hanfu jackets, and coarse woven sandals. On their heads they all wore identical conical straw hats. God alone knew what their lives were like, slaving away in the wilds of Africa without adequate machinery and probably few comforts. It was very difficult getting past some of the convoys as they refused to move over for us or let us in so I could pass them in safe stages. I had to grit my teeth and just go for it when I got a good long stretch of road ahead, while inscrutable oriental faces stared down at us impassively and the girls mostly hid their eyes until we were safely past. It was always a huge relief when I finally overhauled the lead truck and saw clear road ahead. The tanker drivers were better. Using a commonly understood signal, they'd flash their left-hand taillight when it was safe to pass. But I had to be wary, as some were plain malicious, and you'd pull out to find an eight-wheeled behemoth bearing down on you.

Following the route I'd plotted, we kept to a good schedule as we made our way across Tanzania relatively incident free. After Mbeya, our journey took us through Iringa, Morogoro, Korogwe, headed for the border crossing at Taveta and thence to Voi and Mombasa, Kenya, where we hoped to spend a few days R&R over Easter. The girls moaned about missing out on Dar es Salaam, so I promised we'd try and fit it in on the way home. Then they complained about not going via Moshi or Arusha to reach the border, which would have given us a view of Mount Kilimanjaro. I ventured that maybe we could return that way and they were mollified.

One afternoon, as we were doggedly eating up the miles on a dead straight stretch of road, snickering over Mary sleeping with her mouth wide open, we saw a strange, oscillating mirage in the distance. Approaching us was what looked like a cluster of shimmering lights, and it was moving very fast. As it flashed past us, over-revved engine whining its protest, we realized it was a normal vehicle but sporting roof-mounted spotlights as well as blazing headlights, and we could also see that it had decals plastered all over it. Then the penny dropped.

The 1973 East African Safari was the twenty-first rally.

"Rally car," I told the girls, East African Safari. It's famous. That will be a service car caning it to rendezvous with their team. The rally drivers will be on the dirt roads."

We were very impressed, especially when a couple more cars followed the first one at equally blurring speeds that looked suicidal. Not long afterwards, we heard the appalling news that a service car had collided with another during the rally, and eleven people had died. I became even more fastidious about cautious driving.

We left Tanzania with little fanfare and received an unexpectedly warm welcome at the Kenyan border, where I'd once again worked myself up into a lather over our money situation. They couldn't have cared less about the girls having no visible means of support. They looked at their Irish passports and congratulated them for having fought for their freedom, just as Kenyans had, against the British Imperialist oppressors. In my case, they welcomed me as a fellow member of the Commonwealth, and so we were ushered into Kenya in a euphoria of goodwill. Last barrier surmounted.

We drove across Tsavo National Park in pitch darkness which my feeble headlights barely managed to penetrate, only picking up wild animals when we were almost on top of them. At one point we came up behind the backside of a colossal elephant, which obligingly lumbered out of our way, and we saw a pack of wild dogs amongst other game. It was a surreal experience which mesmerized us all and there was a constant background chorus of 'ohs' 'ahs' squawks and squeals which I had to try and ignore as I struggled to follow the vague dirt track.

A couple of hours later, once we arrived in Voi, we got something to eat and then phoned the mission station because we had no clue how to find it. One of the fathers drove into town to meet us, and after introductions we followed him back to the mission in pitch darkness over uneven roads, my feeble headlights again barely coping. He eventually turned off down a very steep, narrow track, with me battling tiredness to concentrate hard on his bobbing red taillights that disappeared abruptly as he made a sharp left turn. I followed suit, into what was an unexpectedly tight and narrow hairpin bend at the top of a steep slope and which I had insufficient room to negotiate. To my horror, I found myself at right angles to the track with the car balanced on the edge of a sheer drop, the front wheels mere inches from disaster. The girls screamed with terror, and I yelled at them to bail out, which they did with unseemly haste. I was hideously aware of the load on the roof and the weight of petrol in the back. Dear old Mary pleaded with me to save myself and abandon the car to its fate, and I think I said something pretty rude to her, for which I had to apologize later. Now alone in the car, I tried desperately to remain calm; I had my foot clamped on the brakes and I yanked the handbrake on as well. Once I'd collected myself, I knew I had to remove my foot from the brake pedal to use the clutch to put the car in reverse. Holding the handbrake so tightly my fingers were losing all feeling, I closed my eyes, prayed, planted one foot on the clutch and the other on the accelerator at the same time as I wrenched her into reverse and eased my death grasp on the handbrake. My heart leaped into my mouth as the car lurched forwards slightly before she shot backwards, nudging the slope behind and I wrenched the wheels around before I repeated my tactics and until a multiple point turn saw me back on the roadway with the bonnet pointing down the slope towards the welcoming sight of lighted windows. The relief was indescribable. To this day, I don't know how I managed it. I believe I had help.

The girls, who'd been standing in a huddle clutching each other while they watched me, erupted into wild cheering and clapping before they jumped back in, and we drove the final stretch to safety. Once I was safely parked, I had to take a moment, just sitting quietly with my forehead resting on the steering wheel, the girls patting me and rubbing my back.

Father, in the middle of setting out cups and boiling the kettle, looked up smiling as we finally entered.

"Cup of tea?"

I felt I needed something a bloody sight stronger than that.

"Could have warned me about the hairpin," I said shakily as I accepted my cup.

"Hmm? Have a spot of bother?"

"You might say that."

Oh God. Tomorrow, I had to deal with that nightmare bend in reverse, but at least I now knew what to expect.

The night spent in Voi was not a restful one, for me anyway, as, although deeply weary, I tossed and turned reliving those nightmare moments when I thought I was going to plunge to my death any second. After a shower and a pleasant breakfast, I steeled myself to tackle the bend from hell once more, but the maneuver went smoothly, helped by daylight. Once again, success depended on coordination of essential factors: unload the passengers, swing just a little bit wide at the right moment, then turn sharply and accelerate at the same time. A terrible disaster had been averted, and as I have at many times in my life, I felt my guardian spirits had watched over me.

The drive to Mombasa was a pleasant two-hour stroll in contrast to the grueling dawn-to-dusk marathons we'd endured thus far. First impressions of the city were enchanting, and we quickly found a cheap, centrally located hotel that accommodated us in a kind of budget bunk room on one side of their flat roof. Shared toilets and baths were on the other side of the roof, and it felt a bit odd crossing back and forth between giant pot plants of brightly colored flowers dotted all over the place, but the digs were clean and comfortable, so we were happy. We freshened up, and went in search of dinner, the friendly locals all greeting us with 'Jambo', Swahili for 'Hello', as we strolled through the city. Because of the dearth of fresh fruit in Zambia, I especially loved the sweet, juicy papaya they served everywhere, always with a wedge of lime. It was delicious for breakfast.

I fell in love with Mombasa, Kenya's main port, instantly, and so did the girls. It had a tropical, exotic feel to it created by palm trees and frangipani, trailing bougainvillea, and beautifully tiled raised porticos fronting its restaurants where you could dine alfresco. Built on a coraline island, for centuries it had been a central part of the Indian Ocean's spice, gold and ivory trade, fought over by the Portuguese, the Arabs and the British, with the British East Africa

Company coming out the clear winners to make the city the first capital of what would become Kenya. Unsurprisingly, Mombasa had become a cultural and racial melting-pot, manifesting all these historical influences in its charming architecture that featured arched doorways, wooden shuttered windows, extending balconies and whitewashed facades.

First stop after a long sleep was the bank to retrieve the girl's money and I was pleased to be reimbursed at last after feeling like the all-dispensing matriarch in the journey thus far.

Typically exotic Mombasa architecture.

In the days that followed, we tried to see and experience as much as we could, which included the famous crisscross elephant tusk arches mounted over the highway, a boat ride on the harbor to watch the graceful dhows, Fort Jesus (built by the Portuguese) with its cannons and commanding view of the sea, the spice market, the old slave market and barracoons, the colorful clothing bazaars, and the stunning beaches. Diminutive Muslim tailors in jelabas and kufis sat hunched over their old treadle Singers on boardwalks outside the clothing stores. For a very modest price, you could choose from their array of beautiful African batik fabrics and have a stunning top or dress made while you waited, or you could choose a ready-made garment from those arrayed in the numerous little shops behind them. The curio markets were superb, too, and once again I sent some pieces to my family, including a magnificent cowhide drum. For the equivalent of $5.00 I bought for myself a piece which is still my favorite African souvenir, a strikingly beautiful head of a Masai warrior, carved in teak.

Mombasa tailor, busy at work.

The visit to the beach, however, set off a bizarre train of events. It was a hot, sunny day and we put on our togs looking forward to a dip. To our dismay, the dazzling white sand that had been so alluring from a distance concealed huge lumps of congealed crude oil flushed out by passing tankers and the horrible burning stuff stuck to our feet like hot tar. This, and a warning from a passing local about sharks, led to us abandoning plans for a swim and strolling along the higher stretches of the beach instead, all agreeing that it was time to find a hotel with a swimming pool. We foolishly meandered about in the sun far too long.

That night not only did Noeline, with her pretty auburn hair and milky skin, have an awful case of sunstroke, but she woozily confessed that she'd got some coral stuck in her foot as well but hadn't wanted to make a fuss. A quick inspection revealed what already looked like a fiery creeping infection in the wound. Clearly, she needed medical assistance, so we helped her into the car, and I drove to the hospital, where they extracted the coral, medicated her, and plastered her with calamine lotion.

Expat Blues

Back at the hotel, we tucked our groggy patient up in bed and promised to return with dinner. Kitty, meanwhile, had decided to change into a dress and as she was doing so, she let out a sharp cry of pain that riveted our attention. Unbeknown to her, a sewing needle had been left in the hem of her dress and, as she put it on, the needle had embedded itself in her thigh before snapping off! We left Mary to keep an eye on Noeline, while I raced back to the hospital with Kitty. We were there for hours, dinner forgotten, while Kitty had emergency surgery, involving quite a big incision plus sutures, to remove the broken needle. By the time all that was sorted, all we could do was collapse into bed, the sounds of rumbling bellies accompanied by whimpering from our two casualties.

Over the following days, the girls improved rapidly. We found a nice hotel with a pool, which assisted their recuperation, as did the attentions of the Indian owners' three young sons! By chance, we met up with two young Irishmen, also teachers from Zambia, who shared a bit of craic with us for a day or two. Declan, the wilder of the two, enjoyed being outrageous. He referred to Mary, who was tall and slim, as 'the big bitch', which did not endear him to her. When I drove him through town one afternoon, he kept sticking his head out the window and bellowing at startled groups of Arabs we passed in his thick Irish accent, "The Catholic Church is the one true church, ye heathens!"

On later reflection, Declan and his friend, who were actually on their way home to Ireland having concluded their tours at a remote bush mission station in Zambia, brought home to me an unsettling truth – how fortunate I'd been to end up in a town like Livingstone. The singles I'd met who, like Declan, had spent close to three years living in the African bush far from any civilized community and facilities were all noticeably troppo. Towards the end of my tour, I recall meeting one young Irishwoman at an isolated mission who had a deranged gleam in her eyes and kept a 'pet' crocodile in a small, dilapidated swimming pool next to her house. Even married couples found remote bush postings a challenge. How would I have fared, I wondered?

Erin Eldridge

We attended Easter Sunday Mass at the stunning Romanesque Holy Ghost Cathedral, and then bade Mombasa farewell as we headed off to Nairobi, where Kitty's priestly relative, Father Tony, was expecting us. After a few days there, we had to think about heading back home. What I hadn't factored in when I planned our trip was that, while the wet season was tapering off in Zambia, up here it was just getting into full swing with April/May being the wettest months, and I was worried about travel issues.

The journey to Nairobi took about seven hours. When we took a break for lunch, a man stopped by our outside table to chat with us, asking the standard questions about our safari, his curiosity spiked by the sight of four young women in a car piled high with luggage. He told us he was a white Kenyan and had lived through all the independence upheaval with the Mau-Mau. To our astonishment, he reached into a pocket and drew out a handgun, assuring us that, even now, he never went anywhere without it.

We found Father Tony's parish that served his Kikuyu flock easily enough, set amongst coffee plantations and surrounded by trees. It was a lovely oasis, and he was a welcoming host. To my delight, we'd no sooner arrived than we had a visit from Sister Jessica, now based at the parish convent, who'd heard that a group of teachers from Livingstone was coming to stay. Of course, she didn't know the girls, but I quickly did introductions, and we all had a cup of tea together while we caught up with each other's news. She had gained weight and was fairly glowing with renewed health in the more temperate climate, which was great to see.

Our stay in Nairobi was a fitting climax to our adventure. We didn't have much to do with the city, which was just another new agglomeration of Western style high rises, but we made lots of forays into the surrounding territory, where we saw the huge flocks of pink flamingoes at Lake Nakuru, met some Masai, who charged us several Kenyan shillings to take their photos, and visited the National Park where we viewed lots of game. I also arranged for the car to have a thorough service in preparation for the return trip.

Expat Blues

A family of Masai in the Rift Valley.

There was an unpleasant incident that occurred when we were driving through a remote little village one morning. A small child, a little girl, suddenly tore out from the huts and ran across the road to crash headfirst into the driver's side front panel of my car. Following the sickening thud, she rebounded to lie prone on her back in the dirt road. The girls all screamed, the volume increasing with outrage as I sped up to clear the scene as quickly as possible. Once they stopped shouting at me to stop and check the child for injury, I explained that I'd been warned that whites who'd done so in similar circumstances had been beaten and robbed or worse. I promised to report the incident at the nearest police station. The girls still weren't happy, especially when we couldn't find a police station, but when they told Father Tony what had happened, he was adamant I'd done the right thing. On inspection, I noticed there was a shallow dent where the child had run into me, and I prayed the little mite was okay. All I could do, really.

On our last day, we attended Mass at the parish church where Father Tony's parishioners played beautiful music and sang like the angels for us, and then the following morning it was time for goodbyes and thanks before we set off on our long journey home. If all went well, we'd be back in Livingstone two or three days before school resumed, affording a chance to rest up before duty called.

The girls wanted to go back via Moshi to get a view of Mount Kilimanjaro, so I obliged them. I think I must have made an error following Father Tony's directions to the border, because I ended up on what was effectively a narrow goat track carved out of a mountainside that didn't even look like it was meant for vehicles. It was easily the most hair-raising drive of the trip, up 'til that point, anyway, over steep, uneven ground studded with rocks, potholes and tufts of coarse grass but there was no turning back; I just had to keep going and pray we didn't meet anyone coming the other way. By the time I reached the bottom, I felt like a wrung-out rag, and it was a tremendous relief to rejoin the main road. The girls had chattered away cheerfully all the way down, oblivious to my personal hell. Honestly! I suppose their confidence in my driving skills was kind of flattering.

Crossing the border went smoothly. I had discovered that the interior door panels on the car unclipped, exposing quite a generous cavity behind them, so I made sure we stowed anything that might possibly get us into trouble inside them. For example, we'd all bought curios and most African countries had strict rules about the import of these items. Best move was to keep them out of sight.

As it turned out, we didn't see much of Kilimanjaro because it was mostly obscured behind mist and cloud. We pushed on to Dodoma and I felt myself becoming increasingly concerned about the intensifying wet, ruling out any detour to Dar es Salaam. One stretch of dirt road was a quagmire with slippery ruts so deep from transiting lorries that it was all I could do to keep the car pressing forwards, and at one point she slewed sideways, beginning a heart-stopping tip before righting herself. Getting back on the tar seal was a huge relief and I told myself it was all smooth going from here. At men's (or women's) plans the gods laugh.

I was driving at a good clip along the main highway when I saw what looked like a long line of stationary vehicles – cars, trucks, tankers etc. all pulled over onto the lefthand side of the road, with lots of people milling about. I slowed right down, and as we drove past the people all started waving and shouting out to us, but we couldn't hear what they were saying, and I just kept driving very slowly, feeling completely baffled. Then an African wearing a uniform, some kind of official, stepped into the lane motioning me to stop and I hit the brakes, rolling my window down as he approached grim faced.

"Madam, you can go no further. The bridge has been washed away."

We looked beyond him and gasped. There was a wide chasm breaching the continuity of the road, bits of timber, torn metal and shredded top seal dangling obscenely into the unnatural ravine. On the opposite side of the severed highway was another long, snaking line of parked vehicles facing us, despondent looking people drifting about aimlessly.

"May we have a look please?"

The girls were already piling out, chattering with excitement.

The official nodded. We were traversing a national park and I think he was a warden. The destroyed bridge most likely spanned a tributary of the Great Ruaha River.

"Yes, madam, but please be quick. You must turn around and go back to the end of the queue."

The girls and I sidled up to and stood on the edge of the dramatic abyss, as close as safety allowed, peering into the seething, muddy brown water far below. It would have been at road level when the flash flood tore the bridge away. I felt sick. Repairing something like this in a third world country would take months – unless they had a Baily Bridge on hand, and I doubted that very much. We were nearly out of money. We had to get back to our jobs. How on Earth did we sort this out?

The warden stood beside me. "Some cars fell in last night," he said softly. "All were swept away."

My blood ran cold. Could have been us travelling in the dark as we had so often done, with our feeble headlights.

"Are there any plans to, um, repair this?"

"Some engineers are coming in the morning. Now, you must move your car."

"Sure. Is there any accommodation near here?"

"Yes." He pointed back the way we'd come. "There is a Game Lodge. You will see the signs."

I gathered up the girls, turned the car around and drove slowly and despondently back to the end of the queue. Leering and beckoning truckies called out to us from their cabs as we passed, the dominant theme being that we were welcome to earn some money during the delay, if we liked. The girls gave them the fingers.

Big chunk of main highway missing!

The Ruaha National Park Game Lodge, set back in the trees not far from the highway, was able to offer us two comfortable twin rooms for the night, and, to our relief, they were not too expensive, this being the off-season. After we'd settled in, we had a meeting to work out a plan of action, and following some discussion, we all agreed to wait for the morning when the engineers arrived to assess the damage before we made any firm decisions. We had a nice dinner and headed off to bed. I was sharing a double room with Noeline and, as we prepared for bed, she pointed out that there was only one mosquito net. I guessed she was worried about bites on her fair skin, still recovering from the sunburn, so I insisted she take the bed with the netting. The mosquitoes were bad because of the wet.

Expat Blues

I slept soundly and, in the morning, noticed that I had numerous red welts, but I wasn't worried. I knew they'd soon fade, and anyway, I was religious about taking my Daraprim. We all were.

After breakfast, we strolled on foot past the, by now, even longer, queue of vehicles, good naturedly fielding the same offers we'd had the day before from the lustful truckies. Most of the backed-up vehicles were lorries or tankers and the drivers were sleeping in their cabs. I had no idea what they were doing for food and water, but we could smell woodsmoke and the savory tang of seared meat coming from somewhere. We'd left our things at the Lodge, assuming we'd probably have one more night there at least.

When we reached the gash in the road there were lots of people gathered there, including some Chinese railway workers in their drab grey uniforms and coolie hats. They made it clear they did not like us taking their photos, glaring our way and turning their backs. On the other side of the divide there was a lot of activity, and we were astonished to see a swarthy young man, clad entirely in skintight denim and wearing knee-high red leather boots, detach himself from the milling throng to saunter to the edge of the ravine on his side, hallooing and waving exuberantly in our direction. Once this flamboyant apparition had our attention, he began to blow ardent kisses towards us, strutting about like a hormonal peacock, sweeping his black Stetson from his head to bow repeatedly to us as he capered and called compliments. Well, we assumed they were compliments because of the kisses and extravagant body language, but we couldn't tell what he was saying. All the onlookers on both sides were laughing and shouting encouragement to him, while we stared in dumb amusement at this bizarre behavior.

"Break it to me," I said to a European standing alongside us, chuckling as he enjoyed the show. "That's the engineer, isn't it?"

"Yes," he answered with a grin. "He's Italian. So's his team."

I turned to the bemused girls. "I think it's time for plan B."

I was really worried now. Finding an alternative route wasn't going to be easy and meant heading off into the unknown wilds of Tanzania, alone and far from any civilization. God alone knew what dangers we'd have to face, and the weather was rapidly deteriorating. Maybe this grand adventure had been a terrible mistake. I felt sick with anxiety.

We left the amorous Italian calling after us in an anguished tone and headed back past the queue. We'd almost reached the side road leading into the Lodge when we had to move well over onto the berm to accommodate an approaching car, three as it turned out, following each other closely. Just another bunch of unfortunates, I thought, who don't know about the washout. The leader braked beside us, and a turbaned head emerged from the window.

"Hello, girls, what's happening?"

As we crossed to the vehicle to respond, I felt a buzz of excitement. They were hard to spot under all the mud splatters, but there was no doubt about the decals, like the big 20 on the door of the lead car, that two of them sported – these were entries from the now-completed East African Safari, the Zambian contingent, and the turbaned driver could only be one man, a legend in the world of rallying and a Zambian hero – Satwant Singh!

The occupants of the other two cars, a young man, Adrian, a young woman, Kay, and an older man, John, got out to join us, and after introductions we gave all of them a brief summary of what we knew.

"The engineers are here," I explained, "but, um, I don't think the road's going to be fixed anytime soon." The girls stifled giggles. "We arrived yesterday, and the washout had happened during the night, with some fatalities, apparently. We urgently need to get back to Livingstone for work."

Satwant nodded. "We're headed back to Lusaka, if we make it," he added with a wry grin gesturing towards the cars. "They're pretty beat up, apart from John's."

The Datsun certainly looked the worse for wear, but Satwant's sleek Mitsubishi Colt Galant was impressively intact, apart from the muck.

Expat Blues

"We got reasonably priced rooms at the Game Lodge last night," I explained. "It's out of season so they might have room for you, too."

"Okay. We'll drive up and have a look at the damage and then meet you there. Hopefully, we can find a solution."

I liked that word 'we'! If the four of us could hook up with these guys, brilliant drivers, going the same way, maybe we'd be all right after all.

Luckily, Satwant and his team were all accommodated at the Lodge, and that night they joined us for dinner, where we were entertained by their stories about the rally. Satwant had finished seventh overall in a starting field of eighty-nine competitors but was endearingly modest about his accomplishment. Adrian, the young man driving the Datsun rally car, claimed Satwant could have finished first had he not lost precious time rescuing a fellow competitor who'd slid down a bank.

Satwant shrugged. "It's the Sikh way. We must help anyone in trouble."

Hope that applies to girls desperate to get home, I thought.

After dinner, at Satwant's invitation, we adjourned to the bar for a nightcap and a discussion about our predicament. Although married, he was something of a flirt who clearly enjoyed the company of women, in the nicest possible way. Our flirt supremo, Kitty, was happy to indulge him. Kay and John, driving in the unmarked private car, were a couple as it turned out, despite the obvious age difference, and had been part of Satwant's service crew during the rally, as was Adrian. Adrian was driving the battered Datsun back to Zambia as a favor for a friend. I explained that we had no more money to spare for accommodation so were feeling pretty desperate. Satwant agreed they were likewise in a predicament and very anxious to get home. He produced a map of Tanzania, and said there was a solution, but it wouldn't be easy. Placing a finger on the map and tracing what looked like a lengthy detour over back roads, he explained his plan.

"We can get around the washout by going inland for about 300kms. We'll come out here back on the main highway again" – he moved the finger – "roughly thirty kilometers beyond the broken bridge. Then hopefully, we have a clear run home."

He smiled, addressing himself to me as the driver of our group. "You can come with us. We'll go in convoy, and we'll get you all home. I promise."

I felt this man would be as good as his word. Anyway, what choice did we have?

"Well, what do you think?" He folded the map.

I looked at the girls who were all nodding their assent.

"Thank you, Satwant. We accept your offer. When do we start?"

"Straight after breakfast."

We opted for an early night, but for a long time I lay staring into the darkness while I listened to the pounding of rain on the Lodge roof. The roads we were about to travel on would present a real challenge, worse than anything we'd encountered so far, and the wet would make them even more hazardous. The rally cars were battered, but they still had special modifications like strengthened suspensions and heavy-duty shock absorbers. My little car had done well, but she wasn't cut out for these conditions. Would we find enough petrol? What if we broke down out in the boondocks? What if we had an accident? What if the alternative road itself turned out to be impassable? In the end my head hurt, and I said some fervent prayers to soothe myself before I finally fell asleep.

In the morning, I had lots more mossie bites, but I ignored them because I had other more important things on my mind.

We set off straight after breakfast and after confirming that not a jot of progress had been made with the washout. The Italian popinjay was nowhere to be seen. Satwant took the lead, and it was decided to lighten my little Mazda's load by dispersing the girls to

Expat Blues

other cars. Kitty stayed with me, Mary joined Adrian in the Datsun and Noeline accompanied Satwant in the Galant.

He came to my driver's side window and said with a reassuring smile, "Just follow me, go at your own pace, and flash your lights if there's a problem. Adrian will keep an eye on you from the rear and so will John. You'll be fine."

I swallowed hard. "Thanks."

And then we were off. We backtracked a short distance along the highway before Satwant signaled a left turn and I followed him into the unknown. What an incongruous sight we must have been! My little car with its stacked roof rack, black polyurethane cover flapping away merrily, two rally cars, one with its back panels vibrating alarmingly, and a big, serene saloon car bringing up the rear.

The roads were every bit as bad as anticipated, especially after the heavy rain of the night before, and the Mazda was soon liberally coated with mud. I did my best to keep up with Satwant's lead car because I didn't want to be a burden to them, but I suspected he was going slower than he needed to just the same. Tanzania was wild and undeveloped, even more so off the beaten track, and I began to stress about access to petrol, too. Fortunately, solitary little bowzers popped up where you least expected them. At one, a little African boy valiantly tried to clean the caked mud off my bonnet before giving up. I redirected him to scrubbing the windscreen and gave him a generous tip. We filled the tank or our jerry cans to capacity at every stop.

Every kilometer passed felt like a victory, but of course it couldn't last. We crested a rise to see a devastating sight. Stretching ahead of us all the way to the next rise, a distance of several hundred meters, was a narrow section of unsealed road hidden under muddy brown water of unknown depth. Completely blocking the flooded dip at the far end of it was a large bus, on a perilous lean, and rendered impassable by the sodden raised berms on either side. The passengers from the bus, Africans of all ages and gender, were standing about in groups looking sullen and despondent. We got out of our cars, staring in dismay at the scene.

Satwant and Adrian set off to have a recce while the rest of us waited. For the life of me, I couldn't see a way out of this impasse. When the two men returned, they both looked grim.

"The bus has been stuck here two days," Satwant informed us. "A grader is supposed to be coming to pull it out, but no one knows how far away it is. The water's not that deep. I think we can get through if they can move the bus."

He sucked on his bottom lip, hands on hips, looking into the middle distance, while we watched him anxiously. We'd seen a lot of graders prowling the roads as we drove through Tanzania. They seemed to be the country's version of random towies.

"All right," he said finally. "We'll give it an hour, then we'll have to find an alternative route. Problem is, I don't think there is one."

There was nothing for it but to sit in our cars and wait. I was actually enjoying a pleasant little doze when someone shouting snapped me out of my reverie and I leaped out of the car. The grader had arrived! Even the tired, dispirited Africans perked up.

Things proceeded quite quickly after that. The bus was not so much towed as maneuvered well over to one side, still listing badly. I think it must have been damaged – broken axle, perhaps. Satwant drove the Galant at a plucky clip through the river of mud, brown waves surging up either side, only to stall at the base of the rise. A group of African men obligingly pushed him up and over onto dry road. Then it was Adrian's turn in the Datsun and he likewise stalled in the mud and needed rescuing. I was next. To my inexpressible delight, the little Mazda outshone them all (John got stuck, too), ploughing through the floodwater and practically skipping up the rise, over it, and out of sight. I say 'out of sight' because I wasn't driving it. I mean, if you've got a famous rally driver on hand who offers to do it for you, why would you not accept? I did my bit by running along the berm, hooting and hollering to provide moral support, much to the stranded Africans' amusement. At least we provided the poor souls with a bit of distraction from their unenviable plight.

Expat Blues

It was a great moment, and later, when we stopped to buy snacks at a little bush general store, Satwant said to me, "Well, Erin, you had the satisfaction today of seeing your car put to shame three vehicles from the East African Safari!"

Okay, the outcome might have been entirely different if I'd been driving, but just the same I had a grin a mile wide for a long time. I also had some great photos.

We continued our journey without any further delays, and the next celebratory moment was when we emerged back onto the main highway, about 30 kms beyond the washout – some detour! Then it was a steady haul onwards to the Tanzania/Zambia border, and we arrived at Tunduma in the wee hours of the morning. Earlier, John bowled a guinea fowl that had wandered onto the road. He tossed it into the boot, claiming they were delicious to eat, and he'd cook it up for us in Lusaka. Dinner taken care of, then.

While we waited for Customs to open, we all snoozed in our cars, and although a poor sleeper in a seated position, I managed to grab forty fitful winks. Getting through both borders in the company of Satwant was a breeze, and we decided to go for broke, straight on to Lusaka, to make up for time lost. The journey was a blur for me, driving twenty-four hours straight, but I fixed my bloodshot, gritty eyes on Satwant's taillights and plugged on. It rained heavily at one point, which, while it didn't help visibility, gave the car a badly needed wash.

When we reached Lusaka, Kay and John kindly invited us to spend the night with them, and so it was time for thanks and farewells to Satwant and Adrian. I found it difficult to put into words the debt we owed to all of them, and it was an emotional parting all round. Satwant shook my hand and told me I was the best woman driver he'd ever come across. Maybe he was simply being nice, but I treasured those words, just the same.

John did indeed cook us the guinea fowl, which was delicious, and even produced some wine to wash it down with. Then our exhausted quartet bunked down for the night on available beds and sofas and slept like babies in the knowledge that we'd be home tomorrow and right on schedule, too.

The drive to Livingstone, after we'd breakfasted and taken leave of our hosts, was a doddle compared to what we'd been through, and the only snag occurred when the car blew a tyre just a few miles out from home. We all pitched in cheerfully to change it and I was appalled by its condition, bald down to the canvas. A quick inspection revealed the other three were much the same. I felt like a mutt as I hadn't given the tyres a thought, really.

So, we limped into Livingstone on a bright, sunny day, deliriously happy to be safely back after what had been, by any standards, an epic adventure. I'd done my dreamed-of big safari and delivered my fellow travelers home unscathed. I was exhausted but very happy.

First stop was the girls' house to offload them and their belongings, and before I left, they invited me to dinner that night. I accepted, knowing my fridge would be bare, and then made my way out to Maramba.

The old place looked just the same as I coasted in through the gates and parked outside my house, journey done, mission accomplished. Now I knew how Odysseus felt when he finally saw Ithaca – well, let's not get carried away. Rather than sprawled on a dung heap like Odysseus' Argus, I spotted Blue over by the fence, investigating something of doggie interest, and called his name. He whipped around, stared at me for a moment, one paw raised, and then barreled across the compound for a joyful reunion that seemed to go on forever, breaking away and then hurling himself back onto me, whining, yelping, and corkscrewing his ears in that unique quirk of his. He looked bonny and in fine fettle. I went over to the Coughlans to get my keys. They'd gone away for a couple of days, but Kuta, their long-suffering houseman, was able to find the keys for me.

I unpacked, every movement closely monitored by Blue, bathed, washed my hair, and put on clean clothes. People drifted in to welcome me back, but typically, were not really interested in hearing anything about my trip. Brendan made one of his trademark spiteful remarks about the colorful top I was wearing, one with a classic African print that I'd purchased in Mombasa, and I let that go. The expat gossip mill had been in overdrive while we'd been away, and apparently the popular story doing the rounds was that we'd all been killed in a car crash somewhere in East Africa, and my reputation as a reckless, rogue individual had been cemented. Some of them seemed disappointed it wasn't true. Great to be home. I borrowed a bit of milk and withdrew to have a quiet cup of tea. That evening, I joined the girls for dinner and took Blue with me, not wanting to leave him again so soon. He didn't enjoy car travel, but he was admirably stoic about it. Kitty, Noeline and Mary had also heard the story of our grisly demise while out shopping, and we had a good laugh about it. That night it felt great to sleep in my own bed again.

The next day, after a good sleep in, I drove into town on my precarious tyres and took the car to the dealership. A thorough inspection showed she'd come through very well, just one broken exhaust bracket, and they put four new tyres on her for me, marveling over the state of the old ones. This was a big expense for me, but when I broached the subject with the girls they stonewalled me, making it clear they would not contribute. Just one of the many hurts from the Irish I found bewildering.

I re-stocked my depleted pantry, sent my film away to be developed, and took it easy for the next couple of days until school started for the second term.

Being notorious had advantages socially. An expat Canadian family I knew invited us all to dinner, eager to hear about our odyssey. Their lovely bungalow was typically well fenced, with a narrow gate leading into the gardens surrounding the house. There was nobody around, so I unlatched the gate and let myself in. As I turned to refasten the gate, I froze – I was wearing shorts, and two wet, cold somethings had pressed into the back of one leg, one at thigh level, the other much lower down. I turned around very slowly, heartbeat accelerating, and found myself confronted by two dogs sharing the same black and tan color scheme – a large Doberman and a small dachshund, who watched me curiously, but without hostility. I could probably take the dachshund, flashed through my mind, but the Doberman? At that moment, the male host came out of the house and called, "Henry, Homer, come here, boys. Inside." Henry (the dachshund), and Homer (the Doberman), were lovely company and made the evening for me.

Before I'd gone away, Berto had invited me to a party at his house on the last Saturday night of the holidays, my understanding being that it was to celebrate his birthday. I only found out later that it was intended to be a double celebration: his birthday and the announcement of our engagement. I hadn't really had much time to think about his proposal, if you could call it that, before I left, but I knew I didn't want to marry him. He'd been kind, generous and protected me from the predators, and I knew I'd want for nothing with him. But there were too many cons. We'd only known each other a couple of months, and I'd never got the feeling he was all that interested in me as an individual human being, more as just potential wife material young enough to breed with. Add to that the age difference, the cultural divide, his game hunting proclivities, his Latin chauvinism and self-absorption. But the bottom line was that we had little in common and I simply was not in love with him. And, God help me, I'm a hopeless romantic.

On Saturday morning, I steeled myself, and drove to his house to return his jerry cans and give him my answer. His obvious joy at seeing me alive and well – he'd also heard the rumors – didn't help matters. Despite my protests, he insisted on cooking me lunch – shallow, I know, but I was going to miss his cooking – and while we sipped coffee afterwards the dreaded moment arrived, and he asked me shyly if I had a response for him. I'd decided to make it swift and brutal, so I told him I was sorry, but I didn't want to marry him, or anybody, for that matter, and that I hoped he found someone worthy of him very soon. He clearly took it hard and became very emotional. After a painful few moments, he insisted that he still wanted me to come to the party. Then he went into his bedroom and closed the door, and I went home.

I should have known better than to go to the party, but I had a small birthday gift for Berto, an ebony carving of an elephant purchased in Kenya that I guess I'd hoped might trigger a change of heart, and I wanted to give it to him and hopefully have closure and no ill feelings. He'd obviously done a lot of planning and gone to a lot of trouble. Trestle tables were set up outside with colorful lanterns strung overhead and a huge haunch of Barotse beef turning on a spit over a cut-down oil drum barbecue. Extra servants bustled about serving nibbles and pouring drinks. The frigidity of my reception, though, was hard to miss. Berto's friends, all of whom I knew well, had been told of my rejection and they froze me out. Berto himself accepted his gift politely but was otherwise cold and remote. The atmosphere was so awkward and horrible that I nibbled a bit from the splendid array of food, made an excuse and fled. Before I did, though, one of his friends took me aside and told me in scathing tones that, while I was galivanting around East Africa, Berto had gone all the way to South Africa to get me a Kimberley diamond, and that I was a very foolish, ungrateful girl. I felt sick with guilt.

A few days later, the Coughlans told me Berto had been up at the Sports Club, horribly drunk, and telling anyone who'd listen that I had broken his heart and that he "would have made a lady" out of me. A little insulting, I thought, as I considered myself a lady already, but perhaps I had underestimated his depth of feeling for me. I felt even worse. Then he disappeared, and I heard on the grapevine that he'd gone back to Italy. When he returned, he had a new wife, a plain little Italian lady who looked closer to him in age, if not slightly older. She had been the spinster sister of one of his Fiat factory pals, who had engineered the rebound union. Both Berto and his wife left Livingstone shortly afterwards, and I never saw him again.

There was another upsetting issue for me to deal with at this point in time – Maggie's hat.

During my first two years teaching back home, in Gore Southland, I'd acquired a lovely dog called Maggie who had a beautiful nature and was my devoted companion. She was a collie/Labrador cross, but I think there may have been a bit of retriever in there as well because she used to bring me gifts and as a result I had accumulated an odd collection of items whose provenance was a mystery: a child's shoe, an old handbag, a blue plastic bowl, a silk scarf, among sundry other jumble. She also brought me a very distinctive dark green felt hat, featuring a rounded crown and wide brim, in excellent condition. When I left Gore, I eventually discarded all her little offerings, but I treasured the hat. I collected all the silver beer can tabs when the teachers went to the pub on a Friday night and made an eye-catching hatband by looping them together. I'd hoped to leave Maggie with my parents when I left for my big OE, but my father, with typical spite, forbade it and so I gave her to a Southland farming family with young kids. It broke my heart. The hat was my precious souvenir of my beloved dog, and I took it to Africa with me, where I hung it on one corner of the mirror sitting on my bedroom dresser. On my return from East Africa, it was gone.

Only the Coughlans had the keys to my house while I was away, to access Blue's food, put him safely inside at night to sleep, and to let Erita in to clean. When I queried them about the missing hat, they looked sheepish. It turned out that Pat O'Connell, one of the two young male teachers at the Christian Brothers' school at Namatama and a good friend of the Coughlans, had visited them a few times during the holidays, and after one boozy evening that raised concern for his driving capabilities, they had let him stay the night in my flat. This was puzzling, since they had two spare bedrooms in their much bigger house. Maybe it gave them a break from letting Blue out early in the morning. The next day, Pat had reappeared wearing Maggie's hat and then left with it. This was such a classic example of the Irish disrespect for a person's property and rights – earlier, Brendan had borrowed my precious chess set and returned it with a piece damaged – and I was, I felt, justifiably angry, exacerbated by Pat and Bernie's marked lack of contrition. I explained why the hat had such sentimental value to me, and Pat drove me up to Namatama to confront his namesake, who shared a house with the other single male teacher, John Clare. Pat O'Connell was defensive and unhelpful. He admitted to 'borrowing' the hat (Catherine told me later that, while I was away, she and Jimmy saw him frequently cruising around Livingstone wearing it), but claimed it had disappeared and he had no idea where it had gone. He had, he vowed, left it on the dining table one night and noticed it missing in the morning. The finger pointed to his sidekick, John Clare, who favored attention-seeking clothing. When I caught up with him, he said his African boyfriend, Godfrey, a Zambian Air Force trainee and thoroughly unpleasant character who spent a lot of time at the house, had taken the hat, but subsequently denied all knowledge of it.

Expat Blues

I never recovered Maggie's hat, and I was gutted. My last link to the dearly loved pet I still grieved for was gone.

Months later, when Kitty, Pat O'Connell, Noeline and I were on holiday in Malawi, Pat bought me a western style straw hat from a roadside stall, claiming he 'owed this lady a hat'. I accepted it without comment. Back in Livingstone, I gave it to Blue, and then sat and watched him destroy it.

I started the second term feeling tired, dispirited and very jaundiced with expat life as a whole. Sister Carmel was relieved to see me back safe and sound, and I told her about the encounter with Sister Jessica and how she'd been looking so well and happy. She said she'd let the other sisters know the good news.

My big safari adventure felt far away and long ago as I threw myself back into my teaching and Head of Department roles, but no amount of distraction could dispel the feeling of malaise that possessed me.

By the end of that first week, I could barely get out of bed and go to school. My head ached, my joints ached, and I had no appetite. After morning break on Friday, I finally admitted defeat and sought out Carmel to tell her I thought I was coming down with 'flu. She immediately sent me home, where I undressed and crawled into bed feeling weak as a kitten. Erita brought me a cup of tea, but I couldn't even manage to drink that.

Pat told Bernie I'd gone home from school ill, and at some point during the afternoon, she came in, looked me over, and said, "I'm almost certain ye've got malaria."

I protested that I'd never missed taking my Daraprim, but she waved a hand dismissively.

"It's good, but it's not infallible. Did ye get bites in East Africa?"

I thought about the Game Lodge, the missing mosquito net, and nodded. "Yes, lots in Tanzania, because of the wet."

Bernie looked grim. "East Africa is the *worst* place to get malaria. I've one chloroquine ampoule at home. I'm going to fetch it."

At this time, quinine was still the standard treatment for malaria, which gave rise to the popular tale about expats drinking lots of gin and tonics because tonic water had quinine in it and kept the malaria at bay. Probably just an excuse for excessive gin consumption!

I didn't know a lot about malaria, just that it was caused by a certain type of mosquito – anopheles – injecting a parasite into your bloodstream, and that it was a serious illness that killed millions every year.

Bernie returned shortly with a small glass phial of chloroquine and a syringe and injected me. Then she fetched me some water, tucked me up and left, promising she'd be back soon.

By the time darkness fell, and Bernie returned with Mary Browne in tow, I was badly delirious and had no flesh left on my right knuckles where I'd apparently been pounding them against the plaster wall, oblivious to the pain. Mary wanted to take me to hospital, but Bernie, who worked there and had nothing good to say about the place, shook her head vehemently.

"They'll do nothing for her, just leave her to die."

Brendan was dispatched to fetch a doctor and lots more chloroquine, and I have a vague recollection of an Indian man leaning over me muttering, "It's bad, very bad."

After that, I became steadily worse. Excruciating pain throbbed in my head, my temperature shot up alarmingly, and I alternated between teeth chattering with cold and feeling I was burning up, sweat pouring off me. Bernie kept up the injections, and they stripped me and sponged me with cold water to try and get my temperature, which was approaching fatal levels, down.

It was a long night. Blue was frantic and kept hurling himself at the front door to try and get to me. His claws did so much damage that afterwards the door had to be stripped, sanded and repainted.

Expat Blues

In my delirium I wasn't aware of any of this, of course. They told me later, when I was recovering, that they had even discussed calling a priest to administer the last rites!

As morning broke, so, miraculously, did my fever, and since I couldn't be left alone, they carried me over to the Coughlans' house, where Bernie could keep an eye on me, and made me comfortable in a spare room. Blue was permitted to settle on the rug beside my bed. We both slept for a long time.

My recovery was slow and difficult. I was badly nauseous and couldn't eat. Just going to the toilet or washing myself exhausted me and I was lightheaded and dizzy. Word of my illness spread quickly amongst the expat community, and I received a steady stream of visitors, which was nice, if rather tiring at times. People were kind and generous, bringing me all manner of treats and special foods like hard-to-get ice cream, and the Coughlans predictably ate and drank all of it. I didn't care. All I could manage for days was sips of Lucozade, anyway. When I finally did feel like eating something I managed half a plate of scrambled eggs. My knuckles scabbed over and healed, the flesh pink and proud.

I was relieved to hear that the other three girls were all well. If only I'd had the common sense to call the desk at the Lodge in Tanzania and ask for another mosquito net, I could have spared myself a lot of suffering.

While I was convalescing, I learned about the horrific deaths of the two young Canadian women who foolishly descended to the Zambesi River for a swim while staying on the Rhodesian side at the Victoria Falls Hotel. Ignoring the warning signs erected by the hotel, they wanted to be able to say they'd swum in the river, so set off in a group of four, the two Canadian women and an American husband and wife. Apart from the danger from crocodiles, The Zambian Army had a contingent of soldiers bivouacked on a bluff overlooking the gorges. They spent their days staring through binoculars at nothing, bored out of their minds, and high on dagga (marijuana) which was supposed to be illegal but never enforced because it was an entrenched cultural norm. The people all grew it in their shambas and authorities turned a blind eye. Many expats indulged, too, since it was cheap and plentiful. The soldiers spotted the group of swimmers, decided they were Rhodesian saboteurs and opened fire to break the monotony. The two Canadian girls, aged 19 and 20, were killed, the body of one never recovered. The American husband sustained a stomach wound and survived, while his wife was unhurt. An engineer at the power station located by the gorges, a British expat, heard all the gunfire and went to investigate. Appalled by what he was witnessing, two young women trying to hide behind rocks as they screamed for their lives, he begged the officer in charge to stop the shooting, but he refused. The engineer subsequently gathered up his family and fled across the border into Botswana, terrified for their safety since he alone knew the truth.

The incident electrified the town, evoked fury from the Rhodesians and was internationally condemned. It reinforced the danger of provoking the soldiers of the Zambian Army who were notoriously unpredictable, ill-disciplined, and trigger-happy.

I knew my family would be shocked to hear about the killings through the media, but, following Sister Carmel's advice, I had warned them early on via mail sent from Rhodesia not to make any references to politics or controversial events when they wrote to me, and I followed the same advice. Our letters, to and from, were opened and checked for any seditious content. Parcels sent from New Zealand, not that I got many, received the same treatment.

Eventually, I was well enough to return home, but not well enough yet to return to school. Sister Carmel told me to take my time, as long as I needed.

"You've the constitution of a horse," she told me. "You beat fearful odds, no doubt about that!"

I knew I'd survived a potentially fatal illness, but her words really brought it home. Cerebral malaria more often than not resulted in death.

"My mum fed me on the best food," I said lamely. "Lots of roasts."

I dropped a lot of weight, and as is common after serious illness, I felt sad and depressed. To this day, I believe Bernie Coughlan saved my life with her prompt diagnosis followed by that one early injection of chloroquine, and I will always be grateful to her for that.

I have an abiding hatred of mosquitoes, and I still get lingering attacks of malaria, though nowhere near as bad as the first one. The worst recurrent attack was in 1980 when I was seven months pregnant with my daughter. The parasite resides in my liver, a malevolent little African souvenir.

One consequence of my illness took me completely by surprise – my hair, which was normally thick and shoulder-length, started to fall out in alarmingly large clumps. At some point, just when I'd resigned myself to imminent baldness, the process arrested itself, and new hair began to grow back in. It was like baby fluff, wild and frizzy, so I pinned the whole wayward mess up in a hair clasp to try and disguise my ruined tresses.

Not yet one hundred percent, I was nevertheless keen to get back to school, so Carmel suggested starting after morning tea, with half a day. The girls spotted me approaching along the pebbled path past the statue of the Virgin Mary, and I froze in my tracks as a spontaneous uproar broke out. They erupted from their desks and rushed to the windows facing the verandah, even classes I didn't teach, cheering, ululating, clapping hands and waving their arms. I recovered, waving and smiling back as I continued to the staffroom, tears blurring my vision. It was an uncharacteristic display of emotion from a traditionally reserved culture and took everyone by surprise, even those like Carmel who'd lived in Africa a long, long time. It was also one of the most profoundly moving moments of my life.

Chapter Eleven: Monkey Bay, The Borders Curse Strikes Again, Apartheid Angst

By now we were well into the dry season, every day the same as the previous one – brilliant sunshine with temperatures around 70 – 73 degrees F, no wind, cloudless skies. School started later and the mornings first thing were crisp and dewy so that up until break time I usually wore a light cardigan. Sleeping at night was a lot easier, as was teaching, the girls being more comfortable and alert.

I struggled that term after my illness, even finding myself sometimes taking a siesta after lunch, which I'd never done previously, although many expats did, according to custom. I felt a bit lost after the breakup with Berto, and although there were other men who paid me attention, I didn't give them any encouragement – especially the married ones, who included a big colored guy, Basil Hendricks, a local businessman, and a German, Jurgen Pfeifer, who drove a Willys Jeep around town and ran a struggling safari company. The latter told me, virtually while his wife was in earshot, that he was going to track me down and find out where I lived. Living in a secure, protected compound was not such a bad idea, after all!

The Coughlans were expecting a child and Bernie was experiencing difficulties with the pregnancy, so I didn't see much of them now as they became quiet homebodies. A lot of expat couples started breeding because maternity care was free and an African nanny/housekeeper could be procured cheaply, allowing the mother a quick return to work. The Gibbons had left of course, and a new teacher arrived, a rather old-fashioned single Irish lass, Fiona, who, to my chagrin, inherited their comfortable house. She was pleasant enough but didn't like the club scene or going out much, so was no fun nor company. I spent most of my leisure time with the girls at St Theresa's – with Noeline and Mary, anyway, Kitty having coupled up with Pat O'Connell. John Clare became ill with hepatitis and ended up in hospital. He was as yellow as a canary. Another teacher I knew, a young British woman, contracted amoebic dysentery and lost kilos in weight. Africa was not for the fainthearted.

Much of my time in Africa is recalled as memorable anecdotes within the larger framework of my two-and-a-half years there, and I often considered recording them as a collection of short stories. However, on reflection, I think they are better embedded in the main narrative, in the context where they truly belong, and so I will recount these vignettes as they crop up.

One anecdote involves a special character I named 'the orange man'.

The orange man was memorable for several reasons. He was elderly, and as I've mentioned earlier, you didn't see many old Africans. He also dressed very distinctively, in a tattered tan safari suit and a battered slouch hat with pinned-up brim, like an Aussie digger's, giving him an incongruously flamboyant air. He never had any shoes, though, and walked everywhere on gnarled, filthy feet. About every three weeks, he would turn up with a burlap bag tied to a pole across one shoulder and give everyone he could accost the hard sell for his single item of merchandise – brittle little green oranges the size of golf balls, completely inedible. I guess selling something – or trying to – preserved his dignity being lost by outright begging. The nuns usually shooed him away as they had their own trees, and then he proceeded on to the teachers' compound, where everybody gave him the bum's rush – except for muggins here. Walking over to my house when school finished, I'd see him squatting on his haunches on my stoop like a skinny mantid, waiting for me, and I'd mutter unkind words under my breath. Of course, I'd always buy a few of the wretched oranges, which he dispensed into the fruit bowl I fetched with an air of aloof condescension, as if he were doing me a huge favor. Still muttering, I'd take them back to the kitchen where they sat on top of the fridge like sad little symbols of indigence, never ripening, just shriveling into dried up pellets before I threw them out.

Then, with me standing in the kitchen, grinding my teeth as I waited, we went through the rest of our well-rehearsed routine.

"Maaadum!" wailed in a voice redolent with self-pity.

Back to the front doorway, hands on hips. "Yes?"

"I am hungry."

"Right."

Back to the kitchen where I viciously slice, butter, and spread jam on two thick pieces of bread. Slap the sandwich on a plate and deliver it.

Some time later. "Maaaaadum!"

"Yes?"

"I am thirsty."

Returns with glass of cordial.

Prepare my own lunch, then go back to check. Plate and glass abandoned on empty stoop. Not so much as a thank you.

The last time I saw the orange man, he was struggling along the Maramba Road carrying what looked like a large piece of stiff cowhide across his shoulders. I stopped and offered him a lift. He refused to put the piece of cowhide, which stank abominably, into the boot, laying it instead across the back seat, to my annoyance. Then he got into the passenger seat and with his customary pomposity directed me further along the road with an imperious wave of one hand. We'd left the tar seal and were on gravel when he held up the hand for me to stop. Having retrieved his malodorous cowhide, he stalked away with great dignity to be swallowed up by the bush, typically without a word or backward glance. I felt a lump in my throat as I watched him. Destitute he may have been, but he bowed to no man – or woman.

Sister Carmel had warned me about the dangers of driving in Zambia when I first arrived, and a lot of expats lost their lives in accidents while I was there. One loss that stands out is the Hogg family. Along with his wife and two little girls, Frank Hogg was Scottish, his accent so broad I found it hard at times to understand him. He loved nothing better than to join us at the Sports Club when the Irish had a singsong, and my abiding image of him is his flushed and smiling face, belting out the songs, always standing erect and with his pint mug of beer clasped to his chest. He was one of those human beings who endear themselves to everyone.

One morning, the Hogg family set off for Lusaka but never arrived. Three days later, their car was found on its roof in the bush that lined either side of the road, the occupants all dead except for one of the little girls, who had miraculously escaped unscathed. The expat community was devastated. Family came out from Scotland to arrange for the bodies to be sent home and claim the surviving child. We had an emotional memorial service in the Cathedral as the Hoggs were Catholic and the girls had attended the church primary school.

Speculation as to what had happened was rife. Many claimed that the sun's glare was a real hazard driving in Africa, causing lack of concentration and sleepiness. Others claimed the monotonously long, straight roads had the same effect. I tended to agree with those who suspected Frank's car had been run off the road by one of the big, aggressive lorries that frequently used it and liked to hog the macadam strip. I'd had to dodge them myself. But, in truth, there were no answers – just another sad loss.

One thing I enjoyed doing on a weekend, usually a Sunday afternoon, was strolling down to the convent and watching the girls at their weekly hairdressing. They'd bring chairs outside into the sunshine and take turns braiding each other's hair into the most intricate cornrow patterns using black cotton thread. Peter Mullins was almost always there, taking photos, which the girls delighted in posing for. He developed them himself and sold them to the girls for a small sum, with Carmel's approval. The girls loved to include them with their letters to friends and family – and boyfriends! They loved writing the letters, too, which was good because letter-writing was included in their English examinations. They always started a letter with a formulaic greeting that cracked me up: 'How are you up there? With me down here fine.'

Receiving letters was the highlight of the girls' week. Saturday morning was letter distribution time and God help the form teacher if he/she was late in doing so! You'd have a deputation of polite but disgruntled girls on your stoop muttering, "Letters, meestress. Letters."

Sometimes the girls had a little pocket money to spend, and they'd often approach me shyly with requests to buy them items from town. Skin creams were popular, especially one called Ambi that lightened the complexion, and I'd sometimes tease them in class when I spotted a kid who'd clearly been applying it too liberally, ending up with a sickly grey pallor.

"Your black skin is beautiful," I reprimanded them. "Why do you want to spoil it?"

It saddened me that they wanted to look white. In the end, I refused to buy it for them.

My wildlife club was going well, and I had to cap the number of members because so many wanted to join. I tried to vary the activities and on one memorable occasion I piled them all into the convent's Kombi van and took them on a field trip to the small local game reserve. 'Reserve' because it was not a game park, just a limited, solidly fenced area with a small population of wild animals, like zebra, rhino and antelope. They had some lions and cheetahs in a caged area, which was a bit sad. The cheetahs were very tame, hand reared, I suspect, and loved to press their heads against the wire, inviting you to scratch and pet them.

The reason for our visit that particular day was to let the girls see the new cubs recently born to the resident lioness. They sang lustily all the way there, and then piled out of the van and ran over to the cages eager to view the babies. The male lion, a formidable creature of enormous size, as big as a donkey, was in a filthy mood, having been separated from his nursing mate and offspring to another cage alongside them. An adult male lion is not necessarily a beneficent patriarch as depicted by Mufasa in the movie, *The Lion King*. Infanticide is common – by both parents – and up to 80% of cubs die before they are two years old, a horrific rate of attrition. Putting aside feelings about animals kept in enclosures, it was heartening to know that these little cubs stood a better chance of survival than their wild counterparts.

So, Dad was pacing back and forth, roaring his displeasure, and after oohing and aahing over the adorable cubs the girls cautiously drew closer to his cage to get a close-up view of his antics. He stopped pacing and slunk up to the wire barrier, watching the girls with his big golden eyes. They were perfectly safe and the thrill of seeing a lion so close provided quite a buzz. They jostled with each other for the best view. The lion waited until there was a dense bunch of them clustered at the front of his cage. He drew a little closer. Then he abruptly turned his back and sprayed them with urine. It was like a hose being turned on. He was a cunning sod, too, lifting his back legs alternately with a subtle swing of the hips to ensure maximum coverage of the target. The girls in the direct firing line screamed and tried to break through the girls behind them, who then got a drenching of their own. It was chaos. We had a very smelly van ride back to school, and no singing. When we reached St Mary's they tumbled out, wailing and lamenting, and made a beeline for the shower block and laundry. That was definitely an experience to be included in their letters! It probably didn't go a long way to endearing them to their wildlife, though.

On another occasion, I took them up to Hillcrest College, the big government co-ed school in Livingstone to watch a documentary on sea turtles in the college's splendid AV theatre. The film focused on the hatchlings' desperate run for the sea, trying to dodge the frigate birds and ghost crabs. It was in the days before controlled breeding and nighttime release, so the carnage was terrible. Africans are largely unsentimental about animals – hence my club's mission – but I must have been getting through as the girls were distraught, and there was a high-pitched, anguished 'Eeeeeeeeee' as a background accompaniment to the action. I found it hard to watch myself.

There was no singing on the way home that day, either!

"Meestress, that was too much sad!" Gertrude chided me.

For our next activity, we pressed flowers.

For me, at least, our most memorable Wildlife Club experience was the time we had a guest speaker, a remarkable man, Graham Dennis, who had worked as a game warden in Africa most of his life, including in Zambia. He was retired, now, and walked with a cane because of terrible injuries he'd sustained to his legs. The girls and I listened spellbound as he explained how he got those injuries.

First, he asked the girls what they considered to be the most dangerous animals in Africa. They came up with the usual suspects: crocodiles, snakes of course, and the hippo. Graham nodded.

"What about the zebra?"

The girls fell silent. Graham rolled up one trouser leg and we all gasped at the sickening sight of scars left by what had clearly been a horrible injury. The flesh on his lower leg was shrunken and distorted.

"The other leg's the same. I'll tell you what happened."

He proceeded to describe the horror that befell him during what he'd assumed was a routine day. He was working with his African helpers to load a zebra onto a truck for transport elsewhere. Suddenly, it broke free of the ropes and charged straight at Graham, knocking him flat on his face. Then it knelt with its forelegs on his back and tore at him with its teeth. Zebras are wicked biters. Graham's boys all ran away in terror and left him to it. By the time he broke free of the animal, he was nearly dead, the most horrific injuries being to his legs where the zebra had torn away both calf muscles.

Graham spent months in hospital, had hundreds of stitches, skin grafts, and underwent numerous surgeries. Everyone thought he was a goner.

"But I survived." He smiled. "And I do not hate zebras. That poor animal was frightened and lashed out. I was just unlucky to be where I was. Now, any questions?"

We all felt honored, and humbled, to have met this remarkable, incredibly resilient man.

I think the saddest story I heard involving wildlife, though, was one told to me by an elderly priest who'd spent many years at a bush mission. He was called out one night to administer the last rites to a little nine-year-old girl who'd been horribly mauled by a hyena. She'd been walking home from school with her two young brothers when they'd spotted the lurking animal. Boys being boys, they picked up rocks and hurled them at the hyena. Instead of fleeing as they believed it would, it turned on them and chased them. The boys escaped, but the hyena brought down the little girl and savaged her with its formidable jaws that have a bite force around 1,100psi. By the time the boys returned with their parents, the child was beyond help. Using its powerful jaws, the hyena had ripped off her entire face.

"She took days to die," my priest friend whispered, his eyes filling up with tears. "It was the most terrible thing I've ever witnessed."

So, yes, lots of anecdotes, but there is just one more story concerning wildlife that begs telling, and it was recounted to me by the same elderly priest. Andy MacDonald was a household name in southern Africa, a star rugby player with South Africa's famous Springboks whom he'd joined on their Australian tour in 1965. Andy had been born in Mufilira, Zambia, but back in the 50s and 60s players from Rhodesia and Zambia were eligible for selection to play for South Africa. Andy MacDonald was a big man and very fit. When not playing rugby, he farmed his spread at Zimba, north of Livingstone. Lions had been causing trouble on his farm and one morning he armed himself and set off to track the culprits. He wounded a lioness which ran into the bush, Andy in pursuit. The lioness pounced on him from behind an anthill and in the ensuing struggle his gun was damaged, rendering it useless. His (armed) foreman having scarpered, Andy was left to fight the animal alone. He managed to get hold of its tongue and held on grimly until the animal died from its wound. His hand almost severed, bleeding from multiple lacerations, covered in mud, he then walked home. A tough breed of man whose like we will not look upon again. Andy MacDonald went to live in Rhodesia, where he and his wife were murdered by rebels in 1980.

By the end of term two I was much recovered from the malaria and feeling a lot better. Noeline, Kitty, and Pat O'Connell asked me to join them on a holiday in Malawi, camping at Monkey Bay by the lake, a favorite destination for expats wanting some rest and recreation in a beautiful area. Kitty and Pat were a strong item by now, and I guess Noeline didn't want to be gooseberry. Mary was going elsewhere to see an old boyfriend. Anyway, I was happy to go. We took two cars – Pat had a white Mazda 1300, same as me – because we needed extra room for the large tent we'd borrowed as well as the equipment required for a two-week campout – plates, pots and pans, utensils, sleeping bags etc. We would be cooking over an open fire, apparently. How romantic. The Mullins kindly offered to look after Blue.

We drove across Zambia eastwards and crossed the border into Malawi at Chipata, where we girls had to swap shorts and jeans for the traditional chitenge, the sarong required by law for women to cover their legs. We also had to submit to compulsory cholera jabs because there was a bad outbreak in the country.

It was driving through Malawi, on a perfectly straight, typically well-made British road that I had the accident Sister Carmel had predicted. I was doing about 120kms, cruising happily, when my right-hand side peripheral vision registered movement, and I turned my head to see an enormous, long-horned African cow burst from the bush line, charging straight towards me. There was nowhere to go. The panicked animal ploughed headlong into the front right-side panel of the car with a sickening crunch, its left horn smashing the driver's window and missing my face by centimeters. I braked savagely and registered Noeline screaming, "Oh my God! Oh my God! The poor cow!"

"Never mind the poor cow!" I bellowed. "What about the *poor car*!"

We established that we were both unhurt. The cow, meanwhile, having rebounded off my car to end up sitting rather comically in a dazed heap in the middle of the road, clambered to its feet, shook its head a couple of times, and ambled off. Pat had been travelling right behind me and he'd braked, too. He and Kitty – I was shocked to see her laughing — ran over, and we stood in a huddle assessing the damage. The body on the Mazda was crap, to put it bluntly and although I recalled the desperate animal trying at the last moment to stall its speed, the damage it had caused was bad. The metal was completely split and had been driven hard up

Expat Blues

against the right front tyre. The driver's window was shattered. We were in the middle of a main highway, so we had to move her somehow. With all of us having a go at tugging and pulling the twisted metal, we freed the tyre and pushed the car to the side of the road. It was definitely drivable, and the engine was unscathed. We cleaned up the glass, took a moment to collect ourselves and resumed the journey. There was no possibility of getting repairs done in Malawi. It would have to wait until I returned to Livingstone. For now, I just had to carry on with a pranged-up vehicle. On reflection I thought it could have been a lot worse, and at least nobody was hurt. The poor beast may have been spooked by a lion and had appeared, thankfully, to be uninjured by the impact.

A happy break for a cold beer…before my accident.
Note the chitenges, compulsory garb for women in Malawi.

I've been camping a few times in my life, and learned the hard way that things generally pan out in a similar fashion – by the end of the trip, no-one is talking to each other. So it was with the sojourn at Monkey Bay. It started well, of course. The camping area by the lake was in a beautiful setting and very peaceful with only a few people staying while we were there. The manager's house and adjoining complex included a bar and a shop for basics, and there were ample toilets and showers dotted around. We all pitched in to erect the tent, which was a tricky beast, and after much cussing and frustration we finally got it up correctly with our sleeping bags and belongings neatly arranged in the interior. There was a little stone fireplace opposite the flap, and we were able to get wood and lighters from a supply beside the shop. The clothing law for women didn't apply here, so we could wear our shorts again, and of course our swimming togs. The sun shone, the lake was lovely for swimming in, and we were assured there was no danger of bilharzia. All good so far.

Cooking over an open fire is definitely NOT romantic. Heat searing your face, greasy smuts on skin and in hair, smoke stinging your eyes and impregnating your clothes, leg muscles cramping as you crouch over the food to monitor, flip or stir – all really aggravating. We took turns – well, some of us did. Every morning, I drove to the nearby village and bought some of their fresh rolls for breakfast. The little village kids would be mustered, eagerly waiting for me and my battered car because I always bought them some sweets to share as well. Fishermen came by our tent to sell us freshly caught fish, and that was great, fried over the coals in a little butter. No matter what you cooked or served up, though, was not good enough for some people. On a few occasions, we went to the nearest town and bought dinner when nobody could face the fire. Evenings spent in the bar were generally pleasant as well.

Every night brought a strange phenomenon, though. While the bay was windless during the day, around midnight a hideous gale blew up for about an hour, pummeling our tent and gusting in dirt and debris under its rim (we had no seamless groundsheet). One night, the entire thing collapsed on us, sliding down the central pole. Poor old Pat, clad only in his red undies, ended up exposed to a trio of unhelpful giggling girls as he desperately stretched upwards lifting the full weight of the tent's roof and trying to secure it again. He was not amused.

Expat Blues

Cooking fresh fish on the open fire at Monkey Bay.

Unsurprisingly, the group dynamics were unravelling. Noeline remains one of the sweetest, kindest people I have met in my life, but she was not herself on this trip, especially compared to our recent safari. She was getting over a failed romance herself, and also feeling glum because her longtime friendship with Kitty was having to adjust to the latter's growing closeness to Pat. She even snapped at me one morning over something trivial, which was totally out of character, but hurtful just the same. Still not a hundred percent over my illness, I felt too weary to be bothered with some of the shallow spite and mockery directed my way by self-centered others in our party. I was informed that my country, New Zealand, was at the 'arse-end of the world'. The only high school teacher in the group, I was derided for not having to work as hard as primary school teachers – which is, of course, nonsense. There were some jibes of a humiliating personal nature, too, that I won't go into. The Irish could make you feel like an outsider as no other expat group could.

Thus, while Noeline languished, listening to songs about unrequited love on the staticky radio, and Kitty and Pat disappeared for lengthy periods, I found myself enjoying time on my own, swimming, sunbathing, joining the friendly local fishermen for rides in their dugout canoes, sitting by the lake in the evening as I watched the sun go down through the lacy branches of the trees, delighting in the little bats that swooped in at dusk, veering away, guided by their infallible sonar, just when you thought they were going to fly into you. Watching the sky change from gold to vermilion to pale mauve before darkness closed in soothed me, body and soul. Then it was good to snuggle up in my sleeping bag and slumber deeply; until the wind started lashing us, anyway.

The village lads waiting for their treats.

One day trip I enjoyed was to the remains of the old Livingstonia Mission above the lake at Cape Maclear. It had been founded in 1894 by the Free Church of Scotland and was characterized by its many distinctive red brick buildings. Above the main entrance to the church was a beautiful stained glass window depicting David Livingstone meeting the local chiefs at Lake Malawi.

The headstones in the cemetery revealed how young most of the missionaries were when they died. Their religious zeal did not protect them from the pitiless ravages of African diseases. Malaria accounted for many premature deaths, as did infestations of worms, which they didn't really understand let alone have the means to treat. Intestinal worms were endemic in Africa and were behind much of the sluggish weariness that debilitated many of the natives. I dosed myself regularly and treated Blue with the same pills I took because the worms afflicted animals, too.

Expat Blues

The fortnight at Monkey Bay passed quickly and it was time to return home. As we headed back through Lilongwe, driving towards the border, two unsettling incidents occurred. The first happened as I rounded a bend to be confronted by the figure of a naked African man standing in the middle of the road. He ran towards us, waving his arms and I swerved around him, speeding away. Noeline, as shocked as I was, agreed that, as in Kenya, stopping was not an option, and apart from his startling lack of clothing, the man appeared okay.

The next incident also occurred as I rounded a bend. Pat was driving ahead of me on this occasion, just out of sight. I was doing a good clip when I noticed a reasonably large-sized boulder squatting in the middle of the lane. A car travelling fast was approaching in the other lane and, realizing I couldn't swerve or brake in time, I had to clench my teeth and drive over the boulder. There was a sickening crunch and I immediately slowed, pulling up on the narrow shoulder of the road and scrambling out to assess this new blow to my already badly damaged car. I was sure the rock had whacked my sump, but I couldn't see any oil pouring out, which was a relief. I heaved the boulder into the bush, and we drove on. By the time we caught up to Pat and Kitty in Lilongwe, I was furious and demanded to know why they hadn't moved the rock when they knew I was right behind them. They both thought it was funny and made it clear they couldn't care less that I was upset or that my car might have sustained more damage. I made a mental note never to travel with either of them again.

That night, we stayed in Lusaka, and in the morning I dreaded what an inspection of my car's undercarriage might reveal, but I was pleasantly surprised. There was no big oil puddle to be seen. Still concerned, though, I promised myself I'd get it checked in Livingstone, and then my heart sank further when I remembered I had to get the panel beating done, too. That was going to take a lot more money than I had, and I knew I couldn't ask my family for a loan. My parents were not hard up; my father owned a successful asphalting business. But I knew better than to ask for help.

As always, it was great to see Blue again and he smothered me with the kind of loving welcome home only a loyal dog is capable of. I gave the Mullins a thank you gift of a little soapstone carving of a leopard I'd bought, and they and others gathered around peering at my smashed-up car. There was only one panel beater in Livingstone, and the business was owned by the married colored guy who had the hots for me. I wasn't looking forward to that encounter.

The following day I drove to the dealership and their mechanics gave the car the once over. The sump was okay, just dented. The body may have been crap, but the engine and component parts were strong. Then it was on to the panel beaters. To my relief, the boss was away in South Africa, and after appraising the damage, his African foreman quoted me K58.00 to repair the front panel and replace the window. I blinked. That seemed ridiculously cheap, especially as the driver's door and rear panel were dented as well – Mr. Cow had bounced off me somewhat – and with a bit of budget trimming I could actually afford it. Luckily, our bursar, Sister Aloysius, was always willing to give you an advance on your monthly salary if you needed it, as long as you didn't abuse the privilege.

We filled out all the paperwork and I left the car there so they could start immediately. There were no courtesy cars, so one of the apprentices drove me home.

I felt bereft without a vehicle and was extremely grateful when an Indian friend, learning of my predicament, offered me the use of his personal car for a couple of weeks, since he also had a company pickup at his disposal. When I used the school phone to ring the panel beaters for an update on the Mazda, Basil, wo had returned to Livingstone, answered my call. Ready for pick-up, he informed me, and Peter Mullins gave me a lift that afternoon. The Mazda was parked in front of reception, and I could see they'd done a great job. Now I just had to get through the payment process with the predatory Basil.

He was sitting at his desk as I entered and rose to come over to the counter, where he deposited my car keys with a flourish.

"Looks good, doesn't she?"

"Yes, thank you." I fumbled for my cheque book. He was a heavyset man with a pocked complexion, a fierce expression, and a cruel mouth that all combined to make him very intimidating. He leaned both hands on the counter and leered at me.

"Do you know that bodywork is very expensive?"

"Um, yes of course," I stammered, not sure where this was leading but experiencing growing unease.

He assumed a pained expression, now. "My foreman misquoted this job very badly. Fifty-eight kwacha, is that right?"

"Yes. That's the figure he quoted me to cover the repairs." I watched him warily.

He gave a sneering laugh. "Ridiculous. That's seriously underquoted. The job is worth three hundred kwacha, minimum."

I felt sick. Two month's salary. "Three hundred kwacha! I – I don't have that kind of money. Can I perhaps pay it off in instalments?"

Basil crossed his arms and leaned on the countertop, fixing me with a penetrating stare. "It's alright," he said softly. "My foreman quoted you fifty-eight kwacha, in good faith, and that is what you will pay. This misunderstanding is not your fault," he purred.

Unnerved, I flung my cheque book down on the counter, gripped the pen with a shaking hand, and wrote the cheque as quickly as I could. Maybe he wasn't such a bad guy after all.

Basil leaned in a little closer, just as I was completing my signature, and I got a strong whiff of garlic. "Don't forget to put your address on the back, and a phone number, if you have one. I'll take the rest out in kind."

At first, I wasn't sure if I'd heard him correctly, but then I stiffened indignantly as full understanding of his meaning dawned. I tossed the cheque at him, snatched up the keys, and started to back towards the door.

"I don't go out with married men! You're wasting your time!"

Then I fled.

For the next few days, I was a nervous wreck, terrified that he would come after me for the rest of the money, or worse, blackmail me into something horrid, but he never did. Basil did not abandon his pursuit, though, and even recruited other people to plead his case to me. But that's another story.

Now, it was back to work for the third and final term of 1973. There'd been some changes in the old compound. The Longs were long gone, likewise Elizabeth, Rahnee and David Paul, and the Gibbons. We had several newcomers: two young African teachers – Lucy and Clotilde, who'd moved into the Pauls' and Elizabeth's vacated flats respectively – Catherine, of course, Fiona, and we'd been integrated further by the transfer of an Indian family, the Matthews, from the 'Indian compound', as it was called, to the Longs' old house. Once again, our compound was suffused with lovely curry smells that had been largely missing since the Pauls left. I was still the only Kiwi in town.

The Matthews had a new baby, a little girl, and as the Indian families customarily did, they invited everyone to a party to celebrate her baptism. These get togethers were very formal. Chairs were arranged in a circle outside and the older female children, all beautifully groomed, their glossy black hair braided and beribboned, served a variety of sweets and savories to the guests, likewise smartly attired for the occasion. I always looked forward to such celebrations because the food was divine: tasty samosas, pakoras, kebabs, and deliciously sweet treats like gulab jamin and jalebi. There was a plantain tree growing in the compound, and Mrs. Matthews made the best 'potato' chips out of the fruit, which needed cooking in some form to be palatable.

Never short of a crisis for long, my stress levels soared anew when, without warning, my toilet became hopelessly blocked. Plunging achieved nothing, and the bathroom was flooded several times – not pleasant. Brother Joe, in charge of all building and maintenance for the Catholic schools, was very slow in coming to fix it, and for about two weeks I was reduced to peeing in a bucket and going door to door, roll of toilet paper clutched in my hand, to beg indulgence from my colleagues when anything more serious was required. Eventually, Brother Joe arrived with his team of African workers and after much serious excavation involving the drains, my toilet was restored.

The next unsettling event was not long in coming. President Kenneth Kaunda was paying a visit to Livingstone, staying at the Intercontinental Hotel. We were warned to keep away from town, including the hotel, because security would be tight, and the place would be swarming with military. A group of us promptly decided to go to the hotel for a drink that evening and hopefully catch a glimpse of the president. On the way, we were stopped by a few soldiers and after some discussion allowed to proceed. I was used to this happening on the Falls Road, especially just before the border with Rhodesia closed, and I was always careful to be polite and co-operative. Everyone knew the story of the young Irish engineer, Paddy Cummins, who'd stood up to them and been badly beaten. After beating him, they'd forced sand into his eyes. He spent quite some time in hospital.

But this night went smoothly. That wasn't so bad, I thought naively as we drove on.

We ordered our beers and decided to sit outside by the pool since it was a pleasant evening. There was no sign of the president or his entourage, so we assumed he'd be a no-show.

Suddenly, there was a terrible commotion and a well-built white man, with a shock of thick red hair and a beard to match, burst through the doors leading from an accommodation block to our left and sprinted along the covered walkway towards the main hotel building. He was naked, except for a pair of red briefs, and he was being hotly pursued by what must have been the security squad. We watched mesmerized as the escapee, howling like a banshee, plunged into the lush shrubbery that bordered the walkway path and disappeared, along with his dogged pursuers. There ensued a great kerfuffle in said shrubbery until the heavily perspiring African bodyguards re-emerged with their struggling quarry, manhandling him back into the building from whence he'd led the charge, the poor man now making an unearthly, high-pitched sobbing sound. In the ensuing silence after the double doors thudded shut, a bubble of conversation arose and gathered volume as the stunned spectators tried to analyze what we'd just witnessed.

A waiter approached to ask if we wanted refills, and we pumped him for an explanation. Who was the semi-naked man? What had happened to him? The waiter was tight-lipped. All he'd admit to was that the red-haired man was a presidential aide. As to what had caused this aide's spectacular melt-down, he had no idea.

"Best forget what you saw," he muttered as he slunk away.

I was feeling increasingly uneasy. "This might not be a good night for whitey to be abroad, guys. Let's get home."

I'd brought the Coughlans, who'd been craving some distraction now Bernie was feeling better, and we'd joined Catherine and Jimmy for drinks. Pat and Bernie agreed with me that we should leave, but Catherine and Jimmy opted to stay a while. We set off back into Livingstone on the dark, deserted highway, and I was just starting to relax when I spotted a purplish light swaying in the middle of the road. The army were notorious for not illuminating their roadblocks properly, so that, some cynics claimed, they could shoot you when you blundered into them. This one was typical of their efforts: a length of dark timber balanced on trestles and placed at right angles across the road with a single feeble light swinging from its middle.

"Roadblock," I murmured, and we were all instantly on full alert. Sure enough, as soon as I slowed, my headlights picked up movement and soldiers swarmed onto the road. That was another tactic. They concealed themselves in the bush. The officer in charge approached my driver's window, one hand raised imperiously, and I wound it down.

"Evening officer. Everything okay?"

He placed both hands on the sill, peering in to check the occupants.

"Where are you coming from?"

There was only one place we could have been. "The Mosi," I said evenly. "Just for a couple of drinks."

"Why did you go tonight?"

I shrugged. "No special reason. We often go there. We work in Livingstone."

He wrenched the door open. "Step out, please. All three."

"Why?" Pat demanded immediately. He'd had a skinful, probably drinking more than he normally would because he didn't have to drive, and he was fiery enough when sober.

I got out and thankfully Bernie encouraged Pat to do the same. When all three of us were standing in the road beside the car, the soldiers moved closer and levelled their guns at us.

If you've never been held at gunpoint, you probably won't understand how terrifying it is, looking down the cold, pitiless eye of the business end on an AK-47 that has the power to kill you in a split second, firing up to 600 rounds a minute. Pat reacted as, with a sense of impending doom, I knew he would.

"Don't point yer feckin' guns at us, ye savages!" he shouted, squaring up to the closest soldier.

I grabbed his arm. Bernie seemed paralyzed at this point. "Pat, calm down. You'll get us all killed."

The officer spread his arms and herded the three of us to the side of the road behind the car, Pat still glowering and breathing heavily. Then he said something over his shoulder to his men, and they lowered their weapons. He turned back to me, his expression apologetic.

"There are threats to the president, and we are looking for white saboteurs, searching for weapons. We are going to take your car apart, now."

"What?" I stared at him aghast. "Take my car apart?" I thought maybe we'd lost something in translation. "Do you mean search us?"

"Yes, and panel beat your car."

Pat exploded. "Ye feckin' eejits! We don't have any weapons! We're teachers working in yer feckin' country! My wife's a nurse at the hospital." He marched to the car door, jerking it open. "Come on, we're leaving!"

It happened very fast, but Pat was summarily seized by two of the soldiers and slammed up against the side of the car.

"Hands on the roof!" they bellowed.

"Don't ye feckin' touch me!" Pat raged.

Oh, sweet Jesus, I thought. We're all going to die.

Bernie began shrieking. "Leave my husband alone!" while simultaneously trying to get between Pat and the soldiers holding him, who elbowed her away.

"Don't ye touch my wife!" Pat roared.

The other soldiers raised their weapons again and I heard safety catches coming off. The situation was deteriorating rapidly.

Meanwhile, the officer and another soldier had opened my boot and were rummaging about in the interior. An excited whoop, and the soldier stepped backwards, triumphantly waving my tyre jack above his head.

Brief explanation about that: my tyre jack comprised a metal tube with holes along its length and a triangular shaped piece of metal at one end with a lever attached. With something approaching nausea I realized that the soldier, in his ignorance, had decided it was some kind of machinegun! I guess if you did stretch your imagination quite a bit it kind of resembled a weapon.

"That's the jack, for changing a tyre," I pleaded.

The officer shook his head, tut-tutting. "Panel beat!" he reiterated firmly.

Then we all froze like rabbits as approaching headlights loomed up out of the darkness and a vehicle slowed and stopped a few meters away. The doors opened either side and Jimmy and Catherine stepped out. Jimmy was in full ZAF uniform, including cap. The officer grinned and greeted him as he approached.

"Captain Patel, good evening."

"Sergeant Mbekwe."

Not only were they brothers-in-arms, but they knew each other!

Expat Blues

The Sergeant saluted and Jimmy touched his own cap. He ran an appraising eye over the situation and then led the chunky little Zambian away a short distance, a fraternal hand on his shoulder as they went into a close huddle talking earnestly. I caught Catherine's eye and she nodded reassuringly. I breathed again.

Poor old Pat was still pinned against the car, snorting furiously. I stood with my arm around an emotional Bernie, making soothing noises.

Jimmy and the sergeant returned.

"Everything is good now," said the latter cheerfully. "Captain Patel has assured me that you are not a danger. You can all go."

Afterwards, I realized how incredibly lucky we were that Jimmy had happened along when he did, and that the debt of gratitude we owed him was fathomless. He had skillfully defused a potentially lethal situation, and his rank and uniform had definitely helped, too. Just one more story of a narrow escape from bored soldiers looking for something to relieve the monotony.

I bought Jimmy many beers at the first opportunity. As for the presidential aide who ran amok, the consensus was that the poor guy, rumored to be Scottish, had a really bad trip on some nefarious substance.

The final term of the year was winding down as teachers worked feverishly to get students exam-ready, write reports, and complete numerous other tasks that are all facets of education everywhere.

The hot season arrived, and I braced myself to contend with the hunting spiders once again. They didn't seem so bad this second year. Blue, now eighteen months old and much bigger, was good at dispatching them. He'd plant a paw on one and hold it down until it succumbed.

Then the rains arrived, anything from a light drizzle to sheeting down like a solid wall, and they brought a whole new set of phenomena. First, were the frogs. Thousands of them. They swarmed over the road into town, and you had no choice but to drive over them. I hated that. Huge toads arrived, too. You'd find them wedged in the oddest places in your house and dislodging them was no mean feat. Blue, always protective of his mum, tried to grab hold of one and promptly dropped it, whimpering and pawing at his muzzle. The toads defended themselves by extruding a very nasty substance through their warty skins. I became adept at winkling them out of their corners to be returned to the outside world. Lightning could be a hazard, too. One evening, when I was walking home from night school just as a deluge descended, a huge blast of forked lightning snaked down and tore up the road only a few meters ahead of me, momentarily paralyzing me with terror as huge clods of earth were flung into the air. Sometimes, I felt as if I were losing my grip on sanity.

Other strange denizens emerged with the rains, not least among them the flying ants that swarmed in large numbers at this time of the year. They congregated in droves around any source of light at night, their long sausage-shaped bodies writhing about on the ground after they'd shed their wings. The local Africans gathered them up by the bucketload, as they were reputedly delicious to eat. I did not attempt to test this theory, but Blue sure loved to snack on them. I liked the dung beetles, though. Hardworking little guys.

I'd been wondering about where I might spend the Christmas break, when Noeline asked me if I'd like to join her and Mary on a trip to South Africa, travelling down on their lauded railway system. We would be accommodated with some nuns in Cape Town, kindly arranged through the sisters at St Theresa's. Putting aside any bad memories or negative feelings towards the apartheid state and always keen for adventure, I was delighted to accept, so Noeline went ahead with organizing the requisite bookings. With only a few weeks 'til departure, she drove out to my house one evening to inform me that I alone in our travelling trio needed a visa and urged me to see to it promptly. The kindly old priest who told me the story about the child mauled by the hyena procured the necessary forms and we filled them out together before posting them to his contact in Pretoria, a fellow priest who would expedite things personally and send a telegram, with, we hoped, good news, as soon as possible. Father told me he didn't like my chances as the cancelled Springboks' tour of New Zealand was still raw in South

Africa, but his forebodings proved ill-founded, and the Pretoria priest's telegram confirmed that the visa had been granted. With snail mail the only option, there now wasn't time for me to post my passport to Pretoria and receive it back again stamped with the visa prior to departure. Father gave me the visa's official number, included in the telegram, on a slip of paper as a contingency, and I placed it carefully in my passport.

"Fingers crossed," he said cheerfully.

Blue seemed resigned to my disappearing from time to time and was happy enough to stay around the compound with whomever was looking after him. This time, the Brownes kindly agreed to take care of him. I drove to the girls' house in the township where I left my car because Father Jude and Father O'Connell had generously volunteered to drive us over the border to Victoria Falls where we would catch the train to Cape Town. Father Matt McCartan (no relation to Noeline) came, too, but I wasn't happy about his presence. I'd disliked him the moment I first saw him, up at the Sports Club, gawping with lust-glazed eyes at curvy Madeleine Murphy as she danced in tight white pants. "Yeah!" he was calling out. He made my flesh crawl. All my life I've had gut reactions to people that have never let me down and as subsequent events proved they didn't let me down with that man.

As mentioned previously, the border with Rhodesia was closed, so we went via Kazungula and Botswana. I always enjoyed crossing the Zambesi on the Kazungula ferry, watching the huge Nile crocodiles lined up in long rows on the banks, formidable jaws agape to allow the little plover birds to clean their teeth. It was an amazing sight, but also unsettling. A white farmer told me he once saw a crocodile take an African mother with a baby on her back as they were crossing a river, leaving barely a ripple in the water.

South African soldiers from Caprivi had a very poorly concealed maimai close to the water's edge on the opposite bank with the barrel of a machine gun and the lens of a film camera protruding through the camouflage netting, just to let us know that they meant business and were keeping an eye on who and what was crossing over from Zambia. We always waved cheerfully at them, often with the addition of a two-finger salute and much derisive hooting and hollering. We'd even considered mooning them on occasion, but today we were on our best behavior, not just because of the presence of our priestly escort, but also because we were en route to their country.

Of course, I started to get my familiar border crossing jitters, but by now I had things down to a pretty fine art, especially my smuggling skills, and all went smoothly. We arrived safely in Victoria Falls where the fathers delivered us to the train station, and we departed on our next big adventure. I sensed that Noeline was missing Kitty, her beloved best friend, who was holidaying elsewhere with Pat. Rumor had it that they'd gone shopping for an engagement ring.

South African Railways had a reputation for excellent service at this time, and we soon learned why. We had a very well-appointed second-class compartment with shower and toilet, and the standard of attention to our care and comfort could not be faulted. All the staff, coloreds and Africans mainly, were smartly dressed in white jackets, dark trousers, and bow ties. While we were at breakfast, our compartment was cleaned and tidied, bunks folded away and bedding stored. When it was time for lunch, we were personally summoned and escorted to our sitting in the dining car, with the same procedure followed for dinner. While we dined, they organized our bunks and bedding for the night. Drinks and treats were offered at regular intervals throughout the day. The quality of the food and wine was superb and I for one was really enjoying the experience of not having to drive for a change. It was lovely to kick back, lulled by the rocking motion of the train, reading my book or snoozing. On one occasion, while we were stopped at a station, I was reclining on the seat with my bare feet resting on the open windowsill that faced the platform when a passing stranger, a young man, stopped and gave me an impromptu foot massage! Very relaxing time. But the prospect of the approaching South African border niggled at me, spoiling my sense of peace.

The train progressed south from Victoria Falls, down through Dete, Gwai, and Bulawayo. We crossed into Botswana at Plumtree without incident and then on to Gaborone. After Gaborone, the next stop of significance was the South African border, at Mafeking. I braced myself.

We arrived at the border at about 5.30 a.m. I was wakened by voices in the corridor and then jumped when there were several sharp raps on our compartment door. The girls barely stirred so I answered it in my nightgown and found myself looking up at the expressionless features of two very tall policemen, their caps pulled so low over their faces I could only see their noses and lips. Both carried guns. The taller of the two had a square-cut Hitler moustache – which didn't bode well.

"Passports!" he barked.

By now the girls were awake and we scrambled to find our documents, which were scrutinized in silence under torchlight. Mary and Noeline's passports were promptly returned with an abrupt, "All good." Then the mustachioed officer turned to me, holding mine aloft delicately by a corner as if it were contaminated.

"You are the New Zealander?"

"Yes."

"Where is your visa?"

"I do have one. I just didn't have time to get the stamp. The number is written on the piece of –"

I didn't get a chance to finish.

"Get dressed, then you will come with us. You are under arrest."

The door closed. Mary and Noeline gasped. Gathering my wits, I quickly used the bathroom before pulling on my clothes and packing up my stuff.

"You two go on to Cape Town," I said firmly to the girls, who were watching me with owlish eyes. "I'll catch up with you there. Everything will be fine."

Then I opened the door, and with everyone gawping through their windows, I was frog marched off the train and along the platform to the station buildings, where I was relieved of my bag, led into the police office and conducted into a small cell. I sat down on the bench provided and waited for them to decide my fate. They did not lock the cell door, which opened directly into their office area, and it was only a few minutes before Mary and Noeline burst in, clearly having dressed in a hurry, and toting their luggage. I groaned. Their loyalty was touching but misplaced. Now we were all in the same boat, except that I was the only one under arrest. The last thing I wanted was to ruin their holiday. In a display of defiant solidarity, they marched into the cell and sat down on the bench either side of me, glaring at my captors. Outside, we could hear our erstwhile train departing the station.

There are two types of white South Africans: descendants of the British colonizers, called the English, and descendants of the Dutch colonizers, called Boers or Afrikaners, who had a more hardline reputation. The taller police officer with the moustache was clearly the latter, his yarpie accent pronounced. The other officer clearly the former. Of the two, he was much less stern and friendlier. He made coffee for me and the girls and explained that we would have to wait for 8 a.m. when they would put a call through to Pretoria to confirm my visa by the number I'd presented.

"If you have no visa. you go straight back where you came from," said moustache gleefully, and I could see how he wanted things to play out. Classic good cop, bad cop!

I glanced at my watch. Six-thirty. The three of us sat in a despondent little cluster in the cell, not talking, counting the minutes. Mary asked if she could smoke, and the nice cop gave her an ashtray. There was no mention of breakfast, though. To rub it in, bad cop sat at his desk, alternately sipping from a big enamel mug full of steaming tea and wresting generous mouthfuls from a giant-sized sandwich. I silently hoped it choked him.

H-hour rolled around, and nice cop made the requisite phone call to Pretoria. Bad cop looked mightily pissed off when they confirmed I had indeed been granted a visa. At his summons, I stood meekly before his desk as he prepared to put the requisite stamp onto a page of my passport, and then I'm not sure why I did what I did next.

Expat Blues

I leaned over and placed my hand over the page just as he was poised to stamp it.

"I want a looseleaf visa," I said firmly. "I don't want a South African stamp on my passport."

This was a fair request, since I worked in a country hostile to his. He went visibly puce from his cap visor downwards, and I feared an implosion, but he had no choice but to comply, and he knew it.

As I picked up my passport, now with two little pieces of paper in it, I asked, "Why do I need a visa, but the girls don't?" I was just curious.

He pushed his cap back a little, and for the first time I met his cold, flinty gaze. "Because your goddammed country makes us get visas. That's why." He leaned a little closer. "If you ever come back this way again, I'll lock you up good and proper."

I opened my mouth to ask, "What? Even with a visa?" but decided I'd best not antagonize him further. Instead, I said cheerfully, "Okay."

Good cop intervened at this point, offering to escort us to the ticket office on the station so that we could arrange for the continuation of our interrupted journey.

South Africa continued to make a bad impression. The young woman in the ticketing office was surly and unsmiling. We made the new bookings for our ongoing journey and were disappointed to hear that we'd have to wait until 6 p.m. for the train to take us to Kimberley, where we had to change once again to travel on to Cape Town. She did allow us to stow our luggage in a corner of the office, though, which was helpful. Bookings completed, we began to walk into town in search of breakfast, a long day of cooling our heels in front of us.

Over tea, toast and scrambled eggs, I asked the girls why they had not gone on without me, and they both insisted there was no way they were ever going to abandon me. We had to stick together. We'd forged bonds on our epic safari to East Africa, I guess, and I was certainly grateful that I had not been left to languish alone in a strange town during this unexpected hiatus in our journey. Ever the history buff, I bored the girls with the story of the relief of Mafeking in the Boer War and the part played by Colonel Robert Baden-Powell, who famously went on to found the Boy Scouts' movement. Mary said drily that the best 'relief' would be leaving the place.

After breakfast, we found the local post office and sent a telegram to our hosts in Cape Town to let them know that we'd be arriving a day late. Then we wandered around the town for a little while and found a bookshop/stationer where we bought some magazines to share around and pass the time with, our books being locked in our bags at the station. When I went up to the cashier's desk, there was a young African man ahead of me. The woman serving looked past him at me and then snapped at the youth to step aside while she served me first. He obeyed instantly, head lowered. I felt absolutely rotten inside. His money was welcome, but he wasn't.

Having been up since 5.30 a.m. we started to wilt a bit, so returned to the station to read or doze on one of the benches along the platform. It was disconcerting to see the signs with 'whites/non-whites' (or 'blankes/nie-blankes' in Afrikaans), on the station's facilities, and we surreptitiously took photos for the record.

Long, weary day in Mafeking. Apartheid signage visible over toilets.

Finally, 6 p.m. rolled around and the train duly arrived. We reclaimed our bags and settled into our compartment, happy to be on the move again. While we waited for the train to depart, a young white policeman suddenly appeared at the window, which we'd opened for fresh air. Seeing three young women, his pimply face broke into a big smile, and he leaned on the sill, to strike up a conversation, asking the usual questions: where were we from, what were we doing in Africa etc. When we told him we all worked as teachers in Zambia, his demeanor changed instantly.

"How do you sit in the bioscope with them, or queue with them at the post office? They stink like cattle. Mind you, I don't mind a bit of blek company after dark." Nod, nod wink wink, was fairly typical of the racist comments he regaled us with. We ignored him and he got the message, muttering to himself as he moved on. Shortly thereafter, the train lurched, steadied, gathered speed and we were on our way. I knew we had to come back through Mafeking on the return journey and the thought brought me no joy. Mary was right. It was a 'relief' to leave!

There was hardly anyone on the train, so we got star treatment. After a fine dinner, the three of us retired early to catch up on lost sleep.

We arrived in Kimberley the next morning and smoothly transitioned to the train that would finally deliver us to Cape Town. This last leg of our journey took us across the famous Karoo, the immense arid region dubbed the heart and soul of South Africa. I was glued to the carriage window, mesmerized by this vast landscape's stark beauty and legendary kopjes that broke up the rolling countryside.

One, Father Leo, an elderly priest, met at us at the station in Cape Town and drove us out to the convent attached to his parish in the suburb of Belleville, where we'd be based for the next two weeks. The sisters, a charitable order who were all Cape colored, welcomed us warmly and one of them, Sister Agnes, introduced herself as our caretaker and liaison person for the duration of our stay. She conducted us to our own personal guesthouse a short distance away in the convent grounds and after showing us around left us to settle in. The guesthouse was charming, built in Dutch Cape style with the distinctive rounded whitewashed gables and shuttered dormer windows. Sister said it was the original farmhouse on a historical estate now owned by the Catholic church and had been converted to accommodate visitors. To my delight, a dog arrived to greet us, a plump old brown and white mongrel called Lassie. She was the sisters' dog, as it turned out, but she spent a lot of time with us whenever we were home over the next fortnight.

The old farmhouse was comfortable and spacious. We each had our own bedroom and there was a lounge, dining room, and kitchen that included a fridge stocked with food. Already, we sensed the hospitality on this trip would prove exceptional.

Our lovely old Dutch farmhouse accommodation in Cape Town.

We unpacked and went for a stroll. The day was bright and sunny with a nice breeze blowing, making a change from the stillness that marked every day in Livingstone. It was the Cape's summertime, and the Mediterranean climate was balmy and relaxing, day after day of glorious clear-sky weather. Locals called the prevailing wind 'the Cape doctor' because it blew any pollution out to sea.

The sisters had left tourist brochures and a map in our house, and we pored over them, planning our itinerary, determined to see as much as we could in our allotted time. There was just one thing niggling me, and I finally broached it with the girls.

"Um, I'm not all that au fait with the race rules here, but I don't think, as whites, we're actually supposed to be in what is clearly a colored area. We, um, could be breaking the law."

Noeline and Mary looked at me aghast. I remembered that the sisters had invited us to dinner with them on this, our first night, so I tried to appear nonchalant about the fact that this time all three of us might end up incarcerated.

"Look, not to worry. We'll ask the sisters at dinner. Clearly, they're not too bothered, and they'll know how the laws here work."

The girls nodded. We set about freshening up and headed off to the convent for dinner. As we dined, I probed sister Agnes about our legal status, and she dismissed any concerns promptly.

"You're temporary visitors, foreign nationals, so it's fine. Don't worry about a thing."

I relayed this to the girls as we prepared for bed, and we decided to just put all that race stuff aside and enjoy our holiday.

Easier said than done. Apartheid proved nerve-wracking.

We packed a lot into our Cape Town stay, doing all the touristy things but also engaging with the human side of life under the apartheid system. We visited the beautiful beaches – whites only, of course, and patrolled by armed police to ensure they stayed that way. On one occasion we were befriended by a glamorous young woman in a dazzling white swimsuit and matching turban who was very eager to have someone to talk to and regaled us in lurid detail about the collapse of her marriage and recent divorce while we simpered and tut tutted with appropriate solicitude during her unburdening. When she learned we were tourists she asked where we were staying and registered immediate alarm when we told her.

"Oh, my gawd, that's a colored area! You shouldn't be there!"

She hurried off, muttering to herself and we thought maybe we should make tracks for home. Father Leo had dropped us off at the beach and given us instructions where to catch the return bus. As we boarded it, we realized that it was full of colored people (Of course it was. It serviced a colored suburb) and froze in an uncertain huddle on the steps. Whites could get into trouble, too, for violating segregation. The driver, a thin middle aged colored man with a world-weary slump, pushed his cap back, ran a jaded eye over us, raised one eyebrow and said, "What are you waiting for, girls? An invitation?"

As I said earlier – apartheid was nerve-wracking. After we'd told the driver our destination, he made a point of dropping us off right outside the convent, acknowledging our words of thanks with a smile and a dismissive wave.

The cable car ride up to the top of Table Mountain was memorable. Sometimes it had a thin layer of cloud on its dramatically flat surface, which the Cape people called 'the tablecloth', but it was clear the day we went, with incredible views. We stood in a cluster, eyes closed facing Robben Island, and said a silent prayer for Nelson Mandela, now in his ninth year of what would be twenty-seven years' imprisonment there and elsewhere.

Another beautiful, breezy Cape Town day.

We went out to the southernmost point of Africa, Cape Agulhas, where the Atlantic meets the Indian Ocean in a wild surge, and spent a beautiful day in Stellenbosch and Paarl, the stunning wine growing areas. Father Leo chauffeured us around willingly and then eventually found us a little car to use while we were there, complete with our own personal guide, a shy gentle young colored man named Gerard. I got to do all the driving, but it wasn't too bad as Gerard gave excellent directions and the speed limits had been lowered to help the nation weather the oil crisis instigated by the Arabs following the October Yom Kippur War with Israel. Gerard often guided us to places where he couldn't accompany us because of the race laws, so we refused to go without him and found other things to do. He introduced us to his family, and they took us on a picnic. We had to travel for hours to reach an area where they could legally relax and spend time, and of course it wasn't very attractive – a lake with leaden water, its shores choked by reeds and bulrushes. No matter, we set up the braii and cooked up a storm. I especially enjoyed the spicy boerewors (farmer's) sausages that came in a glistening coil, at least a foot across, and were served in juicy chunks with a split bun and lots of sauce. Delicious. That was a special day.

Spectacular view of Cape Town from the top of Table Mountain on a hot, hazy day, with our guide, Gerard.

We celebrated Christmas with the nuns, Father Leo and Lassie, attending Mass before enjoying a sumptuous dinner with all the trimmings and then afterwards relaxing with a screening of *Scrooge,* the lovely Albert Finney musical version of *A Christmas Carol.* (There was no TV in South Africa then. One wit claimed it was because you couldn't have black and white on the same screen!). Father Leo, operating the projector and perhaps a little tipsy on Christmas cheer, got the reels in the wrong order, but our post-prandial bliss meant that nobody cared, even when the ending occurred in the middle. The tubby little nun seated next to me became very excited by the phantom-like Ghost of Christmas Yet to Come, shrieking loudly and covering her face. I tried to reassure her that the sinister specter was a benign spirit, on a mission to reform Scrooge, but she was enjoying the terror too much.

As the day drew to a close, the sisters piled us up with leftovers and we tottered off home to sleep off our indulgence.

Father Leo decided we had to go to a proper movie while we were in Cape Town. The bioscope, as it was called all over southern Africa, was a very big deal for city-dwelling South Africans. Trailing wide-eyed into the plush, elaborately furnished theatre behind Father Leo, we quickly realized that, clad in jeans and T-shirts as we were, we were seriously under-dressed. The men and women were all in formal evening wear, gents in tuxes, ladies in long gowns and pearls. They eyed us disapprovingly as they sipped their cocktails at the glittering bar in the foyer.

Father Leo apologized – he had left bookings a little late and this was the only show he could get us into at short notice. It was a nature documentary, which would have drawn a small audience back in New Zealand, but on this night, it was packed to the rafters. The blacks and coloreds had the downstairs stalls, and all the whites sat upstairs in the dress circle. The usherettes, wearing candy-striped mini-skirts and beribboned straw boaters, were all African or colored. It was a truly bizarre experience, but we were getting used to bizarre by this stage.

One of the last outings that Father Leo organized for us was attending a show featuring Rolf Harris (a long time before his fall from grace) and Gerard accompanied us, which meant he'd be seated in the whites only section of the theatre. We were nervous for him, but he reassured us that he often did this when shows came to town and had refined the art of blending in and not drawing attention to himself down to a fine degree. Indeed, he had, and although a few suspicious glances were directed his way

Expat Blues

nobody challenged him. He was with three young white women after all, and he was very well dressed, his posture relaxed, his face expressionless, his manner reserved. We were delighted to see him flout the apartheid system that night.

We were coming to the end of our South African sojourn, and Sister Agnes, who had taken such good care of us, (I remember one morning she brought us mutton chops for breakfast!) invited us to have dinner with her family. She was one of ten siblings so warned us to expect a large turnout. Her family home was in a particularly attractive suburb of Cape Town which was historically a colored area, filled with rows of brightly painted, well-cared for little stucco houses with pretty gardens bordering cobblestoned streets. Sister Agnes said it was under threat because the whites wanted it, so all the coloreds who had lived there for generations were going to be moved out to large estates on the fringes of the city. We'd seen some of these 'estates' – soulless brick monstrosities rearing up out of barren wastelands with no facilities nearby. Sister said she was very concerned about the impact of a move on her elderly father, who was weakened by serious illness.

As we drove to her home, Sister filled us in on her family background. Her father was white and her mother colored. Under the race laws, they could not therefore live in a white area, so her father was registered as colored to enable him to live with his wife in a colored area, which move the authorities considered the lesser of two evils. That was the only way they could be together. Just another example of the insanity that was apartheid. All the children of their union were classified colored.

Sister Agnes, right, with one of her postulants.

We were ushered into a small lounge room packed with people of all ages, all turned out in their best clothes for the occasion, and then conducted to three chairs placed on one side, where we sat awkwardly, feeling like very undeserving VIPs. Sister Agnes introduced each of us in turn to her hushed family, just our names and general background, and then invited us to meet her parents. Her frail, elderly father was in a wheelchair as he was suffering from tracheal cancer and had a little grille in his throat through which he rasped a greeting, squeezing both hands of each of us in turn, smiling his delight at our presence. His wife was a dignified, quiet woman, her long grey hair clasped in a bun on the nape of her neck. They were so deferential and so clearly delighted to have us in their home, while we wondered how they could have such kindly feelings towards any representative of the white race. It was humbling to witness their lack of resentment and their eagerness to differentiate between oppressors and kindred spirits. No racists there. We moved on to meeting the rest of the family one by one, and I gave up trying to remember names after the first half dozen or so. I marveled over how ten children had been raised in such a small home, which was so obviously lovingly cared for. The thought they might lose it was heartbreaking.

Introductions over, we were returned to our seats and subsequently plied with all manner of delicious treats for the rest of the evening, while various family members approached to hear more about our life in Zambia and our impressions of Cape Town. As soon as we emptied a plate, it was filled again, likewise our glasses. The warmth and hospitality were typically overwhelming.

On the drive home, Sister Agnes said she hoped we would continue to bear witness to the truth of what was happening in South Africa, and we promised her we would. We, in turn, thanked her sincerely for what had been a deeply humbling and moving experience, one we'd never forget and always value.

Father Leo delivered us to the train station and saw us safely aboard our carriage. The goodbyes to the nuns had been emotional, and in a final gesture of kindness they'd given us a large cake tin full of food for our journey – sweets, savories, snacks, and even fried chicken.

Expat Blues

If apartheid South Africa had left a bad taste in our mouths, the sisters were determined to banish it! As it turned out, we gave the tin and its contents to an African woman with two small children who approached our window, begging, at a station we briefly pulled into.

On the return journey through Mafeking, I spotted bad cop as he strolled past our carriage window.

"Hey!" I called.

His head swiveled.

"Yes!" he called back, and his lips curved up slightly in a sardonic smile.

Yes, indeed.

Chapter Twelve: Felled Again, a Wise Move, Back to Rhodesia

The big story in the compound after I got home was a very unfortunate incident that had befallen the Coughlans, who were nowhere to be seen. Their baby son had been born by now, of course, and I'd stood as his surrogate godmother, as requested. I'd also bought them a pram, as requested, but I didn't really see much of them anymore. Mary Browne told me the details of the unfortunate incident, which I have always thought would make a very good short story with a strong moral.

But first, some background. Towards the end of 1973, our night watchman had approached the Brownes, who were his unofficial monitors, and asked for a raise as he was sole supporter of a large extended family. Mary and Brendan said they'd call a meeting of all the compound dwellers and run it past them. After a short discussion, we agreed on a K2.00 raise per household, which would give the watchman a nice bit of extra money and hardly inconvenienced us. The Coughlans were the only dissenters, claiming that the watchman was a lazy so-and-so who slept most of the night. Well, maybe he did – who could blame him? In fact, my stoop was his favorite place to bed down for a while, right under my bedroom window, where his loud snoring kept me awake. But, with a couple of good guard dogs like Blue and Kitoga thrown in, he still provided a good deterrent against criminals, and we'd had no problems thus far. To universal disgust, they therefore refused to pay their measly K2.00.

The watchman was given the news, but his delight was tempered by the apology that the raise would have been higher had one household not refused to pay. No names were given, of course, but the compound servants' grape vine was a fertile one and he soon sussed out who had deprived him. By way of revenge, he instituted a policy of avoiding their house on his nightly rounds, and their house was in a very vulnerable, isolated corner of the compound, up against the fence, bush beyond.

Then the Coughlans went away for a weekend to Sesheke. During their absence, in the middle of the night, a group of little African

Expat Blues

kids from the local village tunneled under the compound fence and broke into their house through a window they managed to prise open. All the windows had vertical and horizontal burglar bars, but the little kids were skinny enough to squeeze through a single square. The watchman was nowhere to be seen. It was never established if he was complicit.

Once inside, the hungry little kids made straight for the food sources, namely pantry and refrigerator. In the fridge, they found a large block of what looked like chocolate and devoured it all with gusto. It was laxative chocolate. After they'd gorged on everything edible they could lay their hands on, the laxative took effect. Knowing nothing about flush toilets, they defecated wherever they could, at will and with gay abandon, and wiped their bottoms on bedlinen, towels, clothing etc. Then they pinched a few tawdry items and left.

The Coughlans returned. It took two full weeks for the house and contents to be cleaned and sanitized, involving a whole team of workers, in rubber gloves, masks and coveralls, organized by Brother Joe, while the occupants sought accommodation elsewhere.

I sincerely tried not to smile; but, to my shame, I failed.

There was more drama, too, as the new year unfolded. The bush war came to Livingstone in the form of a parcel bomb sent to the local government offices. The most probable target was the District Commissioner, but it was his secretary who died in the explosion as she opened the package. The news spread like wildfire and Carmel gathered us all to issue a warning not to go near town until things calmed down. The place would be crawling with soldiers.

I had an errand to run, so after lunch I drove into town, using back roads and a roundabout route to reach my destination, a private dwelling. Sister had said restrictions would most likely include a curfew, so I knew I had to get home before dark. For whatever reason, after completing my business, I decided to return home on the fastest route, going straight through town. The town was deserted, eerily quiet, but as I turned onto the road leading to Maramba I was confronted by a roadblock manned by several soldiers. I did a quick U-turn and raced off to the back roads route I'd used coming in. To my dismay, this was now blocked as well, but there was no sign of any soldiers. I approached the barricade slowly and saw that it comprised two short planks of white-painted wood supported on frames, like athletics hurdles, and staggered one behind the other to cover the full road while leaving a sizeable gap between the two barriers. I decided to give it a go and squeeze through. As I inched forwards, I registered a voice screaming at me in a language I didn't recognize, and instantly hit the brakes. The barrel of a gun, probably a Soviet issue AK-47, slid through the open driver's window and rammed into the side of my head while the soldier on the end of it continued to scream abuse at me, emphasizing his outrage with sharp jabs of the muzzle into my temple. I'd forgotten their propensity for concealing themselves in the undergrowth. My life flashed before my eyes.

"Sorry, sorry, sorry, officer. I just want to get home. I teach at St Mary's."

I took my white-knuckled hands off the steering wheel and raised them to shoulder height, all the while repeating those words over and over.

After what felt like a long time, the gun was withdrawn, the screaming stopped. I turned my head and looked into a pair of bloodshot eyes in which rage was gradually dwindling. Without a word, he shouldered his weapon, walked over to the barriers and pulled the second one across the road until it sat squarely behind the other. Then he motioned me through. I fumbled the gears and crept past him, before accelerating away. I half expected a hail of bullets to rip through the rear of the car so he could justify shooting me by saying I'd run the roadblock, but when I glanced in the rear vision mirror, he was busy rearranging its two components to seal off the road again. Once out of sight around a bend, I pulled over, scrambled out, and was violently ill over the road.

I had a reckless streak in those days, and it almost got me killed. When I finally told someone about the incident the person marveled that, given the army's reputation, I hadn't been shot outright. I've always had a first-rate guardian angel.

Expat Blues

The Coughlans' unpleasant experience highlighted an aspect of expat life that intrigued me greatly: the degrees of difference with which people, themselves from humble origins, treated their African domestics – housemen, maids, nannies etc. Most were decent employers, and some even forged close bonds with their domestics, but others were arrogant and demeaning towards those who worked for them.

When I first obtained Erita's services, I was told I should never let her use my toilet. Why, I asked? Because she's probably got VD, I was informed – by a medical professional, no less. I'd seen other servants going off into the bush, clutching rolls of toilet paper and been angered at their humiliation, never mind the risk of snake bite. Kuta, the Coughlans' man, was a good example. I promptly told Erita she was welcome to use my toilet and she nodded her gratitude. Being pregnant, she needed to avail herself of it often, and it was always kept spotless. The ignorance was eye watering. Nobody catches an STD off a toilet seat.

One expat who suffered the consequences of mistreating a houseman was John Clare. He and Pat O'Connell shared a teachers' house at Namatama Christian Brothers' school, and also shared a houseman named Gideon. John's abysmal treatment of Gideon was legendary, as was his exploitation of impoverished African women, and eventually the poor man called it quits and left. His parting shot was that he'd get even with 'Mister John'.

One night while John and Pat were at the Sports Club drinking, their house was broken into. Pat had had the foresight to lock his bedroom door and the thieves failed to break it down. John, who'd taken no such precaution, was robbed blind. The only thing left in his room was his metal bedframe. The culprits were never caught…but you didn't have to be a genius to work that one out.

It did not pay to antagonize the help.

Often, I'd see the compound's African domestics seated on or standing around the bench seat under the mopane tree, having a well-earned laugh and a gossip during a lull in their working day. I'd have loved to know what they thought of their white employers. I bet they had us all well sized up.

The first term of the new year got underway. Exam results for the previous one had been very good, so Sister Carmel urged us on to achieve more of the same. I mostly had senior English classes now, although I did have one junior history class that I enjoyed. A big chunk of their curriculum was devoted to African history, and there was often outrage from the girls when they learned about the battles between European colonizers and the indigenous tribes, especially when the whites were seriously outnumbered. They approved heartily of the outcome of Isandlwana, a Zulu triumph, but vehemently queried the result for Rorke's Drift, where a small garrison of British soldiers had held out against thousands of Zulu warriors.

"Excuse me, meestress, *how* many British soldiers?"

"One hundred and thirty-nine."

"And how many Zulus?"

"Er, four thousand five hundred."

"Eeeeeee!"

Then I got sick again. I'd been warned the malaria could recur, and it did, almost a year to the day of the first attack and laid me out again. It wasn't as severe as the first time, but it was bad enough. There was a new nun at the convent, a young Austrian woman who happened to be a trained nurse, and she brought me chloroquine and tended to me. The Brownes then moved me into their house, where I convalesced.

Once I'd more or less recovered and was back at work, the Irish girls approached me with an offer. Two teachers had now finished their contracts at St Theresa's and returned home. I hadn't really got to know either. That left two vacant rooms and the girls had approached their principal with a request for me to be given permission to move in. It was granted, and Noeline, Kitty and Mary drove out to Maramba to tell me the good news and that Blue was included in the invitation. The timing was perfect, as I was severely disenchanted with life in the compound: my disappointing digs, battling the insects and other wildlife, negotiating the personal politics, and, above all, enduring the loneliness. My principal's blessing was needed next. I ran the offer past Carmel, and she was genuinely pleased for me. I assured her that I loved the school and my job, but I needed the company of single people my own age and she reassured me in turn, insisting that it was a good move for me.

It was sad saying goodbye to Erita, but I wrote her a glowing reference and told her I was sure the flat would soon have another tenant. She nodded her acceptance, but she lowered her eyes and did not smile. Another teacher did arrive, an eccentric single Irishman who was Fiona's boyfriend and who'd transferred from somewhere else in Zambia, but he did not employ Erita.

The weekend after I'd accepted the girls' invitation, I packed up my meagre belongings and Blue and moved into the teachers' spacious, comfortably furnished six-bedroom bungalow attached to St Theresa's. The move coincided with my final payment on my car loan, so I now had extra money as well, which made me feel pretty upbeat and positive about my new circumstances.

My bedroom was clean, bright and comfortable, and unlike the compound where we lived so close to the bush, there were fewer bugs and spiders. Blue was confused and clingy for a few days, but soon settled in. He couldn't come to school anymore, of course, but he had Aclon, our houseman, to hang out with, and he loved joining the kids at break times in the school playground which backed onto the house. He didn't wander and was always waiting on the stoop for me when I pulled up in the car around noon. After dinner, he liked to cuddle with me, keeping one of his paws in my hand so he'd know instantly if I moved. When this endearing habit ceased, I knew he was feeling relaxed and secure.

As far as security went, we had close neighbors, all Indian families, and the street was well lit – especially during Diwali when the candles blazing in the front windows were a sight to behold. There was chain-link fencing across the front of the house with gates that could be padlocked at night, and Blue took his new watchdog duties seriously.

Another young woman joined our household at the same time. Eleanor Brennan was a Protestant from Northern Ireland and taught in a local government school. She'd been living alone, too, in an apartment near town and welcomed the opportunity to join us when a close friend left the house at end of contract. Thus, we were a happy menage of five, quite a change for me after living alone. I still had niggling feelings of being the outsider as the only Kiwi, but I was pretty hardened to that by this stage.

One lunchtime, I remarked, "God, what I'd give for a nice saveloy."

They all looked at me baffled.

"Pink sausage?" I did my best to clarify.

There was a chorus of gagging noises. Yep, cultural differences will out.

The hardest part of moving into the house with the girls was the nocturnal clamor that came from the railway station only one street away. The other girls' bedrooms, on the opposite side of the house's long corridor, all faced towards the school grounds, but mine faced directly towards the railway. Public posturing dictated that Zambia and Rhodesia were sworn enemies, and the border had been shut since early 1973, but economic expediency meant Zambia still needed Wankie coal for its northern copper mines, and this was where African politics got very murky. The Zambians still bought the coal, and the Rhodesians were more than happy to supply it. The subterfuge involved in shunting it across the border under cover of darkness fooled nobody. We all knew what was going on. For night after night the clanking, hissing, graunching locomotives kept me wide awake, rising to face the next day wretched with tiredness, until after a couple of weeks, just as with the nocturnal insect chorus, I never even heard them anymore and slept like a baby.

There were other changes afoot, too. Kitty and Pat had gone off on their own to Rhodesia over Christmas, while we were in South Africa, and had become engaged. The wedding was scheduled to take place in a matter of weeks, and Noeline, who would be bridesmaid, announced she would break her contract and return home to Ireland immediately afterwards. She and Kitty, who'd come to Africa together, had been close for a long time and Noeline was struggling badly with the looming marriage and, as she saw it, the loss of her best friend. Despite her obvious pain, she remained loyal to and supportive of Kitty in every way during the hectic weeks leading up to the nuptials. I felt sad that she was leaving because out of all the people I knew in Livingstone I related to her the best and appreciated the many acts of kindness she'd shown me. She was one of the most genuinely goodhearted, thoughtful people I've ever met, and years later, when I heard of her premature death from cancer, I was gutted.

Before the wedding and her departure for home, Noeline asked me if I would accompany her to Victoria Falls for a last weekend in Rhodesia. It turned out to be a precious memory for both of us. We booked in at one of the beautifully kept but cheap chalets in a pleasant bush setting outside town, before driving down to the Victoria Falls Hotel for dinner. Built above the Zambesi River gorges in 1904, this elegant hotel, featuring lily ponds, arched loggias and broad verandahs, was an outstanding example of British colonial architecture and a popular venue for well-heeled white South African tourists. We chose the Saturday night braii, sitting outside under leafy trees strung with lanterns, sipping a drink, while a glistening haunch of beef turned slowly on a spit, fat dripping off to sizzle on the coals below. As the sun set, everyone went quiet when a horn resounded from somewhere hidden in the bush above the gorges, drums throbbed, and deep African voices floated up, harmonizing in song. Then, one by one, statuesque African men, glistening bodies dressed in full Zulu warrior attire complete with assegais and shields and carrying burning torches, emerged from the bush, chanting, singing and dancing, flowing amongst the guests' tables until they disappeared into the darkness, music and voices gradually fading away. It was spellbinding, breathtaking, a superb way for Noeline to end her sojourn in Africa.

After a sumptuous buffet meal, the band struck up in earnest and two shy, nice-looking young men approached our table to introduce themselves and ask if they could join us. They turned out to be two off-duty South African soldiers, part of a new contingent that had been sent up to Rhodesia to help bolster their border forces. We thought they'd probably leg it when they found out we worked in Zambia, but they were unfazed. Their manners were impeccable, and they insisted on buying us drinks for the rest of the evening. We danced the night away in their company, and when it was time to part, they escorted us to the car and shook hands goodnight. We wished them well and a safe return home. They were so painfully young.

I don't remember much about the wedding. I do remember that drunken Brother Kennedy spilled his beer on the new outfit I'd had made for the occasion, and then insisted on dancing with me, continually squeezing me up against his hard-on until I walked away in disgust. With one or two exceptions, I no longer had any illusions about the male Irish clergy in Livingstone.

After the wedding, there was a mass exodus. Noeline left, of course, followed by the Coughlans, the Mullins, and dodgy Brother Kennedy. Kitty and Pat moved into the Coughlans' old house at Maramba, even though neither was a teacher at St Mary's. I didn't tell them about the shite fest it had hosted. I don't know if anyone else did.

That left me, Mary, and Eleanor in the bungalow, and we were all due to leave at Christmas. Expat communities are fluid by nature. Some people renewed contracts, coming back after a three-month break, but, although I loved the teaching, the salary, given my qualifications, was not sufficient to retain me, plus I had the travel bug. I started applying for jobs elsewhere and was offered a well-paid position at a school in Colombia, South America. Another adventure to look forward to.

The first term was coming to an end, and I began to think about holiday destinations. Catherine was at a loose end as it turned out, Jimmy having flown off to the UK to see family, so she offered to accompany me wherever I chose to go. Mary was likewise keen, so we decided on Rhodesia, going off the beaten track somewhat to the Umtali region in the east, and, hopefully, including an excursion over the border into Mozambique. There was a young Greek man in Livingstone, Panos, whose family ran a clothing factory. He'd got to know the girls when he was going out with one of their colleagues who'd since returned home to Ireland, and when he heard about our trip from Mary, he kindly arranged for us to stay a couple of nights in Bulawayo with two of his elderly relatives. So, we planned our itinerary and set off, taking my car once again. Mary didn't drive, and Catherine was a bit road shy after an awful accident in which she and Jimmy had collided with a herd of cattle in the dark. I didn't mind. The roads were good, I enjoyed driving, and this would likely be my last foray into Rhodesia. Blue was left in the capable hands of Aclon who said he'd use the time to do some 'spring' cleaning. Eleanor was going to be around, too.

We travelled once again via the ferry into Botswana at Kazungula, noting that the South African soldiers still had their maimai on the banks of the river and had expanded their presence there. The bush war was hotting up.

A night spent in Victoria Falls was always a treat, so after we'd checked into one of the comfortable little hill chalets we always patronized when staying overnight there, we went down to the Vic Falls Hotel for dinner, adjourning to the outdoor patio for a quiet drink before calling it a night. The evening deteriorated rapidly when a group of off-duty South African soldiers struck up conversation with us and then became abusive when we told them we worked in Zambia. The racist and sexual innuendos came thick and fast. We quickly finished our drinks and left. The contrast with the enjoyable night Noeline and I had recently spent in the company of the two young soldiers couldn't have been more stark.

The following morning, after a sumptuous breakfast at our favorite café, we decided to spend an hour or so exploring the area a little more instead of just shopping or passing through. I did pause to make one purchase, though – a genuine Rhodesian bush hat, which cost me all of five dollars. It was made of soft buffalo hide with the floppy brim elongated and cross-stitched at the back to protect the neck from sun. I'm wearing it on the cover.

First, we visited an impressive crocodile farm that had been established close to the Zambesi. There were several fenced enclosures featuring concrete lined pools that held crocodiles of all ages, from infants up to mature adults. The biggest crocodile there was a massive seventy-year-old male, weighing 2,000lbs who was used for breeding and, understandably, had his own pen, being notoriously aggressive – not to lady crocs, though. The positive side of all this penning was that the Rhodesian government had established the farm to return the crocodiles to their natural environment in the river as soon as they were mature enough. Our guide, who wielded a hefty staff for warding off any rogue crocs, explained the program: the early white settlers, in their ignorance, had all but wiped out the crocodiles in the area, shooting thousands of them to make the river 'safer'. All they'd achieved was to destroy the river's delicately balanced food chain. The crocs loved to eat catfish, the vundu, rather than the prolific and tasty bream the African fishermen depended upon as a food source, the vundu being regarded as poor table fare. The catfish, in turn, loved to eat bream. With the crocs' numbers depleted, the catfish population soared, decimating the bream, the locals' vital food source. Now, all these years later, those settlers' descendants had grasped their forebears' error and were attempting to redress it.

We were invited to hold a baby croc if we wished. The girls demurred but I cradled one briefly. About ten-months-old, it was cold and tense to the touch, looking up at me with its alien reptilian eyes before hissing in my face like a cat.

It was a bit of a letdown when the guide belatedly admitted they were also farming some of the crocs for export shoes and handbags. Mankind will never change.

Then we progressed on to the local snake park, which boasted a large range of snakes, from harmless house varieties to the deadliest of all, the notorious black mamba. Through the glass of its enclosure, I stared at its hard, pitiless expression, enhanced by a thin cruel mouth and bullet point black eyes. When they open their mouths – which signifies imminent attack – the interior is black as pitch – hence their name. If one bit you, you had about ten minutes to live. They were also very fast and aggressive, able to move at

16kph in pursuit of prey. I recalled that Berto claimed one had chased his land rover!

Again, as our tour concluded – we skipped the python eating his live guinea pig lunch – we were invited to hold a snake – a thoroughly milked one, of course, and used to being handled. The girls unsurprisingly demurred once more, but I was game and nursed a large Gaboon viper while they took photos of me. Again, it was cold to the touch, and I could feel the muscles rippling under its beautifully patterned skin. This species of viper has the largest fangs of any snake and kills its prey by biting and then, instead of disengaging, holding grimly on to pump in a huge volume of venom that ensures death.

It's hard to warm to snakes, but they're still God's creatures, I guess. Like the crocodile farm, the snake park had a more serious mission besides tourism. Resident herpetologists there performed vital work creating anti-venoms with the aim of reducing the numbers of people killed by snakes in sub-Sahara Africa – around 20,000 a year.

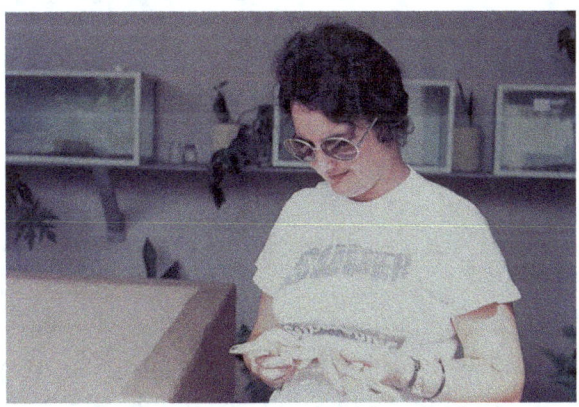

Getting acquainted with a snake.

After all that reptilian education we needed a cup of tea and a sandwich, so returned to the café before driving on to Bulawayo.

The elderly Greek couple who hosted us for the next couple of days were kindness itself and cooked us some lovely Greek food. They were brother and sister and didn't speak much English, but we managed to communicate for the most part. Both expressed their fear of what was coming with the bush war well under way by this time, and we felt concerned for them facing such uncertainty at their time of life.

We drove out to the Matopos Hills, which neither Catherine nor Mary had seen before, and they were as entranced as I had been the first time I visited. I felt nostalgic knowing this would be the last time I'd see this stunning area. Travelling to Rhodesia was becoming increasingly dangerous not just because of the bush war, but because the Zambian authorities were hostile towards white expats touring there.

Stunning World's View, Matopos Hills. My frizzy hair is a legacy of the malaria.

Farewelling our hosts, we travelled east on to Umtali, the main town in Manicaland

province. With a population of only 48,000, Umtali enjoyed a mild, humid climate that encouraged lush tropical growth. After visiting the information center for accommodation options, we opted to stay out of town at an attractive looking motel complex set in the verdant highlands. A phone call confirmed that they could host us, and we followed a map to find the place, which was every bit as pretty as its brochure proclaimed. Our cottage, set amongst exotic blooms, was well appointed and completely self-contained so that we could cook our own meals if we wished. We all agreed that it would make a more than adequate base for the next several days.

Expat Blues

Lying in my very comfortable bed that night, listening to the night noises of the surrounding bush, my overactive imagination conjured fearful images of terrorists creeping through the undergrowth towards us, armed to the teeth with guns and machetes. Prodded into wondering if we were doing the right thing here, the following day I asked the middle-aged widow who ran the place with her African helpers if she had any qualms about being so isolated. She said she did not. But we were only a few kilometers from the Mozambique border with its own terrorist war being waged there as well. I remained privately anxious for the duration of our stay but didn't communicate my fears to the girls.

I knew the situation in Rhodesia was deteriorating despite the best efforts of the Smith government. The white farmers who lived in 'the sharp end', the war zone, all carried Belgian assault rifles while they worked their farms, both men and women and even their older children. Their homes were all safeguarded against guerilla attack by state-of-the-art security fencing, motion activated floodlights, alarms, and radios that connected them to the nearest army patrols. Every farm had its contingent of guard dogs, Rhodesian Ridgebacks the favored breed. Noted for being both loyal and courageous, African legend had it that they were bred from lions with hearts to match. I couldn't imagine what it was like to live that way, on a knife edge, ground down by the continuous stress and vigilance involved. Sometimes, on a Sunday afternoon, I'd listen to the songs request program on the radio for soldiers serving in the bush war against 'the terrs', as they called the African guerillas. It all felt so futile.

One of our goals was to make a foray into Mozambique if we could, so we sashayed up to the border one morning to try our luck. The Rhodesians let us through their border post but warned us not to travel far on the Beira road as it was too dangerous, being subject to attacks by Frelimo guerillas. The Mozambican border post was swarming with Portuguese soldiers, who although friendly and welcoming, gave us the same warning. We insisted we only wanted to go as far as Vila de Manica, the first town just over the border, to sample some nice food and wine. They were happy with that and waved us through with a proviso that we took no photos.

Vila de Manica reminded me of a frontier town of the Wild West, and there was a big military presence there, too. It was lunch time, so we found a nice little restaurant, nothing flash, but clean and inviting with authentic appeal, and ordered a feast of Portuguese food. The standout for me was a bowl overflowing with the biggest, most delicious garlic prawns I've ever tasted, and I could have eaten them five times over. Along with the garlic, I discerned lemon and a hint of chili in the fragrant broth, and they gave me a loaf of the freshest, crustiest bread to tear apart and use to mop up the juices. The food was also ridiculously cheap, as was the wine. Tummies bulging, we did a quick circuit of the town and headed back to Umtali. Dinner was a slice of toast!

A few months after our visit, the Portuguese conceded defeat and Mozambique joined the family of newly independent African nations. Having already lost Guinea-Bissau and Angola, this marked the end of Portuguese influence in Africa, and was a huge blow to white-ruled Rhodesia which could no longer defend its 1300kms border with Mozambique against infiltrating guerillas without Portuguese help. South Africa, too, suffered from no longer being able to channel goods like weapons through Beira to counter international sanctions. Following independence, Mozambique plunged into a devastating civil war that cost over a million lives and manifested such atrocities as child soldiers.

We all enjoyed our time in Umtali (renamed Mutare post-independence), which we found relaxing and recharging. We slept late, went for long walks along the cool highland byways, drinking in the beautiful scenery and heady fresh air, visited numerous cafes and restaurants – some of them deserted, their owners facing ruin, because of the guerilla war – and enjoyed a leisurely drive back to Zambia, spending a last night in Victoria Falls before re-crossing the borders for the final time. As always, I fretted over the danger of the lonely stretch of riverside road linking Vic Falls with the Botswana border, but this time we got an armed escort provided by Rhodesian soldiers patrolling in the area, so the forty-minute drive was nowhere near as nerve-wracking.

Expat Blues

Rhodesia was a superb place for a holiday, provided you put your conscience aside. Sadly, under its new name, Zimbabwe, like so many African states, it has not fared well since independence, fracturing along tribal lines and becoming something of an impoverished international pariah during its period under the tyrannical grip of Robert Mugabe. His nearsighted and vengeful expulsion of the white farmers ensured the collapse of the economy and turned what had been a prosperous country into a ruin.

Chapter Thirteen: Loves and Betrayals, Soccy Rules the Roost, an Errant Priest, Luangwa Valley

The second term got underway, and I was counting down the months until I went home. I don't know why. I had a blind loyalty to my family that wasn't reciprocated, but I felt as if I had a plan: some time spent at home until I departed for Colombia. Home was more than just my family. Robert Frost summed it up: 'Home is the place where, when you have to go there, they have to take you in.' While most of the neighbors around us had come and gone, my parents still lived in the first house they'd bought after marrying. An immutable oasis in a world of terrifying flux.

School kept me busy, although it was never a burden, and Mary and I got along fine most of the time, doing things together. Eleanor tended to have her own friends and interests and shunned the club scene.

I played a lot of squash, and Catherine and Jimmy had become good mates. They often turned up on a Sunday and took me to the Mosi with them for the buffet dinner and movie night, which was very reasonably priced at K15. The buffet was sumptuous, and I had a special fondness for the eggs mayonnaise and the frogs' legs. The movie was always an up to date one.

But I had the expat blues well and truly by now and was growing tired of the mostly married couples and the sexual mores of the place, which felt like they were becoming more and more outlandish. There was a popular belief that if you had any flaws in your character, Africa was going to magnify and unleash them, and just when you thought you'd seen it all, there was a new shock to contend with. The transitory nature of expat communities with their emphasis on increased social interaction and alcohol consumption seems to breed a special sense of hedonistic freedom. After all, you're miles from home and the humdrum routine of life there, with people you'll probably never ever see again if you do happen to blot your copybook, so it's hardly surprising that the accepted social restraints and conventions can go out the window altogether.

By and large, the Irish couples tended towards marital fidelity, maybe because they had so many Catholic clergy breathing down their necks. Although some of those clergy hardly set an example of propriety. Take, for example, Father Lawrence. I first met him at the Gibbons shortly after I came back from Kafue and took an instant dislike to him. Like all the Holy Ghost fathers, he was from a well-to-do Irish family, had his own money, and cruised around on a motorbike when not driving his personal land rover or saloon car. I found him arrogant and patronizing, his attitude mocking when he learned I was a New Zealander.

One night not long afterwards, I was at the Friday night disco at the Mosi, when Father Lawrence strutted in wearing a garish Hawaiian shirt that instantly drew attention and with a scantily clad African beauty on each arm. I blinked, thinking I must be mistaken, but it was him all right. When I mentioned this to someone, the response was eye-rolling laughter, and an oh-yes-everyone-knows-about-Lawrence dismissive lack of interest. The Irish were peculiarly tolerant of aberrant behavior amongst themselves, I found. And, of course, the good old double standard prevailed. Men could get away with things a woman couldn't. One of the first hot items of gossip I'd been told concerned a thirties-something Irishwoman who'd scandalized the community when she became pregnant to and subsequently married a divorced African man, meeting with instant social death.

Unsurprisingly, Father Lawrence soon went full troppo and absconded into the bush with one of his African paramours and their new baby. His family back in Ireland cut him off. I saw him in town one day months later and was shocked by his appearance. He looked very ill, like an incarnation of Kurtz from Joseph Conrad's *Heart of Darkness*. What eventually became of him I do not know.

Marital fidelity amongst the British expats was a different story, and it was hard for the gossip mill to keep up. One story may suffice as a good example. A young British couple arrived who were very attractive, and everybody wanted to be friends with them. The wife was petite with pretty features, a cute bob haircut and a trim figure. Her husband was classically nice looking in a boyish way. Gossip quickly established that they were newlywed and childless. They had only been in Livingstone a few weeks when scandal broke. She had moved in with an Italian working at the Fiat factory, and her erstwhile husband had moved in with the Italian's discarded colored girlfriend. A straight swap as it were. I saw them at the bioscope one night, sitting only a few rows apart with their respective new partners.

That kind of thing happened all the time and was a source of great merriment amongst the expat community. I just found it all sad and dispiriting.

One shattered relationship, though, stands out for its sheer awfulness, and those involved were neither Irish nor British – they were Swedish and, dare I say it, from New Zealand...not me, let's be clear.

I'd just begun teaching what was my form class one morning when Sister Carmel came in followed by a shy white teenaged girl with a mop of beautiful blonde curls. Sister introduced her to me and the class as Ingrid and we found her a spare desk. Her family – mother, engineer father, and a younger brother, had just arrived from Sweden to take up a contract. She was such a sweet kid and coped very well as the only white face in the whole student body. I sometimes saw her up at the Airport Club if I went there with Catherine and Jimmy, and she was always with her family who appeared a happy and close-knit foursome. I was up there one weekend when the club was hosting some unexpected guests.

I often saw the overland safari trucks passing through Livingstone, rugged khaki-colored vehicles, frequently converted Unimogs, taking groups of young people across Africa as part of their big OE adventure. They roughed it, camping out, partying hard, and traveling in the backs of the lorries seated on bench seats under the canopies. One of these trucks suffered a bad breakdown, and while it was being fixed someone in the Airport Club hierarchy gave permission for the group to stay there and use the club facilities – showers, toilets, cooking amenities – for a minimal fee. I noticed

Expat Blues

Ingrid's dad chatting with an attractive young woman from the travelers but thought nothing of it.

Not long afterwards, I arrived at school one morning to be met by a white-faced Carmel. She told me the terrible news that Ingrid's mother had killed herself the night before in the most tragic of circumstances. She'd driven at high speed down the Falls Road and crashed the car into a baobab tree. The impact had been so great that the car was literally wrapped around the tree and had to be prised off with specialized equipment to retrieve the body. Why, I asked? Why would she do such a desperate thing? How did they know it was suicide and not just an accident? Carmel said that was all the information she had, and that of course Ingrid would not be attending school, for a few days at least.

The awful truth was not long in coming out. Ingrid's father and the girl I'd seen him talking to at the Airport Club, a New Zealand woman, had fallen in love. Once the truck had been repaired and the travelers had moved on, they'd kept in touch and decided they had to be together. Ingrid's father had broken this news to his unsuspecting wife of many years, and she had tragically killed herself the same night.

The whole town was agog. Ingrid eventually returned to school, but only briefly. I told her how sorry I was, which sounded so lame. Her father's new woman had flown in before her dead mother barely had time to cool in her grave, and people reported seeing the new 'family' at the airport, prematurely returning to Sweden. Pretty damn raw, even for Livingstone.

The Indian community had its scandals, too, and again there is one story I will never be able to erase from my memory.

There was a sizeable Indian community in Livingstone, and they owned most of the businesses. The majority were decent people, but some of them had a reputation for abusing their African staff and customers, and I'd personally witnessed this on more than one occasion. After Idi Amin expelled all the Asians from Uganda in 1973, Zambia's Indian community started working hard to improve relations with their fellow black citizens.

There was one Indian family that owned a taxi service, comprising three battered blue sedans that I often saw rattling around the township. Like many of their fellows, they had family or contacts in the UK, and a marriage was arranged between their eldest son and the daughter of a comfortably off British Indian family. The son flew off to meet his bride-to-be, wooing her with stories of his family's wealth and social status in Livingstone as owners of an important business. The marriage went ahead, and the happy couple returned to Livingstone to live in the family home.

The first shock for the young woman was realizing that her husband had greatly exaggerated his family's financial status and prestige. Not only was their taxi business minor – it was struggling. Expats and Indians all owned cars. Africans couldn't afford taxis and walked, biked, or bussed. In addition, she became the victim of a common phenomenon in Indian culture – the bullying mother-in-law. The unkindness was relentless. She pleaded with her husband to defend her, but the previously gracious young man who had charmed her now spurned her entreaties and joined his mother in taunting and reviling her. Her life became unbearable, and she started to plot her escape. Only her UK family could rescue her but contacting them proved impossible. She was allowed no money of her own nor access to a phone, writing materials, nor the post office. As her tormentors became aware of her desire to leave the intolerable situation that she found herself in, they cut her off from all human contact lest they lose her dowry which had propped up their faltering business. She was forced to give up a parttime job she'd enjoyed, doing accounts in a local office, and became a virtual prisoner in the house, constantly watched, and monitored. Her mail was confiscated and opened to check the contents, and she had no means of reply.

The young woman believed she was hopelessly trapped, with no prospect of rescue, and spiraled down into the depths of a hopeless despair. She succeeded in getting her hands on a bottle of rat poison kept in the house and drank it all. It took two days for her to die in Livingstone Hospital, only a couple of days before her family arrived from the UK to find out what was going on, why they hadn't heard from her.

Expat Blues

This tragedy has stayed with me ever since I first learned about it. Many will be forgotten in time, but some stories will haunt you forever.

The term ticked along and so did my Wildlife Club. I often wondered if I had managed to instill a more compassionate approach to wildlife amongst my club members, and that speculation had been answered on the first morning of the new term when I'd arrived at school to find a beaming Gertrude, my club president, waiting beside the staffroom with a cardboard box clasped in her solid arms.

She thrust the box towards me and announced, "I have rescued a bird, meestress!"

She placed the box at my feet, and I could hear what sounded like faint clicking sounds coming from it. As I gingerly pulled the top flaps aside, Gertrude breathing excitedly over my shoulder, I saw what looked like a white woolly little – something, glaring up at me with dark baleful eyes while snapping its beak repeatedly to make the clicking noise.

"Er, what exactly is it, Gertrude?"

Gertrude shrugged. Then she looked sad. "All dead but this one, meestress. I rescued him."

"From what?"

Gertrude sighed. "People. They kill them."

She'd brought this little animal all the way from her home village.

I closed the box and stood up, placing a hand on her shoulder. "You've done very well. Great work. I'll get a certificate printed for you."

Gertrude glowed. "You take home now, meestress."

"Take home?"

"Yes," she said firmly. "Yours now. I cannot keep in the boarding, and I know nothing about, but you wildlife teacher. You know."

She sashayed off looking mightily pleased with herself. The beak clicking grew in volume, followed by some hissing. *Oh, God, I'm a victim of my own success. She's probably gone and rescued a bloody vulture!*

I took the box to my classroom and set it on a shelf. Its occupant went strangely quiet, and I checked on him at regular intervals. He appeared to be asleep, propped on what I could only call his 'elbows'. I wondered when he'd last eaten. At end of school, I carried the box to my car and drove home. After lunch, I found a small woven basket in our storeroom, lined it with soft cloth, and lifted the bird into his new home. He settled in happily, with minimal clicking, and dozed off again. Blue was intrigued by him, and the little foundling seemed unperturbed by his inspection, which involved much sniffing, prodding and the odd lick. I knew Blue would not hurt him. A kinder dog would be hard to find. But we also had a house cat, sweet little Brandy, so I shut the sleeping bird in my bedroom for safekeeping, and assuming he was a carnivore, bought some mincemeat from the butcher, reasoning that he needed meat, but finely cut and easily digestible. Gertrude's faith in me was touching, but I really had no idea how to look after a young bird, and there was no Google back then.

After dinner, I told the girls about my unusual day and introduced them to our new tenant, who, darkness having fallen, was now alert and clicking away with renewed menace. He was clearly nocturnal. Eleanor was very interested. She belonged to the local Wildlife Association and informed me they were due to hold their monthly meeting in a couple of days.

"I'll take him along. Bob Dowsett will know what he is and how to care for him."

Of course! Ornithologist Bob! Why didn't I think of that?

"Thanks, Eleanor. I don't know what his chances of survival are, but I'll do my best. He has spirit, that's for sure."

Although a novice, I'd seen enough wildlife documentaries to know that rearing a wild animal was fraught with problems. Even with the best of care, the poor little mite could just suddenly give up on his will to live. I didn't want him to imprint on me either because the plan was to return him to the wild eventually. I vowed that I would keep contact to a minimum and not use my voice around him.

The girls watched in amusement as I gave him a feed of mincemeat using my eyebrow tweezers and he wolfed it all down, puddling into a contented little blob, eyes closed to narrow slits and not a click to be heard.

I kept the chick in my bedroom overnight and fed him every few hours. He let me know when he needed a top-up by clacking his beak furiously until I complied. By the time morning came, I rose feeling dopey with fatigue, while the little harpy now slept peacefully, virtually flat on his back in the basket, legs in the air. This would go on for several weeks until he'd grown substantially and was able to be secluded in the spare room overnight after a late supper. I stopped worrying about finding him dead. He grew stronger every day.

Eleanor was as good as her word and had taken the chick to her Wildlife Association meeting, where he created quite a sensation, squatting in his basket and clicking away at the group of strangers. I learned early that he did not like strangers. I'm sure wariness of humans had been bred into his DNA.

A delighted Bob identified him as a barn owl chick and confirmed what Gertrude had told me. The Africans believed barn owls were ghostly evil spirits, swooping out of the darkness with their pale, heart-shaped faces, and killed them, wiping out whole nests. Didn't bear thinking about. He said I had done a great job by influencing even one child to rescue the little owl as African superstitions ran deep.

So, time to give the owl a name. I referred to him as 'he' because I didn't know his gender and Bob couldn't call it either. I named him Socrates for his ancient symbolism as a wise creature, and he became Soccy for short. Bob was doing an intensive study of bush meat rodents at this particular time, and he supplied me regularly with sealed plastic containers of small, skinned and gutted fieldmice. I kept them in the fridge – to the horror of the girls – and Soccy loved them. They would have been his natural diet, but with the fur on. Bob expressed concern about the lack of roughage, so I rolled each mouse in wheaten cracker crumbs before feeding them to Soccy. Rumors started to spread in the expat community that I myself had gone crackers. I didn't give a toss what they thought.

During the night, Soccy regurgitated the skeletal bones of the mice he'd had for supper, stripped so clean they looked as if they'd been boiled. This was the forerunner of what he would do as an adult, making round pellets of waste material from his gut and expelling them. Bob asked me to let him know when this happened, as he was keen to do a study of owl pellets. Whatever turns you on!

Acron, (pronounced 'Aclon' because of the l/r confusion) our African houseman, was very suspicious of Soccy when he became aware of his presence and referred to him as 'thee chicken'. I knew he'd never hurt him, though. A sweeter, gentler, more self-effacing man would be difficult to find. I explained to him that Soccy was entirely my responsibility and that I would be doing all the feeding, cleaning up etc. The little man was happy with that, and with receiving a share of the mice which were prized bush tucker for Africans, boiled, salted and fire-dried to be eaten with their staple nshima.

Aclon didn't see much of the bird, anyway. Soccy stayed in the spare room until noon, sitting quietly in his basket, and I fetched him out when I got home from school. He was passive during daylight hours but got stroppy from dusk onwards. Aclon worked mornings only. After preparing our lunch, he went home on his trusty bicycle, and we fended for ourselves for dinner, taking turns to cook. Expats in Africa followed the old colonial practice of dining late, which drove me nuts, but which, now I was cooking for others, I had to follow. We ate most nights around 8 p.m., a bit earlier if we were going somewhere. At home, like all Kiwis, we always ate promptly at 6 p.m. (If, by a nanosecond past six no dinner had appeared, my father would be sat at the table in a marked manner, knife and fork gripped vertically in hand, a grim expression on his face, while Mum, aware of his simmering impatience, had panicky conniptions in the kitchen). Anyway, the late dining thing struck me as just another snobbish imperial hangover and I was usually ulcerous with hunger by the time dinner was served. Soccy ate somewhat earlier, and because he was still very young, I dismembered his mice for him, as his parents would have done. Later on, he managed them whole, clutching them in his formidable talons and tearing them apart with his impressive beak. The last bit to slide down, disappearing by degrees, was the mouse's tail, which was a pretty macabre sight, dangling from his face! After supper, he became placid again. At bedtime, he had second supper.

Soccy grew fast, replacing his white, greasy chick down with beautiful plumage, the striking heart-shaped face of his species becoming clearly defined. I took him along to my Wildlife Club and the girls were mostly enthusiastic about him. A few hung back, regarding him with a mixture of fear and uncertainty. I praised Gertrude effusively for her part in his rescue and presented her with a congratulatory certificate and a gift of the candy I knew the girls loved. She visibly swelled with delight, and I had to appear equally delighted when she promised to rescue more owls in the future!

Once Soccy got his adult plumage and settled into his feeding and sleeping routine, the next step was his learning to fly, and I didn't know how I was going to facilitate that. Instinct kicked in and he launched himself, as it were, sweeping items off shelves and leaving pictures hanging askew on the walls as he practiced his circuits and bumps. Once he'd mastered flight, he tended to flit gracefully to select roosts and perch there quite happily for long periods. His favorites were the kitchen door, from which he supervised dinner prep, the lounge door to monitor comings and goings, and the rim of an old-fashioned standard lamp positioned near the dining table – from which he supervised food consumption. He could turn his head a full 180° to keep an eye on everything and the girls said he needed an exorcist! (The horror movie was not long out). He loved to annoy Blue when he was trying to take a nap, and he thoroughly intimidated the cat by rushing at her with his wings spread! When Blue had had enough of his antics, he'd give Soccy a firm but gentle suck on his topknot. I always knew when this happened because the little owl would be sporting a saliva stiffened mohawk.

Soccy supervising dinner prep from the kitchen door, a favorite roost.

Of course, you can't house train an owl, and now that he was on the move, I was grateful for concrete floors that facilitated quick clean-ups using a bit of toilet paper. In the spare room where he went at night, he now perched on the curtain rail, and I spread newspaper on the floor beneath him.

I'd tried hard to prevent Soccy imprinting on me, but it proved impossible. I'd cared for him since his infancy, so he'd bonded to me strongly and liked to show his affection. Since he pretty much free-ranged the house, I couldn't avoid him. He loved to sit on my lap, take a strand of my hair and chirrup softly as he ran it repeatedly through his beak with a dreamy look on his face, while I reciprocated with lots of scritching on his topknot. It was very soothing for both of us. I discovered his ears this way – neat little holes either side of his head. He'd sometimes grip one of my fingers with a talon and the strength was amazing. He never, ever bit me or hurt me.

However, a couple of unfortunate events convinced me that I had to at least encourage him to return to the wild, without outrightly abandoning him. First, the incidents.

We had invited some friends to dinner one night, and my contribution was to make a marshmallow dessert I'd enjoyed in my childhood, and which never failed to please. It set beautifully as I'd hoped, and I topped it all off with whipped cream and tinned fruit. I've mentioned previously that I'd noticed Soccy's aversion to strangers, and when the guests arrived, I observed him tense on his perch on the standard lamp, fluffing out his feathers. He was always a great conversation piece, so once everyone had checked him out, from a distance, we settled down to enjoyment of the evening, me keeping an eye on the feathered one, who was hunched in a glowering, sullen little heap but otherwise tranquil. All went well until I brought out the dessert. At the precise moment that I placed it in the center of the table to accompanying oohs and aahs, Soccy rose into the air and executed a perfect two-point landing in the middle of the pud, wings beating furiously.

The mess was unbelievable. The girls were furious. The guests, liberally splattered, called it a night. I added bathing an owl to my more unusual life experiences repertoire.

The second unfortunate incident occurred when another guest demonstrated the human incapacity to absorb sensible advice. A young Christian brother who sometimes called at the house (especially when Noeline lived there) arrived unannounced one evening. I was sitting with Soccy in my lap, enjoying quiet time, when Mary opened the door to our visitor, who had quite clearly enjoyed a few beers before deciding to call on us. He made a beeline for me, laughing merrily at the sight of woman and owl, and advanced straight into our personal space, bending over to thrust his face into Soccy's, making inane comments along the lines of 'little bubba boidy having cuddles, is he?' I felt the bird tense and put up a hand.

"Back off! Back off now!"

But it was too late. In a heartbeat Soccy had sunk his talons into the young man's face and was literally hanging from his eye sockets. Any socializing was forgotten as we made a fast trip to the hospital with the shocked young cleric who had sobered up fast. He had a couple of lacerations but nothing serious and no permanent damage. Soccy's fearsome reputation grew, along with mine, for unreasonable eccentricity. I heard mutterings that 'the bird' would be 'got rid of'.

After that, I began to work seriously on Soccy's rehabilitation to the wild. The term holidays were looming and there was no one I could trust to look after him if I went away. Bob said he would have but he was going away, too. During the day, I put Soccy outside in the big tree at the front of the house, and he roosted there happily until nightfall when he'd come swooping in to alight on the kitchen door, stomping up and down and screeching for food (barn owls don't hoot). After I'd fed him, I shut him outside. Outraged, he'd beat on the front door with his beak until he got tired of it, and one morning when I drew back my bedroom curtains, he was slumped in a sad little heap on my windowsill, looking pitifully up at me. This was hard. I persevered and at some point, he must have started having forays further afield, possibly hunting, because he'd miss a couple of nights before he turned up again demanding food. He was definitely wilder and had a nasty go at Mary on one occasion, although I could still handle him without incident. Threats about doing him in continued, especially from one source that was causing me serious concern, and not just for Soccy's sake.

Father Matt McCartan, antipathy for whom I expressed earlier, had replaced Father Justinian as the resident priest at a bush mission station some distance from Livingstone. Justinian, a big, jovial bearded fellow in his thirties, always accompanied in his land rover by his beautiful German Shepherd, Sheila, had been a frequent visitor to town, where I often saw him, and to the Irish teachers' bungalow, where I now lived. Rumor had it that he had a fierce crush on Kitty and was none too pleased when she took up with Pat. Then he went home to Ireland and McCartan, probably forty-something, took his place, continuing the tradition of regularly turning up at the bungalow for female company. That would have been fine, but all vows of celibacy aside, he set his sights on Mary, a vulnerable and naïve young woman with a nice figure but a plain face who was desperate for male attention.

At first, I thought I might be misjudging McCartan, but increasingly he began to spend more time at our house than he did at his mission station, always turning up unannounced, spending whole afternoons and evenings with us, including accompanying us out for a drink or to the movies. He made it very clear that I was of no value to him whatsoever beyond preserving propriety and focused all his attention on Mary. He was careful, though, to ensure that we went out as a threesome, and I felt more and more like a chaperone as he ignored me to simper over Mary.

It was chilling to witness what I became certain was a calculated seduction, and I didn't really know what to do about the situation or who to turn to. The Irish were all as tight as tree bark. This shameless predator knew exactly where Mary's weak spots were, using them to gain her trust and affection. He'd talk endlessly to her about her family, or her aspirations for the future, always building her up and playing to her innermost conceits, while Mary, self-absorbed at the best of times, lapped it all up. Then he moved on to prising her away from any influence I might have over her, saying negative things about me which, unbeknown to him, she recounted quite unabashedly to me. Mary always told me everything – and he hadn't counted on that. She said she'd confided to him things she'd never told anyone else. Thus, he added confessor to his role of groomer, strengthening his hold over her. My concern deepened.

Sometimes I found McCartan's behavior in the presence of two young lay women nothing short of shocking. He liked to sing the lyrics of that ambiguous Chuck Berry song, I Want You To Play With My Ding-a-ling, trying to get a reaction – from me, foremost, I think. On one occasion he told us confidentially that a man's most sensitive body parts were his balls. He intimated that he had sex with African women, boasting of one encounter across the hood of his land rover. When Mary and I were alone, I tried to broach my concerns with her regarding what I believed to be seriously aberrant behavior in a priest, but she brushed it all aside and made me feel as if I were over-reacting. I don't think she saw him as a priest anymore – he was always dressed casually, in shorts and open-necked shirt – but as a male admirer whose flattery she was addicted to. I felt increasingly alone in their company.

Then McCartan tried his best to belittle me intellectually. He asked me, one night, if I knew the poem, Lullaby, by W. H. Auden. I said I knew of it, and he quoted the first few lines:

Erin Eldridge

Lay your sleeping head, my love,

Human on my faithless arm

"What does he mean?" he demanded. "Come on, you're supposed to be the literary expert."

I looked him squarely in the eye and said, "The theme of the poem is the shallowness and insincerity of modern love, the transience of human relationships."

He went very quiet. By trying to embarrass me, he had instead been called out. I felt the misogyny radiating off him and I feared for Mary, who was by now totally in this sinister man's thrall. I didn't know who to turn to.

One incident brought home to me how well he was succeeding in advancing me towards irrelevance for his planned twosome. He wanted me sidelined because he knew I saw through him, that I knew what he was.

I was rostered on for evening study at St Mary's on a Friday, and before I left, Mary told me she'd cook something special for dinner. Eleanor was elsewhere, so there would just be the two of us. When I arrived back home after study, tired and very hungry, aching with anticipation for a nice dinner, the first thing I saw was McCartan's blue land rover parked in front of the house, and my spirits plummeted. I opened the door to lovely cooking smells and saw him and Mary seated at the table, eating. They hadn't waited for me, I noted. In fact, they barely looked up as I came in. They were bent over their food laughing and talking, clearly enjoying each other's company.

"Smells lovely," I said. "What is it?"

Without so much as glancing in my direction, Mary forked in another mouthful and said, "Stuffed fillet of steak." She sniggered. "And we've eaten all of it."

Then they laughed.

For a moment, I was too taken aback to respond. Then I found my voice.

"So, there's no dinner for me, even though I contribute to the food costs here?"

No response, just more conspiratorial giggling.

I was so hurt, and so angry, that all I could do was take myself off to bed, hunger unappeased, and try to sleep. I heard McCartan leave much later. Next morning, I wondered if Mary would say anything approximating to an apology. Nothing. She was now wholly his.

If I'd had any doubts about my analysis of McCartan's intrinsic character, they were dispelled by a visit we made to his bush mission station, where I got an additional insight into his baseline nastiness and lack of empathy. It also became the setting for what would be one of the most regrettable incidents of my life.

He'd been issuing invitations to visit him for a while, and since Mary didn't drive, he had no choice but to include me. I had no idea what his motives were, but he may have wanted to impress Mary with his virtuous credentials as the hardworking missionary. We settled on a Saturday, for dinner, and Mary and I made the forty-minute drive out to his mission.

After dinner, at his comfortable house near the church and convent, we were having a final drink before heading home, when I heard a dog bark and sat up straight with surprise.

"Is that Sheila?" I'd assumed Justinian had taken his beloved Shepherd home with him.

McCartan scoffed. "Yes, that's her. She's tied up in the garage, where she barks away happily."

I felt cold. "Can I see her."

"Sure."

He put down his drink and led us through the house to where an interior door opened into the spacious garage, turning on the light. Sheila lay on a blanket, tied by her collar to a rope attached to the wall. She wagged her tail feebly when we entered, and I went straight to her, dropping onto my knees to stroke and pet her. She whined softly, pressing her head into me.

"Why didn't Justinian take her home?"

McCartan shrugged. "Don't know. Wish he had."

"Why don't you take her out with you, the way he did?"

McCartan snorted. "I don't want a dog in my land rover, or my house, for that matter."

At that moment, two nuns came into the garage, one carrying a large enamel bowl full of food, a watery broth with a few bare bones floating in it. She put it down beside the dog, who turned her head away. The nun sighed.

"She's got an infected tick bite, so she's off her food."

"Come on," said McCartan impatiently. Let the sisters take care of her."

I reluctantly left Sheila to the nuns and followed Mary and our host back into the house. Shortly afterwards, we left.

There are times in your life, I believe, when spiritual forces conspire to seek your help, putting you in a time and place where you are given the opportunity to do the right thing, the kind thing. On that occasion, I failed, and failed badly. I should have bundled Sheila up and taken her with me, got her proper vet treatment, and found her a loving home amongst the expats, many of whom would have welcomed the chance to own such a beautiful dog. I was appalled by McCartan's callous attitude, and it cemented my opinion of him. This man, who said Mass every day and partook of the Eucharist, had no empathy for man or beast – or an empty-headed young woman. I was angry with Justinian, too, for leaving Sheila with this monster.

Not long after I returned home that Christmas, I heard that Sheila had died.

Years later, my husband and I adopted a rescued German Shepherd, Tara, and ensured she had a long, happy life. Thus, I absolved myself of some of the guilt I carried over Sheila. It hurts to this day. Some wounds never scab over.

Expat Blues

A few days after our visit to the mission, McCartan made his move.

He'd predictably rolled in one Friday night, as obnoxious as ever, eaten our food, drunk our wine, and collapsed into an armchair chain-smoking, as he did. Tired at the end of a long week, sick of bearing witness to his twisted courtship of my housemate, I retired to bed and slept soundly. I never even heard him leave.

Late Saturday morning, after I'd done some chores (Aclon had weekends off) and was in my bedroom giving it a spruce up, Mary came in, the expression on her face instantly striking me as rather sheepish.

"Erin, I need to talk to you." She held out a folded piece of paper. "Please read this."

I took the piece of paper with building trepidation, opened it and read.

It was a love letter, handwritten by McCartan, the content predictably contrived to play to Mary's weakness and gullibility. I felt sick. From Mary's demeanor, I gathered she, too, finally felt uncomfortable about the situation she found herself in.

I folded the letter, gave it back to her, and squeezed her arm. "Come on. I'll make us a cup of tea and we'll talk."

As I mentioned previously, Mary told me everything, and over a fresh pot of tea, she divulged the events of the previous evening with Father McCartan. After I'd gone to bed, he'd moved from his chair to join her on the couch and had become increasingly amorous, finally pressing himself on her, but prematurely ejaculating before any coupling could take place. Then he'd given her the letter. It took some doing, but I finally managed to get Mary to concede that this was a horrific betrayal in every sense by a so-called man of the cloth, a betrayal with only one likely outcome – misery. She had a good cry and asked me what she should do. Wrestling with simultaneous feelings of pity and anger, I told her to leave it to me, that I'd take care of it. It was time to give the predator priest his marching orders. It wasn't going to be easy. I'd been brought up in a conservative Catholic tradition where priests, and nuns, were revered. This prelate, I reminded myself, deserved no reverence.

We had a peaceful few days before McCartan turned up again, early in the week following his written declaration of love and clumsy attempt at intercourse. I was in the kitchen helping Aclon clean up the lunch dishes. It was his payday, and he'd asked me if I could help him pick up an extra big bag of mealie meal from the warehouse using my car since it would be impossible to carry on his bicycle. Of course, I'd said yes. Poor Aclon. I hated to speculate how many hungry mouths he was feeding, and him such a skinny wee fellow. We were all fond of Aclon.

A peremptory knock on the open front door, followed by a halloo, drew me out of the kitchen to find McCartan standing in the lounge. Blue, who'd been dozing in the sunshine out on the stoop, preceded him in, tail unnaturally flaccid. I'd long before noticed how Blue never greeted him the way he did other regulars to the house, maybe because he knew that the odious man ridiculed him. Blue was very short-haired, and his fine set of testicles were prominently displayed from a rear view. Nobody neutered male dogs back then. It was unheard of, and, besides, expats wanted their male guard dogs feisty. This particular aspect of my dog's anatomy always aroused mockery from McCartan. He'd frequently comment on the size of Blue's testicles and referred to him as 'Balls' or 'Bang' instead of using his proper name. I think he thought he was being amusing, but it was horrible and demeaning, and I hated it. Now, of course, he ran true to form.

"Old Bang's come inside. I suppose that's okay."

It was time. I clenched my fists.

"His name is *Blue*. He's my beloved pet and I named him *Blue*. *He's* always welcome to come into our house."

He froze, staring at me.

"If you're looking for Mary, she's gone out and I have no idea when she'll be home. I have to go out, too. I have a meeting with the *bishop*." (A lie. Sorry, God).

The new bishop for the Livingstone diocese was a native Zambian, a dignified man reputed to be a stickler for piety.

McCartan continued to stare at me, while his pasty complexion turned puce, then he turned on his heel and left.

I sagged. I was shaking. Aclon, who'd heard everything, gave me a megawatt smile.

"We go now, madum?"

"We go now."

We never saw McCartan again for the rest of our tour. Mary started going out with a lovely colored guy, and I started going out with his friend. A happy foursome. Mostly. I resigned from being Mary's minder and wearily let her get on with it. She was, after all, an adult, responsible for her own decisions.

Meanwhile, Mary had received a missive of a different nature. The letter was from an old friend she'd known back in Ireland, Geraldine, who had recently arrived in Zambia with her husband, Tom. They were living in a camp set up in the Luangwa Valley National Park in eastern Zambia, where Irish engineers, Tom amongst them, and Yugoslavian technicians were building a landing strip which, when completed, would enable light planes to bring in groups of tourists directly from Lusaka. Second term school holidays were looming, and Geraldine wanted to know if Mary could pay them a visit. Since she didn't drive, Mary asked me if I'd be interested in accompanying her, and I was delighted to accept. I'd been so lucky to visit Kafue and a chance to include Luangwa Valley, another world class game park, would make for a nice final African adventure before I went home. A swift exchange of letters brought assurances that we were both welcome to stay and dates were quickly finalized. Geraldine included a rough map, which not being blessed with a great sense of direction, I hoped I could follow. The workers' camp was deep inside the park.

The nuns at the cathedral school agreed to feed and look after Blue for the fortnight I'd be away, and I knew Aclon would be coming and going. My big concern was Soccy. Although his visits to the house were becoming less frequent, he still often arrived at dusk, screeching for food, and I still kept mice on hand, either in the fridge or on backup in the freezer compartment.

As Mary and I prepared to leave, a family arrived at the house by invitation of Eleanor, who then promptly left for her own holiday destination. The family, comprising parents and two children, were working and living in Zambia, but they hailed from South Africa and were on their way home for a visit. Just as they reached Livingstone, their Mercedes broke down, so their agreed one-night stay with us became extended. I drove the husband around various garages, but he refused to pay the asking price for the part he needed and decided he'd leave the car at our house and fly the whole family down to South Africa instead, where he could purchase the part cheaply and then return to do the work himself. That made no sense. The flights would surely cost a lot more than the part, but I guess he was also considering the time factor as he said he'd need several days to do the repairs, time they wanted with their southern kinfolk.

The family were still at the house, then, finalizing their new travel arrangements, when Mary and I left. What worried me was the mother of the family's reaction to Soccy the first time he flew into the house while they were there. She became totally hysterical, screaming and flailing her arms around before fleeing to her room. Her husband said she had a bird phobia. Since he seemed okay with the little owl, and the kids were intrigued, I asked him if he'd feed Soccy when and if he flew in while they were there, and he agreed to that. I departed with a sense of unease, just the same.

We travelled to Lusaka and spent a night there in hostel-style accommodation before journeying on to Chipata, near the border with Malawi, (the same route I'd taken for my holiday in Malawi with Kitty, Pat, and Noeline) then turning north to Mfuwe, the town closest to the park. Once in the park, we struck pretty rough dirt roads with really bad corrugations that rattled the little car mercilessly and gave its passengers a bone jarring ride. The heavy rains flooded out the roads in the wet season and they had to be remade every dry. Some people advised you should travel slowly over corrugations to minimize juddering; others said you should go fast for the same effect. I found either strategy was equally bad. You just to grit your (jangling) teeth and bear it.

As dusk drew in and Mary did her best to decipher our rudimentary map, I became afraid we were going to be lost and stranded somewhere in the dark at the mercy of wild animals, but various locals we asked directions from were very kind and helpful, and I breathed a sigh of relief when we finally drove into the camp just as the sun set.

Tom and Geraldine were a delightful young couple, warm and welcoming. Their temporary home was a comfortable bungalow and Mary and I each had a nicely furnished bedroom. We were very impressed to discover the house had air-conditioning, a real luxury. The Yugoslavian workers lived a short distance away in more of a communal bunkhouse set-up. Apparently, most of them had been 'volunteered' by their Communist government, had their passports confiscated as soon as they arrived, and just had to get on with it until the authorities decided they could return home. Theirs was an all-male domestic arrangement, as, unlike the Irish engineers, they were not permitted to have family with them.

Geraldine had cooked a splendid dinner of roast bushbuck (the expats had permission to take occasional game) and we ate heartily before adjoining to another of the engineers' bungalows for an informal welcome. Some of the Yugoslavs attended, too, but only a few spoke or understood English, so I found myself nodding and smiling awkwardly as they repeatedly topped up my glass with the slivovitz that seemed to be in plentiful supply. There was a very convivial atmosphere and everyone, Slav or Irish, seemed to be getting along splendidly despite any language barrier.

Over the next few days, we tried out the camp swimming pool, a little murky but pleasant enough, went game viewing with Geraldine in their land rover (Tom was busy working), and learned about adjusting to the vagaries of camp life in the middle of nowhere with only basic facilities. The setting, close to the meandering Luangwa River with its characteristic dry beds and oxbow lagoons, was outstandingly beautiful and, as with Kafue, I reveled in the feeling of being in the heart of wildest Africa. The park itself covers nearly 10,000 square kilometers in the Rift Valley, comprising woodlands, savannah, thickets and floodplain grassland bordered by riparian forest. Luangwa is home to sixty animal species that include unique varieties like Thornicroft's giraffe, Cookson's wildebeest, and Crawshay's zebra. In addition, there are more than 400 species of bird, including carmine bee-eaters, raptors, lovebirds, weavers, and kingfishers. In the wet season, the entire valley turns beautifully green. Luangwa also has the world's highest population of leopards.

As Geraldine drove us around, Mary and I loved slapping the outsides of the vehicle's doors to make gazelles crossing the roads in front of us pronk high into the air. It worked every time and beautifully displayed their grace and agility. One afternoon, we visited a nearby game lodge where you could sit outside with a cold beer, watching the elephants strolling about in the swampland. I was amused to see a huge, full-color photograph of a snarling leopard suspended above the open bar-cum-food dispensing area, its purpose to dissuade the little vervet monkeys chattering in the shade trees around the forecourt from coming close to steal treats. Apparently, this deterrent worked well. Monkeys are utterly terrified of leopards, even in static images.

Something rather odd happened to me towards the end of our first week in Luangwa. Geraldine complained to Tom that the air-conditioning unit wasn't working properly, so he promised to send over one of the Yugoslavs, a qualified electrician, to have a look at it. I got up latish on this particular morning, had a leisurely bath, and wandered out to the living room to find whoever was up and about. As I walked into the room, I saw a pair of broad shoulders topped by a head of dark curly hair on a man who had his back to me, hunched over the air-conditioning unit, an open toolbox by his side.

Unsure what to do, I coughed lightly and said, "Good morning."

He leaped to his feet and turned around – and then I can't really explain what happened next. I'd never really believed in love at first sight – until that moment, anyway – but something akin to an electrical current rippled across the room between us and I audibly gasped at the effect. I could tell he felt it, too, and we stood there, staring at each other. Smiling and staring. He hadn't been at the welcoming party on our first night in Luangwa. I would have remembered him.

Expat Blues

At that precise moment, Geraldine swept in, and the spell was broken. I don't know if she detected the palpable charge in the atmosphere as well, but she certainly stopped in her tracks, pausing before she said, "Oh, you've met, then. Erin, this is Savo. Savo, Erin."

We stepped towards each other and Savo took my extended hand, squeezing it warmly, his dark eyes fixed on mine.

"Nice to meet you, Erin," he said in a very attractive accent.

"And you," I managed to stammer.

Then Geraldine was chattering away, planning the day, organizing tea and toast while Savo went back to work. The extraordinary moment was over, but I knew I'd always remember the sheer power of that mutual instant attraction. It was bittersweet, though. As I'd shaken Savo's right hand, I'd noticed the heavy gold wedding ring on the third finger, a common practice in Eastern Europe.

That evening, Tom announced over dinner that the Yugoslavs were hosting a big braii on Saturday night, featuring a spit-roasted suckling pig and all the trimmings.

"They have wonderful cooks there," he assured us. "They always put on a great spread."

"Is it for a special occasion?" Mary asked.

Tom shook his head. "Those guys don't need a special occasion to party. We have to make our own fun here, and it's been a while since we had a get together." His pleasant, freckled face lit up. "You two will have a ball with all the single guys."

Hmmm. Only the single ones?

I had a strict personal rule about not getting involved with married men. Ignoring the feelings of guilt, I had to admit that I couldn't wait to see Savo again.

"All the ladies really dress up," Geraldine chimed in. "I hope you brought a posh frock each."

As it turned out, I had. In her letters to Mary, Geraldine had said that the four of us might go for a little break in Malawi, so in deference to the no-legs-showing rule there I'd packed two long dresses I'd bought in Rhodesia. I chose the sleeveless lilac one with the pretty pleated skirt for the braii.

At seven o'clock on Saturday night, the four of us made the short trip over to the Yugoslavs' camp, Tom and Geraldine lighting the way with powerful torches as it was inky black out. Mary and I hoisted up our skirts and took care where we placed our feet. On arrival, it was immediately clear that the men had gone to considerable effort. The fragrant smell of roasting pork wafted towards us on the still night air as the pig turned lazily on its spit over rosy coals, and the barbecue area was beautifully lit up with colorful lanterns and dramatic staked torches. In the communal dining/leisure area within the large barracks-like building, everything was spic and span, ready for the guests and the night's entertainment. The chairs normally placed around the immense dining table were now arranged along the walls, while the table itself was prepared for the buffet with stacks of plates, napkins and cutlery, even a lovely floral centerpiece. On the wooden floor, a space had been cleared for dancing and music played softly in the background.

First up for the evening was drinks and chat and we were invited to select our beverage of choice from the well-stocked bar set up at one end of the table. I decided to pace myself and opted for a lemonade. As I sipped, I looked around for Savo and eventually spotted him in the kitchen. His face lit up as our eyes met and he flashed me a big smile, which I reciprocated, trying hard not to blush. Then he quickly turned back to the task in hand, which looked like salad making. Not only gorgeous, but domesticated, too. Stefano, a strikingly handsome young man, who was single, also treated me to a welcoming smile. I'd met him on our first evening in Luangwa, but conversation had been pretty stymied by the language barrier. He'd come across as a bit grumpy and had told me in his halting English that he hated it here, that he was going to snatch his passport back and take off. That was the gist of

Expat Blues

it, and I'd felt sorry for him being forced to come here against his will by a harsh state. It was good, therefore, to see him smiling.

Sadly, the evening that held so much promise was marred by an unfortunate incident which occurred not long after we arrived. I watched things unfold from a distance and couldn't hear any of the dialogue, but it was reasonably clear what took place and afterwards one of the three Irish engineers filled us in on the details.

Two immaculately dressed young African men arrived at the doors to the venue and stood waiting shyly before entering. A couple of the Yugoslavs spotted them and moved fast to intercept them, blocking their access. Some conversation then took place, and the chatter diminished as people turned to watch. I saw Tom detach himself from a group and walk over to the standoff happening at the entrance. From that point, if the body language were any indication, things ratcheted up and got pretty heated, with Tom getting noticeably emotional, and the Yugoslavs obstinately standing their ground. Eventually, the two young African men accepted defeat and left, the Yugoslavs and Tom watching them go before the argument kicked off again. Then Tom abruptly turned away and it was clear to everyone that he was deeply upset, red-faced and with tears in his eyes. He went over to his wife, spoke to her briefly, and they both left without another word.

I sidled up to Mary, who'd also observed the altercation but was as much in the dark as I was. Paddy, another Irish engineer we'd got to know, took us bewildered girls aside and explained what we'd witnessed in quiet, discreet tones.

The two young African men, both university students, had recently joined the airstrip building squad, working as assistants to the engineering team and forging a positive relationship with them. When Tom learned about the party, he'd invited both of them to come, but without clearing it first with the Yugoslavs. The senior men had objected. The party list was whites only. Tom, one of the best-hearted, kindest people I'd ever met, was shocked and hurt by their attitude, but his pleas on behalf of the two young black men had fallen on deaf ears. Hurt, angry and mortified, he'd gone home, taking a supportive Geraldine with him. Mary and I felt really bad for Tom, but we decided to stay and not inflame the situation or sour the festivities that clearly much work had gone into any further. From what we picked up over the course of the evening, people fell into two camps: those who sympathized with Tom, and those who thought he'd acted unwisely. We remained neutral, but I really admired Tom for the stand he took to support his friends and I felt disappointed by the Yugoslavs' attitude. My sympathies were reserved for the two young men who would be left scarred by what can only be described as deliberate racism, the second such incident I encountered during my tour in Zambia.

Dinner being served distracted everyone, and we helped ourselves to the superb buffet that covered the vast table and comprised delicious, smoky pork, numerous side dishes and some unusual condiments. I especially liked the fiery red pepper relish called ajvar. After dinner, there was more drinking, the music was amped up, and dancing commenced. I hoped Savo might have a dance with me, but he was keeping his distance. I knew why. He was both protecting me and himself. I danced with Stefano and another young man, Marco, for the most part, and as the evening wound down Stefano walked me home. Mary had left sometime earlier to check on her friends.

It was a great evening, despite the drama, and I assumed, that with no more air conditioning units to fix, I probably wouldn't see Savo again.

He turned up the next morning around nine o'clock with Marco in tow, bundled me and Mary into a land rover, and drove us off to lord knows where! By subtle means, he made it clear I was with him, Mary was with Marco.

(When we returned in the evening, Geraldine told us Stefano had come over in the morning looking for me and was really piqued to discover that Savo had beaten him to it).

The day with Savo and Marco was one of the most pleasant I spent during my time in Africa. Once again, I sensed Savo's protectiveness by his inclusion of Marco and Mary to ensure everyone felt comfortable. The two men proved great company, full of interesting local information, non-stop jokers who had us constantly laughing, and both had fluent English, too, which really helped. Marco was very young, early twenties, probably, full of life and enthusiastic about everything. They showed us lots of game, displaying a good knowledge of where to find animals, and some unusual features of the park like the giant sausage trees, named for the shape of their huge, pendulous fruit. Savo said the elephants loved to eat the dangling pods when they were in a fermentation phase and swore that the animals got drunk as a result, staggering around like old inebriates. They both had lots of stories to entertain us with.

When lunchtime came around, they took us to the game lodge and insisted on buying us lunch. After lunch, we sat out in the courtyard area and enjoyed a cold beer while we watched the elephants and giraffes grazing only meters away.

On the way back, after we'd crossed the river by pontoon, Marco found a boat somewhere, a little skiff, and took Mary out on the river for some rowing, while Savo and I called encouragement from the bank. Savo told us a story that when they went out for a night's drinking at the game lodge, Marco wouldn't bother waiting for the pontoon if it had to come from the other side. He swam the river instead! Since the Luangwa was infested with crocodiles, we were incredulous at such foolhardiness, but Marco insisted it was true.

"I reek of whiskey, and crocs don't like that. They leave me alone."

Well, it was an intriguing theory! I hope it held up for any future swims.

We returned to camp at dusk, and Mary and I thanked Savo and Marco for a wonderful day and some outstanding photograph opportunities. They brushed our repeated thanks aside, assuring us they'd enjoyed themselves, too. They'd treated us with warmth and respect, and I felt sad when they drove away. I'd managed to score one nice photo of me and Savo having a chaste hug under a baobab tree. It would be a good memento to have of a special day.

Erin Eldridge

Me and Savo, Luangwa Valley.

With a sigh, I went into the house, where Geraldine and Tom, keen to hear all about our day, had a lovely dinner waiting for us. To cap off our stay in Luangwa, Tom and Geraldine took us to Malawi for a couple of days. Memories of my first journey there were not very positive ones – my accident and smashed up car, the indifferent company, the hazards of camping long term – so at least this was an opportunity to put some unpleasant ghosts to rest. I left my car at the camp, and we travelled in a land rover, Tom doing all the driving, which was a plus.

We only journeyed as far as Lilongwe, but that was a pleasant little town with some nice shops where Tom and Geraldine were able to stock up on a few commodities and get some overdue medical treatment. The highlight for me was a diversion to Vila de Coutinho, in Mozambique. This little town was a real oddity. Although it was in another country, there were no border formalities. You could just drive in and out as you liked from either the Malawi or Mozambique side. It was a sort of no-man's-land. The big attraction in Vila de Coutinho was a warehouse full of beautiful traditional Portuguese glazed terracotta pottery. Tom and Geraldine stocked up on serving ware and Mary and I bought identical casseroles. Mary's pot subsequently shattered in the back of the land rover on the trip back to Luangwa, but I coddled mine in my lap the whole way, swathed in pieces of my clothing, and it survived all the jolting and shaking. The casserole also survived the journey back to New Zealand, served my family well, and I still have it.

A popular form of river crossing in Africa, by pontoon.

On our return to the Luangwa camp, we found it buzzing with terrible news. A licensed white hunter, camping out in the bush, had been attacked and partially devoured by a man-eating lion. It was an old, solitary lion, almost certainly ejected from the pride by a strong young rival, and unable to hunt. Such lions went for easy prey and often became man-eaters. The hunter's guides had legged it leaving him to his fate. Rangers later tracked and shot the lion.

The second item of bad news was the untimely death of a young African ranger who had foolishly antagonized an elephant blocking a road and been trampled to death. Life, human and animal, all too often hung by a thread on this wildest of continents.

Savo joined us for dinner on our last night in Luangwa, and afterwards we cuddled up on the couch to listen to music, have some drinks, and make the most of all the good company. Then it was time to say goodbye, and he and I walked out into the night, pausing in the darkness a short distance from the house. He said he loved me, that he would come to Livingstone to see me, and we exchanged addresses, promising to write to each other. I think he knew as well as I did that this was a final goodbye, so we lingered for as long as we could within the bounds of propriety before he vanished into the darkness. It had been apparent from day one in the camp that the Yugoslavs were subjected to watchful scrutiny and kept rigorously in line. Savo, as a married man, would never have been permitted to leave the camp, especially not to visit me, and his mail, inwards and outwards, was almost certainly intercepted. I wrote to him but never got a reply.

I sometimes think of Savo with his dark curls and radiant smile, and of that moment when we both laid eyes on each other and felt an instant connection. It remains the only time in my life I ever felt so strongly drawn to another human being. I hope he had a good life. It is better not to torture yourself by dwelling on what might have been. Time, place, circumstances frequently taunt us in this way, presenting us with yearnings they then thwart. Better to make the most of what you have, of what is real and present for you within that framework. Loss and missed opportunities are an unavoidable aspect of life.

Not long after we returned to Livingstone, we heard the dreadful news that Stefano had been killed by a local African man in an argument over a woman.

Chapter Fourteen: Homeward Bound

The journey back to Livingstone was uneventful and we still had some holiday time left to rest up and prepare for the new term. I got a rude awakening when I saw Blue. He had lost weight, barely managed a tail wag when he saw me, and his overall demeanor was low-spirited and defeated. He had clearly fretted badly and I burst into tears, which unsettled him further. People told me he had been seen out at Maramba, three kilometers away, doubtless searching for me. I felt terrible, wracked with guilt. Leaving him at the compound had been altogether different; he was a pup raised by a village, knew everyone there, felt at home there, and always understood I'd be back. We hadn't been at the bungalow in town very long, but he'd been fine during my previous trip away. Something had gone wrong this time, and I couldn't get to the bottom of it. Aclon was tightlipped and the nuns weren't forthcoming either. Neglect was the obvious answer, but at the end of the day I alone was responsible for his welfare.

So, I fussed over Blue, fed him up with extra treats, spent lots of time with him and he quickly regained the lost weight, reverting to his happy old self. He'd changed, though, albeit subtly; I felt part of him had withdrawn from me because of the hurt he'd suffered, and it made me very sad.

Then there was my other pet. Aclon shook his head when I asked about Soccy.

"I do not know, madum. I do not see him."

He'd taken all the mice home before they turned bad, he explained, both fresh and frozen. Better that than have them wasted, I agreed.

The South African family returned briefly to collect their Mercedes before returning to their Zambian base. While her husband repaired the car, I broached the subject of my little owl with his ornithophobic wife. She denied having seen any sign of Soccy after Mary and I left for Luangwa. But she didn't look me in the eye when she said it, and I sensed her evasiveness.

Whatever his fate, Soccy never returned to the house again. I liked to picture him in my mind's eye, flying free, hunting, socializing with other barn owls. I hope he made it, that he had a good life and wasn't too shocked when he learned that mice don't come coated in cracker crumbs. I'll never know. Tennyson famously said that nature is red in tooth and claw, but man remains the cruelest predator on the planet.

Zambia celebrated the tenth anniversary of its independence in October and there were morning celebrations, before it got too hot, involving lots of singing, marching, and drumming at the local public reserve which the entire school attended. In the capital, the president had ordered the purchase of 50 brand new Mercedes for a single drive by parade. At the same time, in some of the provinces, the people were reduced to eating grass.

Our girls waiting to perform at Independence Day celebrations.

My last term as a teacher at St Mary's got underway and went quickly. I felt tired and run down, more so after a nasty bout of bronchitis that left me feeling weak and exhausted. Physical weariness aside, my boyfriend drained me emotionally with his inability to sever ties with ex-girlfriends, and I came to the conclusion that I was doomed to be thwarted in affairs of the heart.

Working out what to do with Blue was another painful process. I didn't have the money to take him home, nor the will to put him through miserable months of quarantine, and anyway I saw him as a quintessentially 'African' dog. I felt he needed a stable family with children. He loved kids, as was evidenced by the exuberant way he joined the school youngsters for a romp at every break time. Luck smiled, and a lovely British family, who'd recently lost their beloved but aged bull terrier, agreed to adopt him. They had two young children and spent holidays at home, so Blue, who was given the run of the house from day one, settled immediately and happily into this homely environment. I missed him terribly, but I also felt great relief. Everyone who knew the family told me Blue was doing really well.

I then focused on my packing. I didn't have a lot of personal possessions, just clothes mainly, and not a great deal of them. However, in the course of my tour I had accumulated some lovely pieces of African art, carvings mainly, but also batiks and paintings, and I was loath to abandon them. Eleanor, also planning her return home, told me you could go to the local prison and order a packing case to be made by the inmates for a very reasonable sum, so I quickly organized that. I can't remember who, but somebody supplied us with bags of wadding and once all my treasures were safely packed up, it was just a matter of getting the local customs guys to come for an

inspection and seal the crate. As advised, I made sure I had cold beers on hand for them both, and there were no problems. A friend with a pickup delivered the crate to the airport for me, and that was job done. (The crate made it safely to New Zealand, but I got a real roasting from the MAF boys, especially after they found *one* dead insect, (eye roll) and ended up having to have the crate and all its contents fumigated at a special installation! I'll never forget their faces when they lifted out a very realistic face mask with little carved teeth and stringy hair, dropping it like a hot potato because they thought it was a shrunken head!).

I took home all my books, my tramping pack and my boots – by air, this time! My little paraffin stove I gave to a delighted Aclon. I would miss him, this sweet, obliging man who never turned a hair when Mary ordered him to the shops to buy her sanitary pads, and I worried about him since his job would vanish with the empty bungalow and he had many dependents. I'd always unlocked the door for him every morning when I heard him arrive, crunching his bike across the gravel, taking off as fast as I could because I slept in the nick. I'm sure he caught a flash of naked bum on more than one occasion. I wrote him a brilliant reference and he thanked me humbly with his customary big smile. Jobs working for expats were transient by nature, a sad fact of life. I felt sure, though, that the house would soon host teachers again, perhaps young Zambian women.

One of my last memories of Aclon occurred after he failed to turn up for work one morning. This was totally out of character, and I was very concerned. When I came home at lunchtime, he was waiting for me on the stoop, nursing his youngest child in his arms, a little boy about eighteenth months old. He told me with tears in his eyes that the child was very ill, and he wanted to take him to a private doctor to get the best care for him. I understood. The hospital would be a long wait and indifferent care at the best of times. The baby was coughing and breathing noisily, green snot pouring from his tiny nose. I gave Aclon the money he needed, and he thanked me over and over until I shushed him. I pointed to a malodorous little bag hanging from a cord around the baby's neck. "What's that, Aclon?"

"Witch doctor give me that, madum."

I grinned. Aclon was covering all bases.

The baby made a full recovery.

I kept up my squash playing and my stints with the Sports Club darts team. Swimming remained a favorite pastime and my scruffy little horde of water babies were always waiting for me to show up and pay their way into the pool. I wanted badly to go to Rhodesia one last time, but it was just too dangerous. Instead, I made a trip to Botswana and visited Chobe National Park, where I saw the biggest monitor lizard ever and loads of beautiful Kalahari elephants. I loved Botswana. It had a gentle, rural feel about it, unspoiled and natural. It was one border where I never had any problems! The president, Sir Seretse Khama, was famously married to a white English woman, his beloved wife, Ruth.

Expat Blues

Woman in Botswana busy weaving while she sells her goods at market.

I went down to Victoria Falls to get some last photographs. Now that the wet was starting, increasing the volume of water in the river, the mist, spray and rainbows over one of the Seven Wonders of the World were spectacular, fully justifying Livingstone's comment the first time he saw them: "Scenes so lovely they must have been gazed upon by angels in their flight." I would miss them.

The wet season increasing the flow over the Falls.

With the weather getting hotter now, I also liked to take refuge at the Mosi Hotel on occasion to wallow in the coolness created by their excellent air conditioning. There was a modest café, as opposed to the flash main dining room, which served cheap meals. I was especially fond of a chicken curry they served. It was mild for my taste, but very flavorsome. Thus, I counted down the time to my departure.

Sometimes, young backpackers would arrive at the cathedral seeking accommodation, and Father Jude invariably brought them over to us since we had spare bedrooms. A nice distraction during this final term was hosting two Swedish girls for a couple of nights and then a young Kiwi man who stayed about a week and was very pleasant company. He wanted to go to Rhodesia, so I dropped him off at Kazungula and wished him luck touring through a by now badly war-torn country. I saw him again back in New Zealand, just after I'd become engaged. We'd exchanged addresses back in Zambia and he turned up out of the blue at my parents' home at Christmas at the same time as another old boyfriend. My fiancé was unimpressed!

A few weeks before my departure, the nuns organized a farewell morning tea for me and I was presented with a lovely copper plaque embossed with an elephant, which still has pride of place on my wall. Sister Carmel, who'd written me an outstanding reference, spoke kindly. I remember she said I came across as quiet and reserved when I arrived, but she felt I had come out of my shell very nicely. She added that she was sorry I'd had to deal with some difficult times during my tour, but, in my response, I assured her that I regretted nothing and that I would miss her and St Mary's very much. I knew she wanted me to renew my contract, returning after the statutory three-month break at home, and, if I were honest with myself, I was sincerely conflicted. (After I got home, I wrote her a letter in which I mentioned how much I missed her, the school, the girls etc. and she promptly organized a plane ticket for my return!). Deep down, I knew going back would be a mistake. I'd seen many examples of what happened to those who stayed in Africa longer than their souls could endure. I've held to that principle all my life. Never go back. Always go forwards.

Expat Blues

The girls weren't told I was leaving, and I went along with that. I guess Carmel and I were both keeping our options open at that stage. My thirty months' teaching experience at St Mary's remain my happiest years spent in the profession.

Mary and I organized a farewell party. Eleanor was going home, too, but wanted no part of a potentially boozy get together so absented herself for the weekend. Mary and I cooked up a storm, guests brought food as well, and Jimmy got us cheap alcohol through the Air Force. It was a good do, well attended, and everyone seemed to enjoy themselves. Sister Carmel and a couple of the nuns dropped in briefly to partake of a soft drink and nibble on some food. I put on a Beach Boys record and the dance floor heaved. Apart from the cleanup next morning, not helped by a throbbing hangover, it was a nice note to finish on.

A farewell dance with my mate and best friend. Catherine and Jimmy behind us.

I sold my car to a young African man and was surprised at the wrench I felt parting with her. We'd been through a lot of adventures together and while not the sturdiest vehicle nor one best suited to African conditions, she had always seen me through. I knew she'd no longer be looked after in accordance with my standards – washed once a week, regularly serviced etc., But there was nothing I could do about that. The money, along with the modest gratuity guaranteed by my contract, would give me badly needed funds when I arrived home.

Just before I was due to depart Livingstone, we learned about the dreadful Birmingham pub bombings, blamed on the IRA, which had killed 21 and left 182 injured. On one of my last visits to the Sports Club, I found the British and Irish expats ranged up in silence at opposite ends of the bar, glaring at each other, waiting for one word to ignite hostilities, the bitterness and hatred palpable. It was probably a good time to be leaving.

I flew out of Livingstone mid-morning not long after school finished for the year in early December. The first leg of my journey was to Blantyre, then onwards to Johannesburg, where I spent a night in the airport hotel, then via Perth and Sydney to Christchurch – the old familiar route in reverse, but without the drama. On the last leg, I had a window seat, and I remember gazing down with a lump in my throat at the neat patchwork fields of the Canterbury plains. As I disembarked and walked across the tarmac in the warm sunshine of early summer (no air bridges in those days), I heard a shout and looked up to see my family waving from the terminal roof. I waved back, fighting down tears. I was home.

When David Livingstone died, his faithful African retainers buried his heart under an mpundu tree in a secret place in northern Zambia, and then carried his embalmed remains to the coast from whence they were transported back to England where he was buried in Westminster Abbey in 1874.

I left part of myself in Africa, too. One day, I'd have to return and claim it.

Epilogue

The initial euphoria of being home soon evaporated, and readjusting to life in New Zealand after being away for so long presented some painful challenges. I came very close to returning to Africa, but in the end, I stuck to my resolution of ever onwards, no looking back.

I never made it to Colombia either; I got married instead, ironically, to a man of Italian descent, and we had two children, a son and a daughter. After my husband died prematurely from cancer, I became an expat again, this time in the oil-rich Islamic sultanate of Brunei, Northern Borneo, on one of those lucrative, tax-free contracts teaching English. It was a very, very different experience from Africa, but there were still many aspects that were strikingly the same. Expat communities have their common denominators wherever they are.

And that's another whole story I'd like to tell: Expat Blues #2.

I haven't made it back to Africa yet, but there's still time. Still time.

www.ingramcontent.com/pod-product-compliance
Lightning Source LLC
LaVergne TN
LVHW020422070526
838199LV00003B/244